THE HISTORY OF THE DEVIL

ANCIENT & MODERN

A BIBLICAL AND HISTORICAL ACCOUNT OF SATAN'S DEVICES, FALL, AND ETERNAL JUDGMENT

THE HISTORY OF
THE DEVIL
ANCIENT & MODERN

A BIBLICAL AND HISTORICAL ACCOUNT OF
SATAN'S DEVICES, FALL, AND ETERNAL JUDGMENT

DANIEL DEFOE

Compilation and Biography by Gene Fedele

BRIDGE
LOGOS

Newberry, FL 32669

Bridge-Logos
Newberry, FL 32669

The History of the Devil:
Ancient and Modern in Two Parts
by Daniel Defoe
Compilation, Biography and Edit by Gene Fedele

Republished From the First Edition: LONDON, 1726

Printed for T. WARNER, at the Black Boy, in Paternoster Row

Engravings by Gustave Doré, unless otherwise noted

Printed in the United States of America.

Library of Congress Catalog Card Number: 2021950441

International Standard Book Number: 978-1-61036-273-3

Copyeditor, L. Edward Hazelbaker

Cover/Interior design by Kent Jensen | knail.com

VP 03/2022

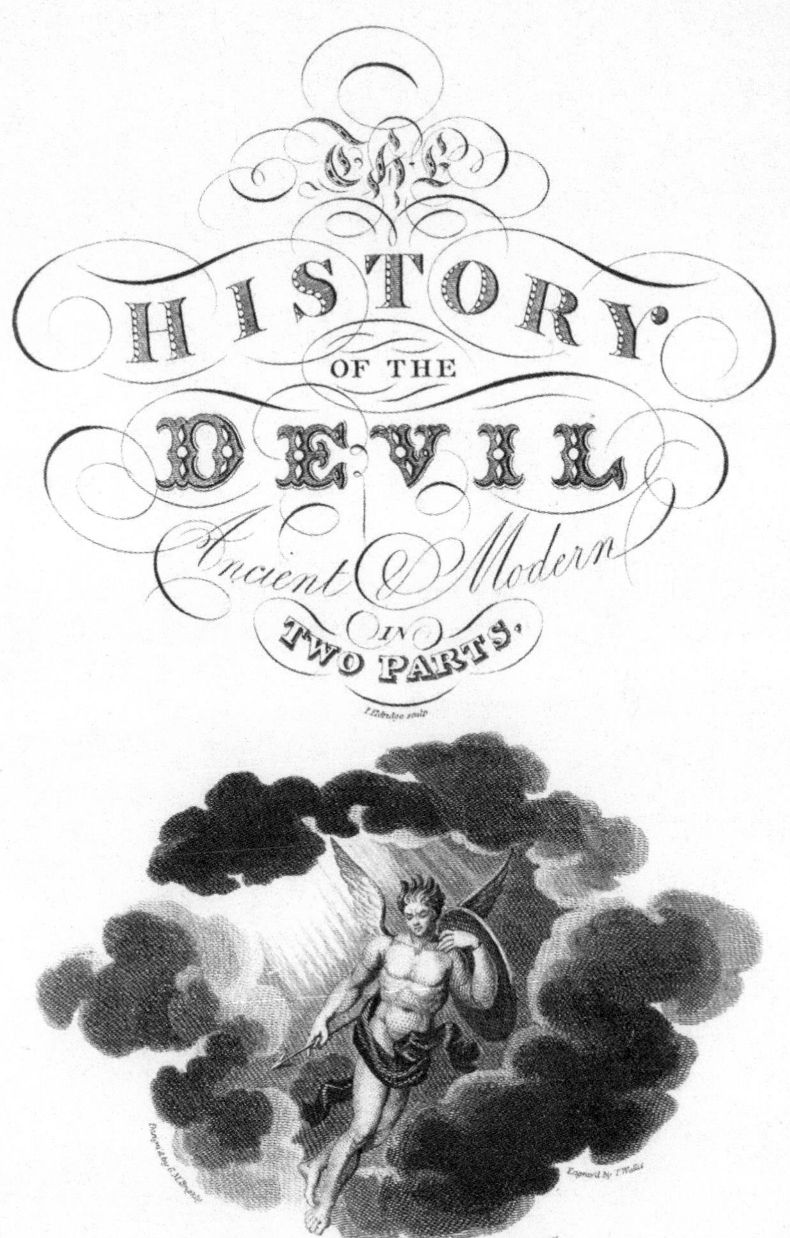

SATAN EXPELL'D FROM HEAVEN.

THE HISTORY OF THE DEVIL, ANCIENT AS WELL AS MODERN: IN TWO PARTS

PART I.

Containing a State of the Devil's Circumstances and the Various Turns of his Affairs, from his Expulsion out of Heaven, to the Creation of Man, with Remarks on the Several Mistakes Concerning the Reason and Manner of his Fall.

Also, his Proceedings with Mankind Ever Since Adam to the First Planting of the Christian Religion in the World.

PART II.

Containing his More Private Conduct Down to the Present Times: His Government, his Appearances, his Manner of Working, and the Tools he Works with.

> Bad as he is, the Devil may be abus'd,
> Be falsely charg'd, and causelessly accus'd,
> When men unwilling to be blam'd alone,
> Shift off those crimes on him which are their own.

ENGRAVING FROM THE FIRST EDITION OF
THE HISTORY OF THE DEVIL (1726).

TABLE OF CONTENTS

PART TWO

THE EDITOR'S INTRODUCTION

The subject of the devil has been as much a fascination as it has been a plague upon mankind, across the earth, throughout all generations since time began. He is known by many names and depicted by many man-made forms, causing much confusion and misunderstanding (surely his intention, no doubt). Yet his true infernal character and behavior and the activities of his host of fallen angels (cast out and condemned with him) upon the physical as well as spirit world are systematically revealed in *The History of the Devil,* penned by the renowned English novelist, Daniel Defoe.

The History of the Devil is a classic historical and religious book widely considered one of Daniel Defoe's greatest works of non-fiction. First published in 1726, it made an immediate impact on English literature, society, and the ecclesiastical community in the early eighteenth century. And today it continues to enrich humanity as a faithful source of historical and biblical truth and wisdom.

While delving deep into the heart and soul of mankind to expose truth through honest, biblical, and sometimes personal inquiry and examination, *The History of the Devil* cleverly unfolds the actions, devices, and evil nature of Satan and his host of devils against God and mankind throughout the history of the world.

Defoe divides the book into two parts: *Ancient*, or the time from before the creation of the universe to the coming of the Messiah, Jesus Christ; and *Modern*, or from the time of Christ and establishment of the Christian Church to the present day. His style is one that uniquely blends serious biblical principles and history with lighter satirical narrative—especially when dealing with mankind's many false presuppositions about the devil—and clearly delineates when each, or both, is applicable to the subject of discussion.

Be that as it may, one might possibly infer a strange and subtle sense of irreverence in *The History of the Devil* if the author's style and intentions are not rightly discerned by the reader early on. Defoe almost dares the reader to question his motives, and yet he incites such a reaction intentionally so as to arouse a sense of deep, honest inquiry and assessment of what is wholly true about God, mankind, and the devil.

In his 1840 edition of this republished work, publisher William Hazlitt elaborates on this in his stellar introduction.

> His work exhibits much and varied reading, strong natural sense, and an intimate knowledge of mankind. His talent for broad-buffeting sarcasm is applied with wonderful effect in exposing the popular delusions, whilst they supply him with materials for insinuating wholesome moral instruction. One of the leading objects is to correct the bad passions of mankind, by tracing them to their proper source, and by showing that they furnish a more accurate representation of Satan than the painted spectres with which the world has

been so long amused and terrified. The matter and mode conjoin to make this a charming performance.

Though *The History of the Devil* is quite comprehensive in its depiction of Satan's influence in the world throughout time, as outlined in Scripture and history, Defoe was also concerned with unveiling the eternal impact such activity and events have on individuals' souls and the sense of urgency required for developing a right understanding about genuine Christian faith and trust in God through Christ as the only defense against *"the fiery darts of the devil"–Defoe* (Eph. 6:16).

Many foundational truths of the Bible regarding the subject of the devil, God, and eternity are revealed by Defoe in his efforts to expose the devil and revere God–and are sometimes even revisited for further proof and commentary.

Some of these truths about the devil revealed in *The History of the Devil* include:

- Satan is a real, singular being–or as Defoe describes, the "monarch of the whole clan of hell." But as seen in Scripture, the devil can be identified as and operate as *many* at times (i.e. Legion). (Mark 5:9; Luke 8:30; Matt. 5:15).
- Satan was once an angel in heaven, where also dwells a significant host of angels. Satan, along with a significant number of angels rebelled against God and were cast out of heaven. (Isaiah 14:12; Rev. 12:9).
- Satan is not an opposite *god* to God but a being created by God, limited by God, and permitted by God in the exercise of any influence he has over the earth and on mankind. The devil has no power over man except that which is permitted by God. (Job 1-2; John 19:11).

- Although his infernal and wicked influence is evident in the lives of mankind throughout history in all ages, Satan does not have a physical body and therefore does not appear in physical or bodily form to people (but can possess and influence people and living creatures).
- Satan and all his demons hate humanity so fervently because a significant number of people are and will be redeemed from the punishment of sin—which is eternal, conscious torments of hell—and inherit their eternal place and positions in heaven that were vacated by their fall.
- His reign has an end, which is destruction of his purposes and being cast into eternal punishment along with all who follow him and deny faith in the One true God through Christ and by the power of the Holy Spirit as recorded in His Word, the Holy Scriptures.
- He constantly seeks to root out true faith and religion in the minds and lives of mankind and leads many to idolatry or "false notions of worship"—the worship of other people, animals, idols—and seeks to convince them that such behavior is genuine worship of the true God.
- No matter how desperate and wicked mankind had fallen at certain seasons in history, there was always a remnant of God's true servants and saints upon the earth.
- His first defeat was the proclamation of the "Seed of the woman"—the prophecy of the coming of the Messiah, as spoken in Genesis 3:15. His second defeat was the actual coming of the Messiah, Jesus Christ, into the world, His death, and His resurrection. His final defeat will be at the second coming of Christ and the final judgment of all men and angels.

- There is a future state for all mankind and angelic beings that is eternal, and there is only one of two places where all will reside for all time—heaven (eternal bliss in the presence of the Holy Trinity, angelic host, and all the saints), or hell (eternal damnation and punishment along with the devil, his host of fallen angels, and all the unredeemed of mankind).
- The majority of mankind naturally supposes the reality of life after death, and that one place is better than the other. As Defoe says:

> Mankind's natural notions necessarily entertain thoughts of things to come; superior or inferior, God or the Devil, which fill up all futurity in our thoughts. And it is impossible for us to form any image in our minds of an immortal or invisible world (we "see as through a glass dimly") but under the notions of extreme felicity [heaven], or extreme misery [hell].

"He has put eternity in their hearts." (Ecclesiastes 3:11)

- Hell is eternal, conscious punishment of the wicked absent from the divine presence and influence of God, Christ, and all His true believers.

In addition, Defoe takes positions on certain issues or beliefs related to these biblical and historical foundations and how they are revealed in the world and in people's lives, including:

- People who engage in ungodly practices are quite susceptible to being "agents" of the devil's antics, many unwittingly.
- Dream disturbances and interpretations are one of the devil's most effective means for influencing and deceiving

men and women. As Defoe states, "By dreams he (the devil) may get inside without opposition . . . insinuates himself within us without our consent, without our knowledge."

- Defoe often references the "cloven foot" relative to physical traits of the devil and how deceived people have ignorantly and erroneously devised such frightful images and placed a visual context on the devil that aligns with his horrid behavior. And that enables many to attempt to evade human responsibility for sinful activity in the world and in individual hearts and lives (e.g. "It's not my fault; the devil made me do it."). But here the author might just as well have chosen the images of horns, forked tongue, or other features commonly accepted, which are all in reality just mere inventions of men. Through his use of the cloven foot imagery, Defoe cleverly points out the absurdity and deception of such physical depictions in reference to the devil and evil activities, and he warns mankind to avoid such notions or be further deceived.
- Another method used by the devil for manipulating people that is often mentioned by Defoe is "oracles," or predictions of the future uttered by psychics, fortune-tellers, false prophets, and false teachers.

> They that know no evil can know no good, so a competent knowledge of the Devil, and all his ways, may be the best help to make us defy the Devil and all his works. —Defoe

I have little doubt and even some suggestive evidence that the renowned Christian author and historian, C. S. Lewis, was very likely intimately acquainted with the works of Daniel Defoe, and in particular *The History of the Devil,* when Lewis penned his classic work on the devil, *The Screwtape Letters.* Though separated by over 200 years, the two present some uncanny similarities in their respective serious inquiry and faithful biblical application to the subject infused with clever satire and sarcasm. In fact, whether coincidence or not, in chapter ten of part 2, Defoe even mentions in an allegorical context a Sir Hellebore Wormwood in reference to man's ease of being influenced by the devil (Wormwood being the same name given to one of the main characters in Lewis' *The Screwtape Letters*).

Throughout the book the reader will notice Defoe's conspicuous reference of the devil as "the Devil," which should not be seen as the author's intention, or mistake, to place the devil on par with God Almighty. His humble reverence for his Lord is never in question. In chapter two and four, Defoe explains his reasoning—that the Devil, or Satan, in the singular and proper form, might be easily distinguished from a more general reference of "devil" describing an evil being or person. Though the Scriptures typically use the lowercase form in reference to the devil, I've chosen to honor the author's intentions and maintain the integrity of this classic work.

In addition, I have added clarification or translation of certain words or phrases, in brackets, where appropriate for ease of reading and to avoid excessive footnotes.

Without doubt, the motivating factors behind the writing of this timeless work were Defoe's resolute faith in God and his Savior, Jesus Christ, and the divine insight the Lord unfolded to him of the operations of good and evil in the history of the world and the society in which he lived. Defoe's Christianity aligned closely with the beliefs of the eminent Puritans and the brave reformers of the Protestant Reformation, and he was a dissenter from the Church of England, which we see consistently and faithfully revealed in the pages of *The History of the Devil,* as it is in many of his other writings.

"Three things," says Defoe, "ought not to be lacking in any man—a reverence of God, a sense of religion, and a profession of the duty we all owe our Maker."

Daniel Defoe (1660-1731) was a prolific English writer with over 500 works to his name. He was a renowned author of many novels including his most famous, *Robinson Crusoe* (1719), *Moll Flanders* (1722), and *Colonel Jack* (1722).

—Gene Fedele
Editor, April 2022

DANIEL DE FOE.

BIOGRAPHY OF DANIEL DEFOE

A religious life is the only heaven on earth. —Daniel Defoe

Wherever God erects a house of prayer,
The Devil always builds a chapel there,
And 'twill be found, upon examination,
The latter has the largest congregation."

—*The True-Born Englishman: A Satire,*
by Daniel Defoe (1701)

Daniel Defoe is considered by many of the most learned and respected historians and scholars to be one of the earliest and most influential English novelists to enrich mankind with numerous classic literary treasures. His most famous works include *Robinson Crusoe* (1719), *Moll Flanders* (1722), *Religious Courtship* (1722), and *The History of the Devil* (1726), among others.

Though he achieved this distinction during his life, as well as even greater recognition posthumously, he battled significant—and sometimes severe—loss, persecution and suffering in his personal and professional life. His successes as a businessman and merchant were juxtaposed at times against seasons of great loss and near ruin. He spent some time in prison for debts he amassed due to unforeseeable business losses and political disfavor from the aristocracy. Additionally, his passions and interests extended into the political and religious realms where he experienced serious opposition to his views and his various writings on related subjects.

Defoe's love for God's Holy Word and his faith in his Savior, Jesus Christ, was a central motivating factor in his writings, political positions, church affiliations, social circles, and business activities, of which he was eminently bold to profess publicly and privately.

Daniel Defoe was born in London, England, of Flemish descent in 1660 to James and Alice Foe (though Defoe biographer Thomas Wright presents supporting information from G. A. Aitken that his true birth date is in 1659). Daniel later changed his name to Defoe as he thought it was more aristocratic.

James Foe was a tallow chandler (candle maker) and member of the Worshipful Company of Butchers, a livery organization that dates back as far as the year 975. The Foes were Presbyterian Dissenters, or Separatists, and were therefore aligned with the non-Conformists with strong Puritan beliefs and influence, and in opposition to the religious and often political dictates of the Church of England.

As a result, Daniel was not able to attend the more renowned schools, academies, or colleges that were generally reserved for those who were more aligned with the Church of England. This persecution in his earlier days likely contributed to Defoe's contempt for the Roman Catholic influence in the English

Church and political leaders of his day—a contempt that we later see clearly and vehemently revealed in many of his writings.

> Alas, the Church of England! What with Popery on one hand, and Schismatics on the other, how has She been crucified between two thieves. NOW, LET US CRUCIFY THE THIEVES! May God Almighty put it into the hearts of all the friends of Truth, to lift up a Standard against Pride and ANTICHRIST! That the Posterity of the sons of Error may be rooted out from the face of this land, forever!
> —*The Shortest Way With Dissenters,* by Daniel Defoe (1702)

When just a boy, one of the tasks given to him by his parents, was to copy out the Bible, which he worked on feverishly, but by the time he finished the Pentateuch, he found himself too exhausted to continue. That introduction to the Word of God took on a renewed vigor in after years and his acquaintance with the Scriptures was phenomenal, leading him to embrace the faith of this parents as his own, and served as the foundation for the stories and lessons within the pages of his timeless literary treasures.

In 1684 Defoe married Mary Tuffley and they had eight children together, but only five would survive into adulthood. They were married 47 years until his death in 1731. Mary followed her husband shortly thereafter in 1732.

Defoe was a self-avowed entrepreneur and savvy purveyor in London's bustling high society and culture, yet he was a man of great compassion for others and was often found hiring the poor or bailing the less fortunate out of debt (even to the detriment of his own finances). The economic crash of 1692 hit his businesses hard and he quickly fell into debt, declared bankruptcy, and eventually landed in debtor's prison. By 1695 he was back in London managing a tile and brick factory, but his aversion to the injustice of religious and political tyranny burned bright in his heart and mind and though he managed to earn favor with King William III and Queen Mary through the publication of some papers supporting the crown, he was committed in his non-Conformist position and influence—serving, in a sense, as a double agent.

In 1697 he published *An Essay Upon Projects,* a series of works promoting economic improvement and cultural advancement, and even included ideas for a national insurance plan.

Defoe was an ardent defender of freedom and liberty in England having viewed it as vital to the health and prosperity of the nation. Amidst political upheaval brewing in Europe, Defoe penned an elegant and persuasive argument within his parliamentary relations; "Liberty and property are the glorious attributes of the English nation; and the dearer they are to us, the less danger we are in losing them; but I could never yet see it proved, that the danger of losing them by a small army was such, as we should expose ourselves to all the world for it. It is not the king that gives laws of peace and war now to Europe; and those who would thus wrest the sword out of his hand in time of peace, bid the fairest of all men in the world to renew the war."

Defoe was also staunch proponent of religious freedom, and in 1701 he began publishing politically charged pamphlets against the policies and affairs of the royals as well as the Church. He published a satirical poem, *The True-Born Englishman* (1701) where he rails on the vices and inbred avarice of the character of Englishmen.

Queen Anne's ascension to the throne of England in 1702

DEFOE LOCKED IN THE PILLORY
FOR HIS NON-CONFORMIST VIEWS AND WRITINGS.

invigorated renewed religious persecution of the non-Conformists, and Defoe became a fresh target. His pamphlet, *The Shortest Way with the Dissenters, or Proposals for the Establishment of the Church,* was initially published anonymously, but his authorship was discovered. He was charged with sedition which landed him in prison for several months and three days locked in the pillory, but instead of the typical public scorn and ridicule from such punishment, the people, in support of this brave dissenter, sang praises from his poem, *Hymn to the Pillory,* and drank health to his name.

Within the sufferings of his confinement, he mustered the deportment to exercise a flare of satire with the flow of his pen, which arose from the unjust circumstances of his situation,

"The first intent of laws
Was to correct the effect and check the cause.
And all the ends of punishment
Were only future mischiefs to prevent:
But justice is inverted, when
Those engines of the law,
Instead of pinching vicious men,
Keep honest ones in awe."

THE GREAT STORM OF 1703.

Within a short time after his release, Defoe found himself a survivor of the Great Storm of 1703, a destructive hurricane that hit England hard with much loss of life and property, and became the source of his following book, *The Storm* (1704), considered by many to be one of the finest works of contemporary journalism. Defoe's literary genius and religious proclivity entitles him to even higher praise from this work. He seizes the opportunity to reveal sober and awesome fundamental truths found in Scripture aligned with the incredible and devastating effects of the great storm, and in particular God's existence, His affairs in mankind, His supreme providence in all events great and small, and the certainty of an eternal destination for all people, either the reward of Heaven or the punishment of hell.

In 1704, Defoe continued with the political pamphlets with the publication of a periodical, *A Review of the Affairs of France,* which was distributed three times a week and ran for over ten years. The Review eventually became a voice for the English government and particularly in regard to the 1707 Act of Union between England and Scotland, which led to the union of the two countries and the formation of Great Britain, chronicled in Defoe's *The History of the Union of Great Britain* (1709).

THE
HISTORY
OF THE
UNION
OF
GREAT BRITAIN.

EDINBURGH,
Printed by the Heirs and Successors of *Andrew Anderson,* Printer to the QUEEN's most Excellent MAJESTY, *Anno* DOM. 1709.

Defoe was a Presbyterian and a Dissenter and suffering greatly in England for these convictions and was therefore given an opportunity to serve as an adviser to the General Assembly of the Church of Scotland, and the committees of the Parliament of Scotland, which were very much favorable to his religious sentiments and political positions.

In a rather sarcastic response to particular political controversies and their respective unjust outcomes, Defoe writes, "Some are advanced without honor, others suppressed without infamy; some are raised with merit, some are crushed without a crime; and no man knows by the beginning of things, whether his course shall issue in a peerage or a pillory."

Defoe was no stranger to opposition, having attacks from his enemies in the political, social, religious, and economic realms—largely sparked by his writings and his often-controversial sentiments. He was also a consummate "equalizer" in numerous heated contests, ready to expose either side for their extremism or error, even if was against the group of which he generally sided. For example, he stood firm with his fellow non-Conformists in exposing their "scandalous practice of occasional conformity."

Amidst insults and railings by his enemies and denunciation by opposing political forces, Defoe published his *Appeal to Honour and Justice,* in 1715, as a genuine and humble account of his conduct and affairs in public life. As Defoe reflected on these preceding years of struggle, persecution and suffering and how he had been maligned and "rewarded," his heart sunk and his health clearly affected by these spiritual attacks, declared, "By the hints of mortality and infirmities of a life of sorrow and fatigue, I have reason to think, that I am very near to that great ocean of eternity, and the time may not be long ere I embark on the last voyage: wherefore I think I should even accounts with this world before I go, that no slanders may lie against my heirs, to disturb them in the peaceable possession of their father's inheritance, his character."

In 1715, he published *The Family Instructor,* which was an instructional manual, of sorts, in three parts (1. Respecting Parents and Children, 2. Masters and Servants, 3. Husbands and Wives), based on biblical truths and practical application of Reformed protestant principles, promoting piety in the home and society as the greatest needs of the day and does the greatest good for mankind. The well-known and admired minister of Black Friars praised the book from the pulpit and reflected on its enduring influence in a letter to the press, stating, "[the book] will last while our language [English] endures; at least, while wise men shall consider the influences of religion and the practice of morals as of the greatest use to society." Defoe later published a second volume with two parts: *Family Breaches, and The Great Mistake of Mixing Passions in the Managing of Children.*

The inspiration for the work was Defoe's keen spiritual insight into the importance of the family for a healthy society and in particular, the need for a commitment to family religion and practice. In Defoe's own home there was family devotions and prayer every morning and evening with an emphasis on the practice of piety and "learning from the Scriptures."

This excerpt from *The Family Instructor* provides insight into the author's intentions: "In the evening, the head of the family calls them all together, reads to them from some good books, and the then sings psalms, and goes to prayers. When that is over, they go to supper, and then spend an hour perhaps, or two, in the most innocent and the most pleasant discourse and conversation imaginable—it is always about something religious—and then everyone retires to their room, and the young ladies spend their time in their closet devotions, til they go to bed."

The whole tenor and style of Defoe in *The Family Instructor* is warm and charming, very much unlike the perceived stiffness of his Puritan doctrinal beliefs. Rather, his religion is one that is clearly genuine, warm and springs from his heart. It is believed that it was Defoe's commitment to the principles he presents in this book within his own home that the Lord used to bring the Gospel and saving faith to his daughters, his youngest daughter, Sophia, being just fourteen—though it's clear from history that his sons continued in their rebellion, causing their father and mother much grief.

The novel that Defoe is most famous for giving the world is his renowned, *Life and Surprising Adventures of Robinson Crusoe,* and reception of the work was amiable and universal. Readers were charmed and entertained by the simple, engaging narrative; its edge-of-your-seat adventure; and a heart-warming instruction of God's long-suffering with and vindication of repentant man. The story is one that Defoe ascribes as a sort of autobiography, more in meaning and purpose than in actual events and history.

Defoe follows up on his success of Robison Crusoe with a second volume of *The Surprise Adventures,* and then in 1720, a third volume titled, *Serious Reflections During the Life of Robinson Crusoe,* along with his *Vision of the Angelick World.* This last in the collection was written with less fable and more instruction in mind, particularly on matters that are less apt to amuse but unfold useful truths and lessons on morality and faith.

Defoe not only declares, in his *Serious Reflections* (*Robinson Crusoe,* pt. 2, ch.1), that *Robinson Crusoe* is an allegory of his own life, though more in meaning and purpose than in actual events in history. Yet he asserts that the narrative extended even to minuteness—that everything, in short, that happened in Crusoe, had its counterpart with Defoe.

Other great novels of the celebrated Daniel Defoe that are of note are outlined by his biographer, George Chalmers (1786):

> "He published, in 1720, *The History of Duncan Campbell.* Of a person who was born deaf and dumb, but who himself taught the deaf and dumb to understand, it is easy to see that the life would be extraordinary. It will be found that the author has intermixed some disquisitions of learning and has contrived that the merriest passages shall end with some edifying moral. *The Fortunes and Misfortunes of Moll Flanders* were made to gratify the world, in 1721. Defoe was aware, that in relating a vicious life, it was necessary to make the best use of a bad story; and he artfully endeavors that the reader shall be more pleased with the moral than the fable; with the application than the relation; with the end of the writer than the adventures of the person. There was published in 1721, a work of a similar tendency, *The Life of Colonel Jack,* who was born a gentleman but was bred a pickpocket. Our author is studious to convert his various adventures into a delightful field, where the reader might gather herbs, wholesome and medicinal, without the accommodation of plants, poisonous or noxious. In 1724 appeared *The Life of Roxana.* 'Scenes of crimes can scarcely be represented in such a manner,' says Defoe, 'but some make a criminal use of them, but when vice is painted in its low-prized colors, it is not to make people love what from the frightfulness of the figures they ought necessarily to hate. Yet, I am not convinced, that the

world has been made much wiser, or better, by the perusal of these lives; they may have diverted the lower orders, but I doubt if they have much improved them; if, however they have not made them better, they have not left them worse. But they do not exhibit many scenes which are welcome to cultivated minds. Of a very different quality are the *Memoirs of a Cavalier*, during the civil wars in England, which seem to have been published without a date. This is a romance most akin to truth that ever was written.'

"It is a narrative of great events, which is drawn with such simplicity, and enlivened with such reflections, as to inform the ignorant and entertain the wise. The moralities of Defoe, whether published in single volumes, or interspersed through many passages, must at last give him a superiority over the crowd of his contemporaries. The approbation which has been long given to his *Family Instructor*, and his *Religious Courtship*, seem to contain the favorable decision of his countrymen.

"Defoe's classic work of non-fiction, *The History of the Devil* (1726), was not his only writing on the subject of good and evil, heaven and hell, God and the devil. In his *The History of Apparitions*, he reveals his belief in his 'appointed, deputed sort of stationary spirits in the invisible world.' These spirits having given hints, because they are not able to speak plainly, then man has to do his part to lift up his voice to heaven and ask 'for direction and counsel from that hand, who alone can both direct and deliver.'

"It's important to remember that though Defoe imports a good measure of his Defoe-an sarcasm in his narrative in

FRONTISPIECE FROM AN EARLY EDITION
OF *THE HISTORY OF THE DEVIL*. ENGRAVING BY T. WALLIS

The History of the Devil, and other writings on this subject, he was an intensely committed Christian and Bible scholar and believed he was accompanied by good spirits and ministering angels, guiding him in his life and work."

Chalmers continues in his estimation of Defoe's influence and lasting imprint he left in the hearts and minds of mankind.

"As a novelist, everyone will place him in the foremost rank. Who considers his originality, his performance, and his

> purpose? Who, like Defoe, has ever carried his reader to the sea, in order to mend the heart and regulate the practice of life, by showing his readers the effect of adversity, or how they might be called to sustain his hero's trials, as they sailed around the world. The writings of no author since have run through more numerous editions. And he whose works have pleased generally and pleased long, must be deemed a writer of no small estimation.
>
> "As a commercial writer, Defoe is entitled to stand in the foremost rank of his contemporaries, whatever their performance or fame. He foresaw that man's conduct must finally be directed by his principles... and that when he writes on commerce he seldom fails to insinuate some axiom of morals or to inculcate some precept of religion.
>
> "As an historian, it will be found, that Defoe had few equals in the English language, when he wrote. With extraordinary skill and information, he relates, not only the event, but the transactions which preceded, and the effects which followed. He is at once learned and intelligent. Considering the factiousness of the age, his candor is admirable, and his moderation is exemplary."

Defoe is described as a man full of wit and wisdom combined with a deep commitment to the Word of God and his faith in Christ. He was a man with an exceedingly broad sphere of talents and enterprising interests spanning religion, history, business, politics and economics along with a resolute determination of seeing justice served faithfully in society. He possessed an amiable character and clear sense, but with an ingenuity in conversation that unveiled brutal honesty in matters of man's motives and behavior, which was not always well-received within the various circles of influence Defoe engaged. Of his own character and behavior he confessed himself, "God, I thank thee, I am not a drunkard, or swearer, or a whore master, or a busy-body, or idle, or revengeful; and though this be true, and I challenge all the world to prove the contrary, yet, I must own, I see small satisfaction in all these negatives of common virtues; for thankfully I have not been guilty of any of those vices, nor of any more."

"Defoe was above all, the Man of God," say his biographer, Thomas Wright, "In his Religious Courtship, the dialogue that forms the greater part of it might have been written by John Bunyan, Rowland Hill, Isaac Watts, or Hannah More.

"What I mean is, not that he never sinned, or that all which he did was right, but that his aims and desires were right. His was a great soul, and little souls should beware of measuring him by their own standard. An Achilles in the field who feared not the face of any man, Daniel Defoe before his God was a humble, tearful penitent. To use his own words, 'he was often heard to pray to God in his solitudes very audibly and with great fervency.' The prize of fame he constantly coveted, and it has been awarded to him; but above all things he valued 'the prize of the high calling of God in Christ Jesus.'"

Defoe's Christian faith is reflected in his self-professed favorite verses, which include, "Blessed are those who hunger and thirst after righteousness, for they shall be filled" (Matt. 5:6); and Philippians 4:8, to which Defoe says, "Whatsoever things are honest, pure, lovely, and of good report, think of these things, for the practice of such results in a gentleman and a Christian."

THE CHIEF WRITINGS OF DANIEL DEFOE

NOVELS

- *The Consolidator, or Memoirs of Sundry Transactions from the World in the Moon: Translated from the Lunar Language* (1705)
- *Robinson Crusoe* (1719)—originally published in two volumes:
  - *The Life and Strange Surprizing Adventures of Robinson Crusoe, of York, Mariner: Who Lived Eight and Twenty Years* (1719)
  - *The Farther Adventures of Robinson Crusoe: Being the Second and Last Part of His Life*
- *The King of Pirates* (1719)
- *Serious Reflections During the Life and Surprising Adventures of Robinson Crusoe: With his Vision of the Angelick World* (1720)
- *Captain Singleton* (1720)
- *Memoirs of a Cavalier* (1720)
- *A Journal of the Plague Year* (1722)
- *Colonel Jack* (1722)
- *Moll Flanders* (1722)
- *Roxana: The Fortunate Mistress* (1724)

NON-FICTION

- *An Essay Upon Projects* (1697)
- *The Storm* (1704)
- *Atlantis Major* (1711)
- *The Family Instructor* (1715)
- *Memoirs of the Church of Scotland* (1717)
- *The History of the Remarkable Life of John Sheppard* (1724)
- *A Narrative of All the Robberies, Escapes, &c. of John Sheppard* (1724)
- *A Tour Through the Whole Island of Great Britain, Divided into Circuits or Journeys* (1724–1727)
- *A New Voyage Round the World* (1724)
- *The Political History of the Devil* (1726)
- *The Complete English Tradesman* (1726)
- *A Treatise Concerning the Use and Abuse of the Marriage Bed* (1727)
- *A Plan of the English Commerce* (1728)

PAMPHLETS OR ESSAYS (PROSE)

- *The Poor Man's Plea* (1698)
- *The History of the Kentish Petition* (1701)
- *The Shortest Way with the Dissenters; Or Proposals for the Establishment of the Church* (1702)
- *The Great Law of Subordination Considered* (1704)
- *Giving Alms No Charity, and Employing the Poor* (1704)
- *The Apparition of Mrs. Veal* (1706)
- *An Appeal to Honour and Justice, Though it be of His Worst Enemies, by Daniel Defoe, Being a True Account of His Conduct in Publick Affairs* (1715)
- *A Vindication of the Press: Or, An Essay on the Usefulness of*

Writing, on Criticism, and the Qualification of Authors (1718)
- *Everybody's Business, Is Nobody's Business* (1725)
- *The Protestant Monastery* (1726)
- *Parochial Tyranny* (1727)
- *Augusta Triumphans* (1728)
- *Second Thoughts are Best* (1729)
- *An Essay Upon Literature* (1726)
- *Mere Nature Delineated* (1726)
- *Conjugal Lewdness* (1727)

PAMPHLETS OR ESSAYS (VERSE)

- *The True-Born Englishman: A Satyr* (1701)
- *Hymn to Pillory* (1703)
- *An Essay on the late Storm* (1704)

THE AUTHOR'S PREFACE

The subject of this history is singular, and it has been handled in a singular manner. The wise part of the world has been pleased with it. The merry part has been diverted by it and the ignorant part has been taught by it. None but the malicious part of the world has been offended at it. Who can wonder, then, that when the Devil is not pleased, his friends should be angry?

The strangest thing of it all is to hear Satan complain that the story is handled profanely. But who can think it strange that his advocates should be what he was from the beginning?

The author affirms, and has good vouchers for it (in the opinion of such whose judgment passes with him for an authority), that the whole tenor of the work is solemn, calculated to promote serious religion, and capable of being improved in a religious manner. But he does not think we are bound never to speak of the Devil except with an air of terror, as if we were always afraid of him.

It's evident the Devil, as subtle and as frightful as he is, has played the ridiculous and foolish part as much as most of God's creatures, and daily does so. And he cannot believe it's any sin to expose him for a foolish Devil, as he is, or show the world that he may be laughed at.

Those who think the subject is not handled with enough gravity have all the room given them in the world to handle it better. And as the author professes, he is far from thinking his piece to be perfect, so they ought not to be angry that he gives them permission to mend it. He has had the satisfaction to please some readers and to see good men approve it, and for the rest, as my Lord Rochester says in another case:

"He counts their censure fame."

As for a certain reverend gentleman, who is gravely pleased to dislike the work, he hopes rather for the author's sake than the Devil's, the author only says, let the performance be how it will and the author what he will. It is apparent he has not yet preached away all his hearers.

It is enough to me, says the author, that the Devil himself is not pleased with my work, and less with the design of it. Let the Devil and all his fellow complainers stand on one side, and the honest, well meaning, charitable world who approve my work on the other, and I'll count noses with Satan, if he dares.

THE AUTHOR'S DEDICATION

AS CONCERNING A DEDICATION

It is case before me to determine who has the most right to a dedication of this work.

Ancient usage would have directed a solemn author to address these sheets to the great Majesty of heaven in congratulation of His glorious victory over the Devil and his angels, but I decline that method as profane.*

The same reason forbids me from addressing it to Him who conquered him on earth and who, when the Devil was so insolent as to assault Him, made him fly like a vanquished rebel with merely the word, *Get thee behind me.*

I then had some thoughts of inscribing it to Satan himself, but I did not really know how to relish holding a parley with the Devil, talking to him in the first person, and, indeed as it were, making all my readers do so too. And besides, since I knew there was so very little in the whole work that Satan would be pleased with, I was loath to compliment him while I was exposing him, which would be to imitate the very hypocrisy by which he is

* Irreverent, unworthy

distinguished and, you might say, I played the devil with the Devil.

With these difficulties presented, I think giving my reasons for making no dedication is dedication enough.

SATAN CAST OUT OF HEAVEN

PART I

THE HISTORY OF THE DEVIL

1

BEING AN INTRODUCTION TO THE WHOLE WORK.

I doubt not but the title of this book will amuse some of my reading friends a little at first. They will hesitate, perhaps, as they do at a witch's prayer, and spend some time resolving whether they had best look into it or not lest they should really raise the Devil by reading his story.

Children and old women have told themselves so many frightful things of the Devil, and they have formed ideas of him in their minds in so many horrible and monstrous shapes, that really it would be enough to frighten the Devil himself to meet himself in the dark dressed up in the various figures that imagination has formed for him in the minds of men. And as for them, I cannot think by any means that the Devil would terrify them half so much if they were to converse with him face to face.

It must certainly therefore be a most useful undertaking to give the true history of this tyrant of the air, this god of the world, this terror and aversion of mankind, which we call Devil, to show what he is and what he is not, where he is and where he is not, and when he is in us and when he is not. For I cannot doubt but that the Devil is really and in fact in a great many of our honest weak-headed friends, when they themselves know nothing of the matter.

Nor is the work so difficult as some may imagine. The Devil's history is not so hard to come by as it seems to be. His origination and the first rise of his family is recorded. And as for his conduct, he has acted indeed in the dark as to method in many things. But in general, as cunning as he is, he has been foolish enough to expose himself in some of the most considerable transactions of his life, and he has not shown himself a politician at all. Our old friend, Machiavel, outdid him in many things. And I may in the process of this work give an account of several of the sons of Adam, and some societies of them too, who have outwitted the Devil—indeed, who have out-sinned the Devil and, I think, may be seen as out-shooting him with his own bow.

It may perhaps be expected of me in this history that since I seem inclined to speak favorably of Satan, to do him justice, and to write his story impartially, I should take some pains to tell you what religion he is of. And even this part may not be so much a jest as at first sight you may take it to be; for Satan has something of religion in him, I assure you. Nor is he such an unprofitable devil that way as some may suppose him to be. For though in reverence to my brethren I will not reckon him among the clergy, yet I cannot deny that he often preaches. And if what he preaches is not profitable to his hearers, it is as much their fault as it is by his own design.

It has indeed been suggested that he has taken orders, and that a certain pope famous for being an extraordinary favorite of his gave him both institution and induction. But as this is not in the record, and therefore we have no authentic document for the audition, I shall not affirm it for a truth. For I would not slander the Devil.

It is said also, and I am apt to believe it, that he was very familiar with that holy father, Pope Silvester II. And some charge him with impersonating the infamous Pope Hildebrand on an extraordinary occasion and seating himself in the apostolic chair in a full congregation. And you may hear more of this hereafter. But as I do not see Pope Diabolus among the list in father Platina's *Lives of the Popes,* so I am willing to leave it as I find it.

But to speak to the point, and a nice point it is I acknowledge, namely, what religion the Devil is of, my answer will indeed be general yet not at all ambiguous; for I love to speak positively and with undoubted evidence.

1. **He is a believer.** And in saying so, if it should follow that even the Devil has more religion than some of our men of fame can at this time be charged with, I hope my Lord____ and his Grace, the____ of____, and some of the upper class in the Redhot Club will not wear the coat regardless of how well it may fit them, or challenge the satire as if it were pointed at them, because it is due to them, in a word (whatever their lordships are), that I can assure them the Devil is no infidel.

2. **He fears God.** We have such abundant evidence of this in sacred history that unless I were (in common with a few others) talking to an infidel-sort of gentleman with whom those remote things called Scriptures are not allowed in evidence, I might say it were sufficiently proved. But I don't hesitate in the process of this undertaking to show that the Devil really fears God, and in a different way than he ever feared St. Francis or St. Dunstan. And if that be proved, as I take upon myself to advance, I shall leave it to judgment who is the better Christian, the Devil, who believes and trembles, or our modern gentry of those who believe neither God nor Devil.

Having thus brought the Devil within the pale, I shall leave him among you for the present—but only so I may examine in its order who has the best claim to his brotherhood, the papists or the protestants, and among the latter, the Lutherans or the Calvinists. And so descending to all the several denominations of churches, I do this to see who has less of the Devil in them and who has more, and whether less or more, to see if the Devil has not a seat in every synagogue, a pew in every church, a place in every pulpit, and a vote in every synod, even from the Sanhedrin of the Jews to our friends at the Bull and Mouth, and so forth, from the greatest to the least.

It will, I confess, come very much within the scope of this part of my discourse to give an account, or at least make an essay toward the share the Devil has had in spreading religion in the world, and especially in dividing and subdividing opinions in religion to perhaps make it reach the farther. And also to show how far he is or has made himself a missionary of the famous clan *de propaganda file*, it is true that we find him heartily employed in almost every corner of the world *ad propagandum errorem* [to propagate an error]. But that discourse may require a history by itself.

As to his propagating religion, it is a little hard indeed at first sight to charge the Devil with propagating religion—that is to say, if we take it literally and in its totality. But if you take it as the Scots insisted, to take the oath of fidelity, viz., with an explanation, it is clear that Satan has very often had a share in the method, if not in the design, of propagating Christian faith. For example:

I think I do no injury at all to the Devil to say that he had a great hand in the Holy War, as it was ignorantly and enthusiastically called, and in stirring up the Christian princes and powers of Europe to madly run after the Turks and Saracens and make war with those innocent people over a thousand miles away only because they entered into God's heritage when he had forsaken it, grazed upon his ground when he had fairly turned it into a common, and laid it open for the next comer. They spent the nation's treasure and embarked their kings and people, I say, in a war over a thousand miles away, filling their heads with that religious madness called in those days, "holy zeal," to recover the *terra sancta*, the sepulchers of Christ and the saints, and as they called it falsely, the "holy city," though true religion says it was the accursed city and not worth spending one drop of blood for.

This religious bubble was certainly of Satan, who (as he craftily drew them in like a true Devil) left them in the lurch when they came there, turned about to the Saracens, animated the immortal Saladin against them, and managed so dexterously that he left the bones of about thirteen or fourteen hundred thousand Christians there as a trophy of his infernal politics. And after the Christian world had run *à la santa terra*—or in English, a sauntering of about a hundred years—he dropped it to play another game less foolish but ten times wickeder than that which went before it, namely, turning the Crusades of the Christians one against another. And as Hudibras said in another case, he,

> Made them fight like mad or drunk,
> For dame Religion as for puck.

Of this you have a complete account in the history of the popes' decrees against the Count de Toulouse, the Waldenses, and the Albigenses, with the Crusades and massacres that followed them. To do the Devil's politics some justice, he met with all the success he could desire, and the zealots of that day executed his infernal orders most punctually and planted religion in those countries in a glorious and triumphant manner through the destruction of an infinite number of innocent people whose blood has fattened the soil for the growth of the Catholic faith in a manner very particular and to Satan's full satisfaction.

To complete this part of his history, I might give you the detail of his progress in these first steps of his alliances with Rome and add a long list of massacres, wars, and expeditions in behalf of religion, which he has had the honor to have a visible hand in, such as the Parisian massacre, the Flemish war under the Duke d'Alva, the Smithfield fires in the Marian days in England, and the massacres in Ireland, all which would most effectually convince us that the Devil has not been idle in his business. But I may meet with these again in my way. While I am discussing things in general only, it is enough to mention them thus in a summary way. I say, it is enough to prove that the Devil has really been as much concerned as anybody in the methods taken by some people for propagating the Christian religion in the world.

Some have rashly, and I almost said maliciously, charged the Devil with the great triumphs of his friends the Spaniards in America and would place the conquest of Mexico and Peru to the credit of his account.

But I cannot join with them in that at all. I must say, I believe the Devil was innocent of that matter. My reason is because Satan was never such a fool as to spend his time or his politics or embark his allies to conquer nations who were already his own. That would be Satan against Beelzebub, a making war upon himself, and at least doing nothing to the purpose.

If they should charge him with deluding Phillip II of Spain

into that preposterous attempt called the Armada (Anglicè, the Spanish Invasion), I should indeed more readily join with them. But whether he did it weakly in hope that it should succeed, which was not likely, or wickedly to destroy the great fleet of the Spaniards and draw them in within the reach of his own dominions (this being a question which authors differ exceedingly about), I shall leave it to decide itself.

But the greatest piece of management that we find the Devil has concerned himself with of late in the matter of religion seems to be that of the mission into China. And here indeed Satan has acted his masterpiece. It was no doubt much for his service that the Chinese should have no insight into matters of religion, I mean that we call Christian. And therefore, though popery and the Devil are not at so much variance as some may imagine, yet he did not think it safe to let the general system of Christianity be heard of among them in China. Hence, when the name of the Christian religion had just been received with some seeming approbation in the country of Japan, Satan immediately, as if alarmed at the thing and dreading what the consequence of it might be, armed the Japanese against it with such fury that they expelled it at once.

It was much safer to his designs when he (if the story is not a fiction) put that Dutch witticism into the mouths of the States' commanders when they came to Japan. Having more wit than to present themselves as Christians in such a place as that, when the question was put to them they answered negatively, that they were not, but were instead of another religion, called Hollanders.

However, it seems the diligent Jesuits outwitted the Devil in China and, as I said above, overshot him with his own bow. For the mission being in danger by the Devil and the Chinese emperor joining together, with them in danger of being wholly expelled there too as they had been in Japan, they cunningly fell in with the ecclesiastics of the country. And by joining the priestcraft of both religions together, they brought Jesus Christ and Confucius to be so reconcilable that the Chinese and the Roman idolatry appeared capable of a confederacy, of going on hand in hand together, and consequently of being very good friends.

This was a masterpiece indeed, and as they say, it almost frightened Satan out of his wits. But being a ready manager and particularly famous for serving himself with the rogueries of the priests, he faced about immediately to the mission. And making a virtue of necessity, he clapped in to the proposal with all possible alacrity.[1] So the Jesuits and he formed a hodgepodge of religion made up of popery and paganism. And they calculated to leave the latter rather worse than they found it by blending the faith of Christ and the philosophy or morals of Confucius together and formally christening them by the name of religion. By that means the political interest of the mission was preserved, and yet Satan lost not one inch of ground with the Chinese, no, not by planting the gospel itself, such as it was, among them.

Nor has it been much advantage to him that this plan or scheme of a new-modeled religion would not go down at Rome, and that the Inquisition damned it with bell, book, and candle. Distance of place served his new allies, the missionaries, and provided them protection from the Inquisition. And now and then a rich, well placed present found them friends in the congregation itself. And where any nuncio with his impudent zeal pretended to take such a long voyage to oppose them, Satan took care to get him sent back *re infecta* or inspired the mission

1 N.B. He never refused setting his hand to any opinion which he thought it for his interest to acknowledge.

to move him off the premises by methods of their own—that is to say (being interpreted) to murder him.

Thus, the mission has in itself been truly devilish, and the Devil has interested himself in planting the Christian religion in China.

The influence the Devil has in the politics of mankind is another special part of his history and would require, if it were possible, a very exact description. But here we shall necessarily be obliged to inquire so carefully into the arcana[2] of circumstances and unlock the cabinets of state in so many courts, canvass the councils of ministers and the conduct of princes so fully, and expose them so much, that it may, perhaps, cause a combustion among the great politicians abroad. And in doing that we may come so near home, too, that though personal safety and prudence forbid our meddling with our own country, we may be taken in a double entendre and fall unpitied for being only suspected of touching truths that are so tender whether we are guilty or not. For these reasons I must meddle less with that part, at least for the present.

Be it that the Devil has had a share in some of the recent councils of Europe, influencing them this way or that way to his own advantage, what is it to us? For example, what if he has had any concern in the late affair of Thorn? Why should we blame him, seeing his confederates the Jesuits with the assessorial tribunal of Poland to take it upon themselves? I shall leave that part to the issue of time. I wish it were as easy to persuade the world that he had no hand in encouraging the injured protestants to commit the arbitration of that affair to the very party and leave the justice due to the cries of Protestant blood to the arbitrement

2 Arcana—plural of *Arcanum*, mysterious or specialized knowledge, language, or information accessible or possessed only by the initiate. (Ed.)

of a popish power, who dare say that the Devil must be in it if justice should be obtained that way. I should rather say, the Devil is in it, or else it would never be expected.

It occurs next to inquire into whether or not the Devil has more influence or less influence in the affairs of the world now than he had in former ages. And as we go along, this will depend on comparing his methods and way of working in past times and the modern politics through which he acts in our days with the differing reception he has met with among the men of such various ages.

But there is so much to inquire into about the Devil, that before we can bring his story down to our modern times we must for the present let that drop and look a little back to the remoter part of his history, draw his picture that people may know him when they meet him, see who and what he is, and see what he has been doing ever since he got permission to act in the high station he now appears in.

In the meantime, if I might be permitted to present an humble petition to Satan, it should be that he would, according to modern usage, oblige us all with writing the history of his own times. It would, as well as one that preceded it, be a devilish good one. For as to the sincerity of the work, the authority of the particulars, and the justice of the characters, and so forth, if they were no better supported as true, no more consistent with themselves, with charity, with truth, and with the honor of an historian than the last of that kind that was circulated among us, it must be a reproach to the Devil himself to be author of it.

Were Satan to be brought under the least obligation to write truth, and that the matters of fact which he should write might be depended upon, he is certainly qualified by his knowledge of things to be a complete historian. Nor could the bishop himself, who by the way has already given us the devil of a history, come up to him. Milton's *Pandemonium,* though an excellent dramatic performance, would appear a mere trifling sing-song business beneath the dignity of Chevy Chase. The Devil could give us a true account of all the civil wars in heaven, how and by whom, and in what manner he lost the day there and was obliged to quit the field. His narrative being his refusing to acknowledge and submit to the Messiah upon Him being declared generalissimo of the heavenly forces (which Satan expected himself as the eldest officer), and his not being able to bear another to be put in over his head.

I say, a fine-spun thought of Mr. Milton would appear to be strained too far and only serve to convince us that he (Milton) knew nothing of the matter. Satan knows very well that the Messiah was declared to be the Son of God with power, fulfilled after the resurrection from the dead, and that all power was then given him in heaven and earth. So Satan's rebellion must derive from other causes and upon other occasions, as he himself, if he likes, can doubtless give us an account of—which we shall speak further about in his history.

What a fine history might this old gentleman write of the antediluvian world and of all the weighty affairs as well as of the state of religion that happened during the fifteen hundred years of the patriarchal administration!

Then who like him could give a full and complete account of the deluge, whether it was a mere vindictive blast from heaven wrought by a supernatural power in the way of miracle, or whether according to Mr. Burnet's theory it was a consequence following antecedent causes by the mere necessities of nature seen in composition, natural position, and the unavoidable working of things, as by the theory published by that learned enthusiast it seems to be?

Satan could easily account for all the difficulties of the theory and tell us why if there was a natural necessity for the deluge there is not the like necessity and natural tendency for [another] conflagration at last.[3]

If the Devil were to exert himself as an historian for our improvement and diversion, how glorious an account he could give us of Noah's voyage round the world in the famous ark! He could resolve all the difficulties about building it, furnishing it, and laying up of provisions in it for all the collection of animals. He could tell us whether all the creatures came voluntarily to him to go into the ark, or whether he went a-hunting for several years in order to bring them together.

He could give us a true relation of how he beguiled the people of the next world into the absurd, ridiculous undertaking of building a Babel, how high that stupendous staircase (which was in imagination to reach up to heaven) was built before it was interrupted and the builders confounded, how their speech was altered (how many tongues it was divided into or whether they were divided at all), and how many subdivisions or dialects have been made since then by which means very few of God's creatures, except the brutes, understand one another or care one farthing whether they do or not.

In all these things, Satan, who no doubt would make a very good chronologist, could settle every epoch, correct every calendar, and bring all our accounts of time to a general agreement, since to this day the Grecian Olympiads, the Turkish Hegira, the

3 For God promised never to again destroy the world with a flood; see Genesis 9:11-16 (Ed.).

THE TOWER OF BABEL AND THE CONFUSION OF TONGUES (GENESIS 11).

Chinese fictitious accounts of the world's duration, and our blind Julian and Gregorian accounts put the world in such confusion, that we neither agree in our holy days or working days, fasts or feasts, nor keep the same Sabbath in any part of the same globe.

This great expert of antiquities could bring us to a certainty in all the difficulties of ancient story and tell us whether the tale of the siege of Troy and the rape of Helen was a fable of Homer, or a history, whether the narratives of the poets are formed from their own brain or founded in facts, and whether letters were invented by Cadmus the Phœnician or dictated immediately from heaven at Mount Sinai.

Indeed, he could tell us how and in what manner he beguiled Eve, deluded Adam, put Cain into a passion till he made him murder his own brother, and made Noah, who was above five hundred years a preacher of righteousness, turn sot in his old age, dishonor all his ministry, debauch himself with wine, and by getting drunk and exposing himself become the jest and laughingstock of his children and of all his posterity to this day.

And if Satan were to enter into the characters of the great men of his age according to the modern practice of the late right reverend historian, how might we be diverted with the just history of Adam in Paradise and out of it, his character, how he behaved at and after his expulsion, how Cain wandered in the land of Nod, what the mark was that God set upon him, whose daughter his wife was, and how big the city was that he built there according to a certain poet of noble extraction.

How Cain in the land of Nod
When the rascal was all alone
Like an owl in an ivy tod
Built a city as big as Roan. —ROCH

He certainly could have drawn Eve's picture, told us every feature in her face and every inch in her shape, whether she was a perfect beauty or not, and whether with the fall she grew crooked, ugly, ill-natured, and a scolder, as the learned Valdemar suggests to be the effect of the curse.

Descending to the characters of the patriarchs in that age, he might, no doubt, give us in particular the characters of Belus (worshipped under the name of Baal, Saturn, and Jupiter), who his successors were, and how they behaved, along with all the Pharaohs of Egypt, the Abimilechs of Canaan, and the monarchs of Assyria and Babylon.

Hence, also, he is able to write the lives of all the heroes of the world, from Alexander of Macedon to Louis XIV, and from Augustus to the great King George. Nor could the bishop himself go beyond him for flattery any more than the Devil himself could go beyond the bishop for falsehood.

I could enlarge with a particular satisfaction upon the many fine things which Satan, rummaging through that inexhaustible storehouse of slander, could set down to blacken the characters of good men and load the best princes of the world with infamy and reproach.

But we shall never prevail upon him, I doubt, to do mankind so much service as resolving all those difficulties. For he has an indelible grudge against us since he believes, and perhaps is sure, that men were at first created by his Sovereign with the intent that, after a certain state of probation in life, such of them as shall be approved will be appointed to fill up those vacancies in the heavenly host that were made by the abdication and expulsion of him and his angels.

So man is appointed to come in Satan's stead to make good the breach and enjoy all those ineffable joys and beatitudes which Satan enjoyed before his fall. No wonder, then, that the Devil swells with envy and rage at mankind in general, and at the best of them in particular. Indeed, acknowledging this point is giving an unanswerable reason why the Devil practices with such unwearied and indefatigable application upon the best men to, if possible, disappoint God Almighty's decree that He should not find enough among the whole race to be proper subjects of His clemency and qualified to succeed the Devil and his host, or fill up the places vacated by the fall!

It is true, indeed. The Devil, who we have reason to say is no fool, ought to know better than to suppose he could by the success of his wickedness thwart or disappoint the determined purposes of heaven if he could seduce the whole race of mankind and make them as bad as he is. Notwithstanding all that the Devil and all the host of hell can do to prevent it, those who are appointed to inherit the thrones that he and his followers abdicated and were deposed from shall certainly be preserved in spite of all his devices for that inheritance and shall have the possession secured to them.

But he knows the certainty of this and that when he endeavors to seduce the chosen servants of the Most High, he fights against God himself, struggles with irresistible grace, makes war with infinite power to undermine the Church of God and faith in Him, which are fortified with eternal promises of Jesus Christ that the gates of hell—that is to say, the Devil and all his power—shall not prevail against them (Matt. 16:18). I say, he knows how impossible it is that he should obtain his ends. Yet he is so blind in his rage, and so infatuate is his wisdom, that he cannot refrain from breaking himself to pieces against this mountain and splitting against this rock, *qui Jupiter vult perdere hos dementat* [who Jupiter desires to destroy these is mad].

But to leave this serious part, which is a little too solemn for the account of this rebel, seeing we are not to expect him to write his own history for our information and diversion, I shall see if I cannot write it for him. In order to do this, I shall extract the substance of his whole story from the beginning to our own times, which I shall collect out of what is come to hand. (Whether it come by revelation or inspiration, that is nothing to him.) I shall take care to improve my intelligence in such a way as may make my account of him authentic and, in a word, such as the Devil himself shall not be able to contradict.

In writing this uncouth story, I shall be freed from the censures of the critics (in a more than ordinary manner) upon one account especially—that my story shall be so just and so well grounded, and all the good things I shall say of Satan will be so little to his satisfaction, that the Devil himself will not be able to say I dealt with the Devil in writing it. I might, perhaps, give you some account of where I received my intelligence and how all the arcana of his management have come into my hands; but pardon me, gentlemen, this would be to betray conversation and to reveal my agents. And you know statesmen are very careful to preserve the correspondence they keep in the enemy's country lest they expose their friends to the resentment of the powers whose councils they betray.

Besides, the learned tell us that ministers of state make an excellent plea of their not betraying their intelligence against all party inquiries into the great sums of money pretended to be paid for secret service—whether the secret service was to bribe people to betray things abroad or at home, and whether the money was paid to somebody or to nobody and employed to establish correspondences abroad or establish families and amass treasure at home. And in a word, whether it was to serve their country or serve themselves, it has been the same thing, and the same plea has been their protection. Likewise, in the important affair I am undertaking, it is hoped you will not desire me to betray my correspondents; for you know Satan is naturally cruel and malicious, and who knows what he might do to show his resentment? At least it might endanger a discontinuance of our intelligence for the future.

And yet, before I finish, I shall make it very plain that however my information may be secret and difficult, yet I came very honestly by it and shall make a very good use of it. For it is a great mistake to think that an acquaintance with the affairs of the Devil may not be made very useful to us all. They that know no evil can know no good. And as the learned tell us, a stone taken out of the head of a toad is a good antidote against poison. So a competent knowledge of the Devil and all his ways may be the best help to make us defy the Devil and all his works.

2

OF THE WORD "DEVIL," AS IT IS A PROPER NAME TO THE DEVIL, AND ANY OR ALL HIS HOST, ANGELS, ETC.

It is a question not yet determined by the learned whether the word Devil is a singular, that is to say, the name of a person standing by himself, or a noun of multitude. If it is a singular, and so must be used personally only as a proper name, it consequently implies one imperial devil, monarch, or god of the whole clan of hell—justly distinguished by the term, The Devil, or as the Scots call him, The muckle-horned Dee'l, or as others in a wilder dialect, The Devil of Hell—that is to say, The Devil of a devil, or (better still) as the Scripture expresses it by way of emphasis, the great red dragon, the Devil, and Satan.

But if we take this word to be, as above, a noun of multitude, and so to be used ambidextrously, as occasion presents (singular or plural), then *the Devil* signifies Satan by himself, or Satan with all his legions at his heels, as you please, more or less. And this way of understanding the word, as it may be very convenient for my purpose in the account I am now to give of the infernal powers, is not altogether improper in the nature of the thing. It is thus expressed in Scripture, where the person possessed (Matt. 4:24) is first said to be possessed by the Devil, singular. And our Savior asks him, as speaking to a single person, *"What is thy name?"* But it is answered in the plural and singular together, *"My name is Legion; for we are many"* (Mark 5:9 NKJV). (See also Luke 8:30).

Nor will it be any wrong to the Devil, supposing him a single person, seeing that it entitles him to control all his inferior agents. And he will take that as an addition to his infernal glory rather than a diminution or lessening of him in the extent of his fame.

Having thus articled with the Devil for liberty of speech, I shall talk of him sometimes in the singular, as a person, and sometimes in the plural, as a host of devils, or of infernal spirits, just as occasion requires and as the history of his affairs makes necessary.

But before I enter upon any part of his history, the nature of the thing calls me back, and my Lord B ____ of ____ in his recent, famous orations in defense of liberty, summons me to prove that there is such a thing or such a person as the Devil. And in short, as my Lord ____ said very well, unless I can give some evidence of his existence, I am talking of nobody.

> "D—mn me, sir," says a graceless comrade of his to a great man. "Your Grace will go to the Devil."
>
> "D—mn you, Sir," says the Devil. "Then I shall go nowhere. I wonder where you intend to go?"
>
> "Indeed, to the Devil too, I suspicion," says Graceless; "for I am almost as wicked as my Lord Duke."
>
> DEVIL. You are a silly, empty dog, says the Devil, and if there is such a place as a hell, though I believe nothing of it, it is a place for fools, such as you are.

GRACELESS. I wonder, then, what heaven the great wits go to, such as my Lord Duke? I don't care to go there, no matter where it is; for they are an excessively tiresome kind of people. There's no bearing them. They'll make a hell wherever they go.

D. Please, hold your fool's tongue. I tell you, if there is any such place as we call *nowhere,* that's all the heaven or hell that I know of or believe anything about.

GR. Very good, my Lord ____. So heaven is nowhere, and hell is nowhere, and the Devil is nobody, according to my Lord Duke!

D. Yes, sir, and what then?

GR. And you are to go nowhere when you die, are you?

D. Yes, you dog! Don't you know what that incomparable noble genius, my Lord Rochester, sings about the subject? I believe it unfeignedly.

(sings)
After death nothing is,
And nothing death.

GR. You believe it, my Lord! You mean you would fain believe it if you could. But since you put that great genius, my Lord Rochester, upon me, let me play him back upon your grace. I am sure you have read his fine poem about Nothing, in one of the stanzas of which is this beautiful thought:

And to be part of thee[4]
The wicked wisely pray.

4 Meant of nothing (Defoe).

D. You are a foolish dog.

GR. And my Lord Duke is a wise infidel.

D. Why! Is it not wiser to believe no Devil than to be always terrified by him?

GR. But shall I toss another poet upon you, my Lord?

> If it should so fall out, as who can tell,
> But there may be a God, a heaven, and hell
> Mankind had best consider well, for fear
> 't should be too late when their mistakes appear.

D. D—mn your foolish poet, that's not my Lord Rochester?

GR. But how must I be damned if there's no Devil? Is not your grace a little inconsistent there? My Lord Rochester would not have said that and if it please your grace.

D. No, you dog, I am not inconsistent at all, and if I were in charge of you, I'd make you aware of it. I'd make you think yourself damned for lack of a devil.

GR. That's like one of your grace's paradoxes, such as when you swore by God that you did not believe there was any such thing as a God or Devil. So you swear by nothing and damn me to nowhere.

D. You are a critical dog. Who taught you to believe these solemn trifles? Who taught you to say there is a God?

GR. Indeed, I had a better schoolmaster than my Lord Duke.

D. Why, who was your schoolmaster pray tell?

GP. The Devil, and if it please your grace.

D. The Devil! The devil he did! What! You're going to quote Scripture, are you? Please don't tell me of Scripture. I know what you mean; *"the devils also believe and tremble"* (James 2:19). Why then, I have the whip-hand of the Devil, for I hate trembling, and I am delivered from it effectually. For I never believed anything of it, and therefore I don't tremble.

GR. And there, indeed, I am a wickeder creature than the Devil, or even than my Lord Duke, for I believe, and yet don't tremble either.

D. Nay, if you are come to do your repentance, I am done with you.

GR. And I think I must be done with my Lord Duke, for the same reason.

D. Ay, ay, pray do, I'll go and enjoy myself. I won't throw away the pleasure of my life. I know the consequence of it.

GR. And I'll go and reform myself, else I know the consequence too.

This short dialogue happened between two men of quality, and both men of wit too. And the effect was, that the Lord brought the reality of the Devil into the question, and the debate brought the profligate to be a penitent. So in short, the Devil was made a preacher of repentance.

The truth is, God and the Devil, however opposite in their nature and remote from one another in their place of abiding, seem to stand pretty much upon a level plane in our faith. For as to our believing the reality of their existence, he who denies one generally denies both, and he who believes one necessarily believes both.

Very few, if any of those who believe there is a God and acknowledge the debt of homage that mankind owes to the supreme Governor of the world, doubt the existence of the Devil, except here and there those whom we call practical atheists. And like my Lord Duke, it is the character of an atheist, if there is such a creature on earth, to believe neither God nor Devil.

As the belief of both of these stands upon a level plane, and that God and the Devil seem to have an equal share in our faith, so the evidence of their existence seems to stand upon a level plane, too, in many things. And as they are known by their works in the same particular cases, so they are discovered after the same manner of demonstration.

Indeed, in some respects it is equally criminal to deny the reality of them both, only with this difference: To believe the existence of God is a debt to nature, and to believe the existence of the Devil is a similar debt to reason. One is a demonstration from the reality of visible causes, and the other a deduction from the similar reality of their effects.

One demonstration of the existence of God is from the universal, well-guided consent of all nations to worship and adore a supreme power. One demonstration of the existence of the Devil is from the avowed, ill-guided consent of some nations who, knowing no other god, make a god of the Devil for lack of a better one.

It may be true that those nations have no other ideas of the Devil than as of a superior power. If they thought him a supreme power it would have other effects on them, and they would submit to and worship him with a different kind of fear.

But it is plain they have right notions of him as a devil, or evil spirit, because the best reason (and in some places the only reason) they give for worshipping him is that he may do them no harm. Having no notions at all of him having any power, much less any inclination, to do them any good, they indeed make a mere devil of him while at the same time they bow to him as to a god.

All the ages of paganism in the world have had this notion of the Devil. Indeed, in some parts of the world they also had some deities they honored above him, as being supposed to be beneficent, kind, and inclined as well as capable of giving them good things. For this reason, the more polite heathens, such as the Grecians and the Romans, had their Lares, or household gods, who they paid a particular respect to as being their protectors from hobgoblins, ghosts of the dead, evil spirits, frightful appearances, evil geniuses, and other noxious creatures from the invisible world—or to put it into the language of the day we live in, from the Devil in whatever shape or appearance he might come to them, and from whatever might hurt them.

And what was all that but setting up devils against devils and supplicating one devil under the notion of a good spirit to drive out and protect them from another whom they called a bad spirit—the white devil against the black devil?

This proceeds from the natural notions mankind necessarily entertains of things to come. Superior or inferior, God and the Devil fill up all futurity in our thoughts, and it is impossible for us to form any images in our minds of an immortality and an invisible world except under the notions of perfect felicity or extreme misery.

Now, as these two respect the eternal state of man after life, they are respectively the object of our reverence and affection, or of our horror and aversion. But notwithstanding, they are placed thus in a diametrical opposition in our affections and passions.

They are on an evident level plane as to the certainty of their existence, and, as I said above, they bear an equal share in our faith.

It being then as certain that there is a Devil as that there is a God, I must from this time forward admit no more doubt of his existence nor take any more pains to convince you of it but—speaking of him as a reality in being—proceed to inquire into who he is and whence he came in order to enter directly into the detail of his history.

Now, not to enter into all the metaphysical trumpery of the schools nor wholly confine myself to the language of the pulpit—where we are told to think about God and the Devil—we must endeavor first to form ideas of those things that illustrate the description of rewards and punishment.

In the One (the eternal presence of the highest good and, as a necessary attendant, the most perfect, consummate, durable bliss and felicity springing from the presence of that Being in whom all is possible), supreme blessedness is inexpressibly present, and that in the highest perfection.

And contrariwise, to conceive of a sublime fallen archangel attended with an innumerable host of degenerate, rebel seraphs or angels cast out of heaven together—all guilty of inexpressible rebellion and suffering from that time and to suffer forever the eternal vengeance of the Almighty in an inconceivable manner—his presence (though blessed in itself) is to them the most complete article of terror. They are in themselves perfectly miserable. And to be with whom forever adds an inexpressible misery to any state as well as place fills the minds of those who are to be, or expect to be, banished to them with inconceivable horror and amazement.

ANGELS BATTLE IN THE CLOUDS

But when you have gone over all this and a great deal more of the like, though language that the passions of men collect to amuse one another with is less intelligible, you have said nothing if you omit the main article, namely, the personality of the Devil—nothing till you add to all the rest some description of the company with whom all this is to be suffered, viz., the Devil and his angels.

Now, as to who this Devil and his angels are, what share they have either actively or passively in the eternal miseries of a future state, and to what extent they are agents in or partners with the sufferings of the place, they are difficulties yet not fully discovered by the most learned. Nor do I believe one is made less a difficulty by their meddling with it.

But to come to the person and origin of the Devil, or as I said before, of devils, I concede him to have come from an ancient family, for he is from heaven. And more truly than the Romans could say of their idolized Numa, he is of the race of the gods.

That Satan is a fallen angel, a rebel seraph cast out for his rebellion, it is the general opinion, and it is not my business to dispute things universally received since he was tried, condemned, and the sentence of expulsion was executed on him in heaven, that he is in this world like a transported felon, never to return. His crime, whatever particular aggravations it might have, is certain to amount to high treason against his Lord and governor, who was also his maker, and against whom he rose in rebellion, took up arms, and in a word, raised a horrid and unnatural war in his dominions. But being overcome in battle and made prisoner, he and all his host, whose numbers were infinite—all glorious angels like himself—lost at once their beauty and glory with their innocence and commenced being devils, transformed by crime into monsters and frightful objects. To describe such, human fancy is obliged to draw pictures and descriptions in such forms that are most hateful and frightful to the imagination.

These notions, I doubt not, gave birth to all the beauteous images and sublime expressions in Milton's majestic poem, where though he has played the poet in a most luxuriant manner, he has sinned against Satan most egregiously and done the Devil a manifest injury in a great many particulars, as I shall show in its place. And as I shall be obliged to do Satan justice when I come to that part of his history, Mr. Milton's admirers must pardon me if I let them see that, though I admire Mr. Milton as a poet, he was yet greatly out in matters of history, and especially the history of the Devil. In short, he charged Satan falsely in several particulars, and so he did the same to Adam and Eve too. But that I shall leave till I come to the history of the royal family of Eden, which I resolve to present to you when the Devil and I have finished with one another.

But not to run down Mr. Milton either (whose poetry nor his judgment can be reproached without injury to our own), all those bright ideas of his that make his poem so justly valued, whether or not they are capable of proof as to fact, are, notwithstanding, confirmations of my hypothesis and are taken from a supposition of the personality of the Devil, placing him at the head of the infernal host as a sovereign, elevated spirit and monarch of hell. And as such, it is why I undertake to write his history.

By the word *hell*, I do not suppose, or at least not determine, that his residence or that of the whole army of devils is yet in the same local hell to where the divines tell us he shall be at last chained down or at least confined to. For we shall find he is at present a prisoner at large. I shall take occasion to speak of both circumstances of Satan in its course.

But when I call the Devil the monarch of hell, I am to be understood, as suits the present purpose, that he is the sovereign of all the race of hell—that is to say, of all the devils or spirits of the infernal clan—let their numbers, quality, and powers be what they will.

Upon this supposed personality and superiority of Satan, or as I call it, the sovereignty and government of one devil above all the rest. I say, upon this notion are formed all the systems of the dark side of futurity that we can form in our minds. And so general is the opinion of it that it will hardly bear to be opposed by any other argument—at least an argument that will bear to be reasoned with. All the notions of a parity of devils, or making a commonwealth among the black counsel, seem to be enthusiastic and visionary. But with no consistency or certainty, and so generally exploded, we must not venture so much as to debate the point.

Taking it then, like the generality of mankind do, that there is a grand Devil, a superior of the whole black race, and that they all fell together with their general, Satan, at the head of them, even though he, Satan, could not maintain his high station in heaven, he yet continued his dignity among the rest who are called his servants (in Scripture, his angels), so that he has a kind of dominion or authority over the rest, and that they were all at his command (however many millions in number) and employed by him in all his hellish designs and in all his wicked contrivances for the destruction of man and for the establishment of his own kingdom in the world.

Supposing then, that there is such a superior master-devil over the rest, it remains that we inquire into his character and something of his history. In that, though, we cannot perhaps produce such authentic documents as in the story of other great monarchs, tyrants, and furies of the world. Yet I shall endeavor to speak some things that the experience of mankind may be apt to confirm, and which the Devil himself will hardly be able to contradict.

It being then granted that there is such a thing or person as a master-devil (call him what we will)—that he is thus superior to all the rest in power and in authority, and that all the other evil spirits are his angels, or ministers, or officers to execute his commands, and are employed in his business—it remains to inquire whence he came. How did he come hither into this world? What business is he is employed in? What is his present state, and where and to what part of the creation of God is he limited and restrained? What are the liberties he takes or is allowed to take? In what manner does he work, and how are his instruments likewise allowed to work?

What has he ever done since he commenced being the Devil, and what is he now doing? And what may he yet do before his last and final confinement? Also, what can he not do, and how far may or may not we be said to be exposed to him or have or have not reason to be afraid of him? These and whatever else occurs in the history and conduct of this arch-devil and his agents that may be useful for information, caution, or diversion, you may expect in the process of this work.

I know it has been questioned by some with more face than fear how it is that after a complete victory over the Devil, which they say was at first obtained by the heavenly powers over Satan and his apostate army in heaven when he was cast out of the holy place and dashed down into the abyss of eternal darkness as into a place of punishment (a condemned hole, or place of confinement to be reserved there to the judgment of the great day)—I say, how it is after that entire victory that he could be let loose again and given liberty to range about God's creation like a thief that has broken out of prison, and there to continue his rebellion, commit new ravages and acts of hostility against God, make new efforts at dethroning the Almighty Creator, and in particular, fall upon the weakest of His creatures, man (how after Satan being so entirely vanquished he should be permitted to recover any of his wicked powers and find room to do mischief to mankind).

But they also go further and suggest bold things against the wisdom of heaven in exposing mankind (weak in comparison of the immense extent of the Devil's power) to so manifest an overthrow in so unequal a fight in which mankind is sure, if alone in the conflict, to be bested—to leave man such a dreadful enemy to engage with and so ill furnished with weapons to resist him.

I shall give as good an answer to these objections as the case will admit in their course but must adjourn them for the present.

We have evidence enough to confirm that the Devil is not yet a confined prisoner. I will not suggest that, like our Newgate thieves (to bring little devils and great devils together), he is let out by connivance and has some little latitudes and advantages for mischief by that means and returns at certain seasons to his confinement again. This might hold were it not that the comparison must suggest the power that has cast him down could be deluded, and that the under-keepers or jailers, under whose charge he was in custody, could wink at his excursions and the Lord of the place knows nothing of the matter. But this requires further explanation.

3

OF THE ORIGIN OF THE DEVIL, WHO HE IS, AND WHAT HE WAS BEFORE HIS EXPULSION OUT OF HEAVEN, AND IN WHAT STATE HE WAS FROM THAT TIME TO THE CREATION OF MAN.

To come to a regular enquiry into Satan's affairs it is needful we should go back to his original as far as history and the opinion of the learned world allow us.

It is agreed by all writers, the sacred as well as the profane, that this creature we now call a devil was originally an angel of light, a glorious seraph, and perhaps the choicest of all the glorious seraphs. See how Milton describes his original glory:

Satan, so call him now, his former name
Is heard no more in Heaven; he of the first,
If not the first archangel, great in power,
In favour and preeminence.
—Par. Lost, lib, v.

And again, the same author, and upon the same subject:

Brighter ones amidst the host
Of angels, then that star the stars among.
—*Ib.* lib. vii.

The glorious figure that Satan is supposed to make among the thrones and dominions in heaven is such as we might suppose the highest angel in that exalted train could make. And some think, as above, that he was the chief of the archangels.

Hence that notion (and not ill founded), namely, that the first cause of his disgrace, and on which ensued his rebellion, was occasioned upon God proclaiming his Son *generalissimo* (with him, Supreme Ruler in heaven, giving to Him the dominion of all his works of creation—that already finished as well as that not yet begun), which post of honor, say they, Satan expected to have conferred on himself as next in honor, majesty, and power to God the Supreme.

This opinion is followed by Mr. Milton, too, as appears in the following lines, where he presents all the angels attending at a general summons and God the Father making the following declaration to them:

Hear all ye angels, progeny of light,
Thrones, dominations, princedoms, virtues, powers!
Hear my decree, which unrevok'd shall stand.
This day I have begot whom I declare
My only Son, and on this holy hill
Him have anointed, whom you now behold
At my right hand; your Head I him appoint;
And by myself have sworn to him shall bow
All knees in heaven, and shall confess him Lord;
Under his great vice-regent reign abide
United, as one individual soul,

Forever happy: him who disobeys,
Me disobeys, breaks union, and, that day
Cast out from God and blessed vision, falls
Into utter darkness, deep ingulf'd, his place
Ordained without redemption, without end.

Satan, was affronted at the appearance of a new essence or being in heaven, called the Son of God. For God himself, says Mr. Milton (though erroneously), declared at that time, saying, "This day have I begotten him," and that He should be set up above all the former powers of heaven, of whom Satan (as above) was the chief and who expected if any higher post could be granted, it might be his due. I say, affronted at this, he resolved:

With all his legions to dislodge, and leave
Unworship'd, unobey'd, the throne supreme
Contemptuous.
—Par. Lost, lib. v.

But Mr. Milton is grossly erroneous in ascribing those words, *"This day have I begotten thee,"* to that declaration of the Father before Satan fell, and consequently to a time before the creation, since it is by interpreters agreed to be understood of the incarnation of the Son of God, or at least of the resurrection. See Matthew Pool, on Acts 13:33.[5]

---

5 Mr. Pool's words are these: "Some refer the words, this day have I begotten thee,' to the incarnation of the Son of God, others to the resurrection. Our translators lay the stress on the preposition of which the verb is compounded, and by adding 'again,' (viz.) 'raised up Jesus again' (Acts 13:33), intend it to be understood of the resurrection. And there is ground for it in the context, for the resurrection of Christ is that which St. Paul had propounded in v. 30 of the same chapter as his theme or argument to preach upon.

"Not that Christ at his resurrection began to be the Son of God, but that he

In a word, Satan withdrew with all his followers, malcontent and chagrined, resolved to disobey this new command and not yield obedience to the Son.

But Mr. Milton agrees in the opinion that the number of angels that rebelled with Satan was infinite and suggests in one place that they were the greatest half of all the angelic body or seraphic host.

But Satan with his powers,
_____an host
Innumerable as the stars of night,
Or stars of morning, dew drops, which the sun
Impearls on every leaf and every flow'r. —*Ib.* lib. v.

Be their number as it is, numberless millions and legions of millions, that is not part of my present enquiry. Satan, the leader, guide, and superior (since he was author of the celestial rebellion), is still the great head and master-devil as before. And they still act under his authority—not obeying, but carrying on the same insurrection against God they began in heaven—still making war against heaven in the person of his image and creature man. And though vanquished by the thunder of the Son of God and cast down headlong from heaven, they have yet resumed, or rather not lost either the will or the power to do mischief.

The fall of the angels, with the war in heaven that preceded it, is finely described by Ovid in his *Metamorphoses*, in the war of the Titans against Jupiter, casting mountain upon mountain and hill upon hill (Pelion upon Ossa) in order to scale the adamantine walls and break open the gates of heaven till Jupiter struck them

was manifested then to be so (Rom. 1:4), which before, while He was in a suffering condition, was not so apparent. Some of the ancients have understood these words of the eternal generation of the Son of God, eternity being an everlasting point and one and the same day forever." (Defoe).

with his thunderbolts and overwhelmed them in the abyss.

Vide Ovid. *Metamorphoses.* New translation:

Nor were the Gods themselves secure on high,
For now the Giants strove to storm the sky,
The lawless brood with bold attempt invade
The Gods, and mountains upon mountains laid.
But now the bolt, enraged the Father took,
Olympus from her deep foundation shook,
Their structure nodded at the mighty stroke,
And Ossa's shattered top o'er Pelion broke,
They're in their own ungodly ruins slain.—Lib. i. p. ix.

Then, again, speaking of Jupiter resolving in council to destroy mankind by a deluge and giving the reasons for it to the heavenly host, he says thus, speaking of the demigods and alluding to the good men below:

Think that they in safety can remain,
When I, myself, who o'er immortals reign,
Who send the lightning, and heaven's empire sway,
The stern Lycaön[6] practiced to betray?—*Ib.*

Since, then, so much poetic liberty is taken with the Devil relating to his most early state and the time before his fall, allow me to make a similar excursion relating to his history immediately after the fall and till the creation of man—an interval in which I think much of the Devil's story is to be seen and of which Mr. Milton took little notice, at least it does not seem completely filled up. After that I shall return to honest prose again, and pursue the duty of an historian.

---

6 Satan.

Satan, with hideous ruin thus supprest,
Expell'd the seat of blessedness and rest,
Look'd back and saw the high eternal mound,
Where all his rebel host their outlet found
Restor'd impregnable: the breach made up,
And garrisons of angels ranged a top;
In front, a hundred thousand thunders roll,
And lightnings temper'd to transfix a soul,
Terror of Devils. Satan and his host,
Now to themselves as well as station lost,
Unable to support the hated sight,
Expand seraphic wings, and swift as light
Seek for new safety in eternal night.
In the remotest gulf of dark they land,
Here vengeance gives them leave to make their stand;
Not that to steps and measures they pretend,
Councils and schemes their station to defend,
But broken, disconcerted, and dismay'd,
By guilt and fright to guilt and fright betray'd;
Rage and confusion every spirit possess'd,
And shame and horror swell'd in every breast;
Transforming envy to their essentials burns,
And beauteous angels frightful devils turns.
Thus Hell began; the fire of conscious rage
No years can quench, no length of time assuage.
Material fire, with its intensest flame,
Compared with this can scarce deserve a name;
How should it up to immaterials rise?
When we're all flame, we shall all fire despise.
This fire outrageous and its heat intense
Turns all the pain of loss to pain of sense.

The folding flames concave and inward roll,
Act upon spirit and penetrate the soul
Not force of devils can its new powers repel,
Where'er it burns it finds or makes a hell;
For Satan flaming with unquench'd desire
Forms his own hell and kindles his own fire;
Vanquish'd, not humbl'd, not in will brought low,
But as his powers decline his passions grow;
The malice, viper like, takes vent within,
Gnaws its own bowels, and bursts in its own sin:
Impatient of the change he scorns to bow,
And never impotent in power till now;
Ardent with hate, and with revenge distract,
A will to new attempts, but none to act;
Yet all seraphic, and in just degree,
Suited to spirits' high sense of misery,
Derived from loss which nothing can repair,
And room for nothing left but mere despair.
Here's finish'd Hell! what fiercer fire can burn?
Enough ten thousand worlds to overturn.
Hell's but the frenzy of defeated pride,
Seraphic treason's strong impetuous tide,
Where vile ambition, disappointed first,
To its own rage and boundless hatred curst;
The hate's fann'd up to fury, that to flame,
For fire and fury are in kind the same;
These burn unquenchable in every face,
And the word 'endless' constitutes the place.
O state of being! where being's the only grief,
And the chief torture's to be damn'd to life;
O life! the only thing they have to hate;

The finish'd torment of a future state,
Complete in all the parts of endless misery,
And worse ten thousand times than not to be!
Could but the damn'd th' immortal law repeal,
And devils die, there'd be an end of hell;
Could they that thing called 'being' annihilate,
There'd be no sorrows in a future state;
The wretch, whose crimes had shut him out on high,
Could be revenged on God himself, and die;
Job's wife was in the right, and always we
Might end by death all human misery,
Might have it in our choice, to be, or not to be.

4

OF THE NAME OF THE DEVIL, HIS ORIGIN, AND THE NATURE OF HIS CIRCUMSTANCES SINCE HE HAS BEEN CALLED BY THAT NAME.

The Scripture is the first writing on earth where we find the Devil called by his own proper distinguishing denomination, Devil, or the Destroyer.[7] Nor indeed is there any other author of antiquity or of sufficient authority who says anything of that kind about him.

Here he makes his first appearance in the world, and on that occasion he is called the serpent. But the serpent, however (since made to signify the Devil when spoken of in general terms), was but the Devil's representative, or the Devil *in quovis vehiculo* [in any vehicle] for that time, clothed in a bodily shape and acting under cover and in disguise—or, if you will, the Devil in masquerade. But if we believe Mr. Milton, the angel Gabriel's spear had such a secret powerful influence that it make him suddenly strip, and with a touch, to unmask and stand upright in his naked original shape a mere devil without any disguises whatsoever.

Now as we go to the Scripture for much of his history, so

7 The meaning of the word Devil, is *destroyer*. See Pool, upon Acts 13:10. (Defoe).

we must go there also for some of his names. And he has a great variety of names indeed, as his several mischievous doings guide us to conceive of him. The truth is, all the ancient names given him, of which the Scripture is full, seem to be originals derived from and adapted to the several steps he has taken and the several shapes he has appeared in to do mischief in the world.

- Here he is called the serpent, Gen. 3:1.
- The old serpent, Rev. 12:9.
- The great red dragon, Rev. 12:3.
- The accuser of the brethren, Rev. 12:10.
- The enemy, Matt. 13:39.
- Satan, Job 1; Zech. 3:1,2.
- Belial, 2 Cor. 6:15.
- Beelzebub, Matt. 12:24.
- Mammon, Matt. 6:24.
- The angel of light, 2 Cor. 11:14.
- The angel of the bottomless pit, Rev. 9:11.
- The prince of the power of the air, Eph. 2:2.
- Lucifer, Isa. 14:12.
- Abaddon, or Apollyon, Rev. 9:11.
- Legion, Mark 5:9.
- The god of this world, 2 Cor. 4:4.
- The foul spirit, Mark 9:5.
- The unclean spirit, Mark 1:27 ["unclean spirits," *pl.* referencing devils].
- The tempter, Matt. 4:3.

But to sum them all up in one, he is called in the New Testament plain Devil.

All his other names are varied according to the custom of

speech and the dialects of the several nations where he is spoken of. But in a word, *Devil* is the common name of the Devil in all the known languages of the earth. Indeed, all the mischief he is empowered to do is placed to his account in Scripture under the particular title of the Devil and not of *devils* in the plural number, though they are sometimes mentioned too. But in the singular it is the identical individual Devil, in and under whom all the little devils, and all the great devils, if there be such, are supposed to act and be governed and directed by him.

Thus, we are told in Scripture of the works of the devil, 1 John 3:8; of casting out the devil, Mark 1:34; of resisting the devil, James 4:5; of our Savior being tempted of the devil, Matt. 4:1; of Simon Magus, a child of the devil, Acts 13:10; and of the devil coming down in a great wrath, Rev. 12:12; and the like. And according to the usage in speech we go on to this day, all the infernal things we converse with in the world are fathered through the Devil, as one undivided simple essence by however many agents are working.

Everything evil, frightful in appearance, wicked in its actions, horrible in its manner, and monstrous in its effects is called the Devil. In a word, *Devil* is the common name for all devils, that is to say, for all evil spirits, all evil powers, all evil works, and even all evil things. Yet it is remarkable *Devil* is no Old Testament word, and we only find it used in all the Old Testament four times,[8] and then not once in the singular number, and not once to signify Satan as it is now understood.

It is true, the learned give a great many differing interpretations of the word *Devil.* The English commentators tell us it means a destroyer—others that it signifies a deceiver. And

8 Lev. 17:7; Deut. 32:17; 2 Chron. 11:15; Psalm 106:37.

the Greeks derive it from a *calumniator,* or false witness; for we find that Calumny was a goddess to whom the Athenians built altars and offered sacrifices during some solemn occasions. And they call her *Diabole,* whence came the masculine, *Diabolos,* which we translate Devil.

Thus, we take the name of Devil to signify not persons only, but actions and habits, making imaginary devils, and transforming that substantial creature called Devil into everything noxious and offensive. Thus, St. Francis, being tempted by the Devil in the shape of a bag of money lying in the highway, and the saint having discovered the fraud, whether seeing his cloven foot hang out of the purse or whether he distinguished him by his smell of Sulphur (or how otherwise, authors are not agreed), but, I say, having discovered the deception and outwitted the Devil, the saint took occasion to preach that eminent sermon to his disciples, where his text was, *Money is the Devil.*

Nor, upon the whole, is any wrong done to the Devil by this kind of treatment. It only gives him the sovereignty of the whole army of hell and makes all the numberless legions of the bottomless pit servants, or, as the Scripture calls them, angels to Satan, the grand devil. And all their actions, performances, and achievements are justly attributed to him, not as the prince of devils only but the emperor of devils, the prince of all the princes of devils.

Under this denomination then of *Devil,* all the powers of hell, all the princes of the air, all the black armies of Satan are comprehended, and in this manner they are to be understood in this whole work, *mutatis mutandis* [things having been changed that have to be changed], according to the several circumstances in which we are to speak of them.

This being premised, and my authority being so good, Satan must not take it ill if I treat him after the manner of men and give him those titles that he is best known by among us. For indeed, having so many, it is not very easy to call him out of his name.

However, as I am obliged by the duty of an historian to decency, as well as impartiality, I thought it necessary, before I used too much freedom with Satan, to produce authentic documents and bring antiquity upon the stage to justify the manner of my writing and let you see I shall describe him in no colors, nor call him by any name, but what he has been known by for many ages before me.

And now, though writing to the common understanding of my reader, I am obliged to treat Satan very coarsely and to speak of him in the common acceptation, calling him plain Devil, a word that in this mannerly age is not so sonorous as others might be, and which by the error of the times is apt to prejudice us against his person. Yet it must be acknowledged that he has a great many other names and surnames by which he might be known of a less obnoxious import than that of Devil, or Destroyer, and so forth.

Mr. Milton, indeed lacking titles of honor to give to the leaders of Satan's host, is obliged to borrow several of his Scripture names and bestow them upon his infernal heroes, whom he makes the generals and leaders of the armies of hell. And so he makes Beelzebub, Lucifer, Belial, Mammon, and some others, to be the names of particular devils, members of Satan's upper house, or Pandemonium, whereas, indeed, these are all names proper and peculiar to Satan himself.

The Scripture also has some names of a coarser kind by which the Devil is understood. Particularly, as is noted already in the Apocalypse, he is called the Great Red Dragon, the Beast, the Old

Serpent, and the like. But take it in the Scripture, or where you will in history (sacred or profane), you will find that in general *the Devil* is, as I have said above, his ordinary name in all languages and in all nations–the name by which he and his works are principally distinguished.

Also, besides that the Scripture often gives him this name, it speaks of the works of the devil, of the subtlety of the devil, of casting out devils, of being tempted by the devil, and of being possessed with a devil. And so many other expressions of that kind, as I have said already, are made use of for us to understand the evil spirit by, that in a word, *devil* is the common name of all wicked spirits. For Satan is no more the devil as if he alone is so and all the rest were a diminutive species who did not go by that name, but I say, even in Scripture every spirit, whether under his dominion or out of his dominion, is called devil and is as much a real devil (that is to say, a condemned spirit) and employed in the same wicked work as Satan himself.

His name, then, being thus ascertained and his existence acknowledged, it should be a little inquired as to what he is. We believe there is such a thing, such a creature as the Devil, and that he has been, and may still with propriety of speech and without injustice to his character, be called by his ancient name, *Devil.*

But who is he? What is his origin? Whence came he? And what is his present station and condition? For these things and these inquiries are very necessary to his history. And indeed, no part of his history can be complete without them.

That he is of an ancient and noble origin must be acknowledged, for he is heaven-born and of the angelic race, as has been touched upon already. If Scripture evidence may be of any weight in the question, there is no room to doubt the genealogy of the Devil. He is not only spoken of as an angel, but as a fallen angel, and one who had been in heaven, had beheld the face of God in his full effulgence of glory, and had surrounded the throne of the Most High. Whence, commencing to be a rebel and being expelled, he was cast down, down—down to where God and the Devil himself only know; for indeed we cannot say that any man on earth knows it. But wherever it is, he has, ever since man's creation, been a plague to mankind, been a tempter, a deluder, a calumniator, an enemy, and the object of man's horror and aversion.

As his origin is heaven-born, and his race angelic, so the angelic nature is evidently placed in a class superior to the human, and this the Scripture is expressive also. When speaking of man, it says He *"made him a little lower than the angels"* (Psalm 8:5).

Thus, as mean thoughts as you may have of him, the Devil is of a better family than any of you, indeed, than the best gentleman of you all. What he may be fallen to is one thing, but what he is fallen from is another. And therefore, I must tell my learned and reverend friend J. W., LL.D.,[9] when he spoke so rudely of the Devil lately, that in my opinion he abused his betters.

Nor is the Scripture more help to us in the search after the Devil's origin than it is in our search after his nature. It is true, authors are not agreed about his age, what time he was created, how many years he enjoyed his state of blessedness before he fell, or how many years he continued with his whole army in a state of darkness before the creation of man. It is supposed it might be a considerable space, and that it was a part of his punishment too, being all the while inactive, unemployed, having no business, nothing to do but gnawing his own bowels, and rolling in the

9 LL.D—doctor of laws (Ed.).

agony of his own self-reproaches—being a hell to himself in reflecting on the glorious state whence he had fallen.

It is true we have no light from history into how long he remained thus, and but little from tradition. Rabbi Judah says the Jews were of the opinion that he remained twenty thousand years in that condition, and that the world shall continue twenty thousand more, in which he shall find work enough to satisfy his mischievous desires. But he shows no authority for his opinion.

Indeed, let the Devil have been as idle as they think he was before, but it must be acknowledged that now he is the most busy, vigilant, and diligent of all God's creatures, and very full of employment too, such as it is.

Scripture indeed gives us light into the enmity there is between the two natures, the diabolical and the human, the reason of it, and how and by what means the power of the Devil is restrained by the Messiah. And to those who are willing to trust in gospel light and believe what the Scripture says of the Devil, much of his history may be discovered. Therefore those may go there for a fuller account of the matter.

But to reserve all Scripture evidence of these things—as stored in a magazine for the use of those with whom Scripture testimony is of force—and now directing my story to an age wherein to be driven to Revelation and Scripture assertions is esteemed giving up the dispute, I must for the present turn to other inquiries. People now-a-days must have demonstration. And in a word, nothing will satisfy the age but such evidence as perhaps the nature of the question will not admit.

It is hard, indeed, to bring demonstrations in such a case as this. *"No man has seen God at any time,"* says the Scripture (1 John 4:12). So the Devil, being a spirit incorporeal, an angel of light [before his fall], and consequently not visible in his own substance, nature, and form, it may in some sense also be said that no man has seen the Devil at any time. I shall examine, and perhaps expose by themselves all those pretenses of frenzied and fanciful people who tell us they have seen the Devil.

It might take up a great deal of our time here to inquire whether the Devil has any particular shape or personality of substance that can be visible to us, felt, heard, or understood, and which he cannot alter—and then, what shapes or appearances the Devil has at any time taken upon himself and whether he can really appear in a body that might be handled and seen, and yet so as to know it to have been the Devil at the time of his appearing. But this also I defer as not of weight in the present enquiry.

We have divers accounts of witches conversing with the Devil, with the Devil in a real body with all the appearance of a body of a man or woman appearing to them. There are also accounts of having a familiar spirit, as they call it, an incubus, or little devil that sucks their bodies, runs away with them into the air, and the like. Much of this is said, but much more than it is easy to prove, and we ought to give but a just proportion of credit to those things.

As to his borrowed shapes and his subtle transformations that we have such open testimony of, there is no room for any question for that. And when I come to that part, I shall be obliged rather to give a history of the fact than enter into any dissertation upon the nature and reason of it.

I do not find in any author whom we can call creditable that even in those countries where the dominion of Satan is more particularly established, and where they may be said to worship him in a more particular manner as a devil (which some tell us the

Indians in America did, who worshipped the Devil that he might not hurt them)—I say, I do not find that even there the Devil appeared to them in any particular constant shape or personality peculiar to himself.

Scripture and history, therefore, giving us no light into that part of the question, I conclude and lay it down, not as my opinion only but as what all ages seem to concur in, that the Devil has no particular body, that he is a spirit, and that though he may, Proteus-like, assume the appearance of either man or beast, yet it must be some borrowed shape, some assumed figure, *pro hac vice* [by this time], and that he has no visible body of his own.

I thought it needful to discuss this as a preliminary, and that the next discourse might go into a certainty in this grand point, namely, that however he may for his particular occasions put himself into a great many shapes and clothe himself, perhaps, with what appearances he pleases, the Devil is himself yet still a mere spirit, that he retains the seraphic nature, is not visible by our eyes, which are human and organic, and he cannot act with the ordinary powers or in the ordinary manner as bodies do.

Therefore, when he has thought it fit to descend to the meannesses of disturbing and frightening children and old women by noises and knockings, dislocating the chairs and stools, breaking windows and suchlike little ambulatory things (which would seem to be below the dignity of his character, and which in particular are ordinarily performed by organic powers), yet even then, he has thought it fit not to be seen and rather make the poor people believe he had a real shape and body, with hands to act, mouth to speak, and the like, rather than give proof of it in common to the whole world by showing himself and acting visibly and openly, as a body usually and ordinarily does.

Nor is it any disadvantage to the Devil that his seraphic nature is not confined or imprisoned in a body or shape (supposing that shape to be whatever monstrous thing we would). For that would indeed confine his actions within the narrow sphere of the organ or body to which he was limited. And though you were to suppose the body to have wings for a velocity of motion equal to spirit, yet if it had not a power of invisibility, too, and a capacity of conveying itself undiscovered into all the secret recesses of mankind, and if it had not the same secret art or capacity of insinuation, suggestion, accusation, and so forth, by which his wicked designs are now propagated and all his other devices assisted, and by which he deludes and betrays mankind—I say he would be no more a devil (that is, a destroyer), no more a deceiver, and no more a Satan (that is, a dangerous arch-enemy to the souls of men). Nor would it be any difficulty to mankind to shun and avoid him, as I shall make plain in the other part of his history.

Had the Devil from the beginning been embodied as he could not have been invisible to us whose souls, equally seraphic, are only prescribed by being embodied and incased in flesh and blood as we are, he would have been no more a devil to anybody but himself. Had the powers of that body been all that we can conceive to make him formidable to us, the imprisonment in a body would yet have been a hell to him.

Consider him as a conquered, exasperated rebel retaining all that fury and swelling ambition, that hatred of God and envy at his creatures that dwells now in his enraged spirits as a devil. Yet suppose him to have been condemned to organic powers, confined to corporeal motion, and restrained like a body must be supposed to restrain a spirit. It must at the time suppose him

SATAN HIDES IN PARADISE

to be effectually disabled from all the methods he is now allowed to make use of for exerting his rage and enmity against God (any further than as he might suppose it) to affect his Maker second hand by wounding His glory through the sides of His weakest creature, man.

He must certainly be thus confined, because body can only act upon body, not upon spirit. No species is empowered to act out of the compass of its own sphere. He might have been empowered, indeed, to have carried out terrible and even destructive things upon mankind, especially if that body had any powers given it that mankind had not, by which man would be overmatched and not be in a condition of self-defense. For example, suppose him to have had wings to have flown in the air, or to be invulnerable, and that no human invention, art, or engine could hurt, ensnare, captivate, or restrain him.

But this is to suppose the righteous and wise Creator to have made a creature and not be able to defend and preserve him, or have left him defenseless at the mercy of another of his own creatures whom he had given power to destroy him. This, indeed, might have occasioned a general idolatry and made mankind, as many do to this day, worship the Devil so he might not hurt them.

But supposing the Devil to have had malice equal to his power, it could not have prevented the destruction of mankind. For he would need to put on a new nature, be compassionate, generous, beneficent, and steadily good in sparing the rival enemy he was able to destroy, or else he would need to have ruined mankind. In short, he would have ceased to have been a devil and would have resumed his original, angelic, heavenly nature filled with the principles of love to delight in the works of his creator, and be bent on propagating His glory and interest, or else he would have put an end to the race of man, whom it would be in his power to destroy, and oblige his Maker to create a new species or fortify the old with some kind of defense that must be invulnerable, and which his fiery darts could not penetrate.

On this occasion, suffer me to make an excursion from the

usual style of this work and with some solemnity to express my thoughts thusly:

How glorious is the wisdom and goodness of the great Creator of the world in thus restraining these seraphic outcasts from the power of assuming human or organic bodies, which, could they do, would invigorate them with the supernatural powers they now possess and might exert as seraphs and angels. They would then be able even to frighten mankind from the face of the earth and destroy and confound God's creation. Indeed, even as they are, were not their power limited they might destroy the creation itself, reverse and overturn nature, and put the world into a general conflagration. But were those immortal spirits embodied, even though they were not permitted to confound nature, they would be able to harass poor, weak, and defenseless man out of his wits and render him perfectly useless either to his Maker or himself.

But the dragon is chained. The Devil's power is limited. He has indeed a vastly extended empire, being prince of the air and having, at least, the whole atmosphere to range in, and how far that atmosphere is extended is not yet ascertained by the nicest observations.

But let his power be what it will there, we are sure it is limited here, and that in two particulars: First, he is limited, as above, from assuming body or bodily shapes and substance, and secondly, from exerting seraphic powers and acting with that supernatural force that, as an angel, he was certainly vested with before the fall, and which we are not certain is yet taken from him. Or at most, we do not know how much it may or may not be diminished by his degeneracy and by the blow given him at his expulsion. This we are certain, that whether his power is greater or less, he is restrained from the exercise of it in this world. And he, who was once equal to the angel who killed a hundred and eighty thousand men in one night, is not able now, without a new commission, to take away the life of one Job nor to touch anything he had.

But let us consider him then limited and restrained as he is. He yet remains a mighty, terrible, immortal being infinitely superior to man in the dignity of his nature as well as in the dreadful powers he still retains about him even though the brainsick heads of our "enthusiastics" paint him blacker than he is. And, as I have said, they represent him clothed with terrors that do not really belong to him as if the power of good and evil was wholly vested in him. They assume him placed in the throne of his Maker to distribute both punishments and rewards, terrifying and deluding fanciful people about himself till they turn their heads, and frightening them into a belief that the Devil will let them alone if they do such and such good things, or carry them away with him they know not where if they do not obey.

Thus, for example, a poor deluded country fellow in our town, who had lived a wicked, abominable, debauched life, was frightened with an apparition, as he called it, of the Devil. He fancied that he spoke to him. And telling his tale to a good honest Christian gentleman, his neighbor, who had a little more sense than he, the gentleman asked him if he was sure he really saw the Devil. "Yes, yes, sir," says he, "I saw him very plainly." And so they began the following discourse.

GENT. See him! See the Devil! Are you sure of it, Thomas?

THO. Yes, yes, I am sure enough of it, master. To be sure, it was the Devil.

GENT. And how do you know 'twas the Devil, Thomas? Had you ever seen the Devil before?

THO. No, no, I had never seen him before, to be sure, but for all that I know, it was the Devil.

GENT. Well, if you are sure, Thomas, there's no contradicting you. Tell me, what clothes had he on?

THO. No, sir, don't jest with me. He had no clothes on, He was clothed with fire and brimstone.

GENT. Was it dark or daylight when you saw him?

THO. Oh! It was very dark, for it was midnight.

GENT. How could you see him then? Did you see by the light of the fire you speak of?

THO. No, no, he gave me no light himself, but I saw him for all that.

GENT. But was it within doors, or out in the street?

THO. It was within. It was in my own chamber, when I was just going into bed, that I saw him.

GENT. Well, then, you had a candle, hadn't you?

THO. Yes, I had a candle, but it burnt as blue and as dim!

GENT. Well, but if the Devil was clothed with fire and brimstone, he must give you some light. There can't be such a fire as you speak of, except it must give a light with it.

THO. No, no, he gave no light, but I smelled his fire and brimstone. He left a smell of it behind him when he was gone.

GENT. Well, so you say he had fire but gave no light. It was a devilish fire, indeed. Did it feel warm? Was the room hot while he was in it?

THO. No, no, but I was hot enough without it, for it put me into a great sweat with the fright.

GENT. Very well, he was all in fire, you say, but without light or heat. Only it seems he stunk of brimstone. Tell me, what shape was he in? What was he like? For you say you saw him.

THO. Oh! sir, I saw two great staring saucer eyes, enough to frighten anybody out of their wits.

GENT. And was that all you saw?

THO. No, I saw his cloven-foot very plainly. T'was as big as one of our bullocks that goes to plough.

GENT. So, you saw none of his body but his eyes and his feet? A fine vision, indeed!

THO.No, that was enough to send me going.

GENT. Going! What! Did you run away from him?

THO.No, but I fled into bed in one jump, and sunk down, and pulled the bedclothes quite over me.

GENT. And what did you do that for?

THO. To hide myself from such a frightful creature.

GENT. Why, if it had really been the Devil, do you think the bedclothes would have secured you from him?

THO. No, I don't know, but in a fright, it was all I could do.

GENT. Indeed, 'twas as wise as all the rest. But come, Thomas, to be a little serious, tell me, did he speak to you?

THO. Yes, yes, I heard a voice, but who it was the Lord knows.

GENT. What kind of voice was it? Was it like a man's voice?

THO. No; it was a hoarse ugly noise, like the croaking of a frog, and it called me by my name twice, "Thomas Dawson, Thomas Dawson!"

GENT. Well, did you answer?

THO. No, not I. I could not have spoken a word for my life. Why, I was frightened to death.

GENT. Did it say anything else?

THO. Yes, when it saw that I did not speak, it said "Thomas Dawson, Thomas Dawson, you are a wicked wretch. You lay with Jenny S_____ last night. If you don't repent, I will take you away alive and carry you to hell, and you shall be damned, you wretch.

GENT. And was it trite, Thomas? Did you lie with Jenny S___ the night before?

THO. Indeed, master, it was true. But I was very sorry afterward.

GENT. But how should the Devil know it, Thomas?

THO. Indeed, he knows it to be sure. Why, they say he knows everything.

GENT. Well, but why should he be angry at that? He would rather bid you lie with her again and encourage you to lie with forty whores, than hinder you. This can't be the Devil, Thomas.

THO. Yes, yes, sir, 'twas the Devil to be sure.

GENT. But he bid you repent too, you say?

THO. Yes, he threatened me if I did not.

GENT. Why, Thomas, do you think the Devil would have you repent?

THO. Why, no, that's true too. I don't know what to say to that. But what could it be? 'Twas the Devil to be sure. It could be nobody else.

GENT. No, no, 'twas neither the Devil, Thomas, nor anybody else but your own frightened imagination. Thomas, you had lain with that wench, and being a young sinner of that kind, your conscience terrified you, told you the Devil would fetch you away, and said you would be damned. And you were so persuaded it would be so, that you at last imagined he had come for you and indeed, that you saw him and heard him. Whereas you may depend on it, if Jenny S___ will let you lie with her every night, the Devil will hold the candle or do anything to forward it but will never disturb you. He's too much a friend to your wickedness. It could never be the Devil, Thomas. 'Twas only your own guilt that frightened you, and that was devil enough, too, if you knew the worst of it. You need no other enemy.

THO. Why that's true, master. One would think the Devil

should not have me repent; that's true. But certainly, 'twas the Devil for all that.

Now Thomas was not the only man who, having committed a flagitious crime, had been deluded by his own imagination and the power of fancy to think the Devil had come for him. Whereas the Devil, to give him his due, is too honest to pretend to do such things, it is his business to persuade men to offend, not to repent, as he professes no other. He may press men to this or that action by telling them it is no sin, no offence, no breach of God's law, and the like, when really it is both. But to press them to repent when they have offended, that is quite out of his way. It is none of his business, nor does he pretend to it. Therefore, let no man charge the Devil with what he is not concerned with.

But to return to his person, notwithstanding his lost glory, he is, as I have said, a mighty, a terrible, and an immortal spirit. He is himself called a Prince, the Prince of the Power of the air, the Prince of Darkness, the Prince of Devils, and the like. And his attending spirits are called his angels. So however Satan has lost the glory and rectitude of his nature by his apostate state, yet he retains a greatness and magnificence that places him above our rank, and indeed above our conception. For we know not what he is any more than we know what the blessed angels are, of whom we can say no more than that they are ministering spirits, and so forth, as the Scripture has described them.

Two things, however, may give us some insight into the nature of the Devil in the present state he is in, and in these we have a clear discovery of the whole series of his conduct from the beginning.

1. That he is the vanquished but implacable enemy of God his creator, who has conquered him and expelled him from

the habitations of bliss on which account he is filled with envy, rage, malice, and all uncharitableness. And he would dethrone God and overturn the thrones of heaven if it were in his power.

2. That he is man's irreconcilable enemy—not as he is a man, nor simply on his own account, nor for any advantage he (the Devil) can make by the ruin and destruction of man, but in mere envy at the felicity man is supposed to enjoy as Satan's rival, and because he is appointed to succeed Satan and his angels in the possession of those glories from which they are fallen.

And here I must take upon myself to say, Mr. Milton makes a wrong judgment of the reason of Satan's resolution to disturb the felicity of man. He tells us it was merely to affront God his maker, rob Him of the glory designed in His new work of creation, and to disappoint Him in His main design, namely, the creation of a new species of creatures in a perfect rectitude of soul and after his own image, from whom He might expect a new fund of glory should be raised, and who was to appear as the triumph of the Messiah's victory over the Devil. In all which Satan could not be fool enough not to know that he should be disappointed by the same power that had so eminently counteracted his rage before.

But I believe the Devil had a much more probable reason. And though he may be said to act upon a meaner principle than that of pointing his rage at the personal glory of his Creator, yet I hold that, in my opinion, it was by the much more rational undertaking (and what was more likely to succeed). And that was, that whereas he perceived this new species of creatures had a sublime as well as human part, and were made capable of possessing the mansions of eternal beatitude whence he (Satan) and his angels were expelled and irretrievably banished, envy at such a rival moved him by all possible artifice (for he saw himself deprived of capacity to do it by force) to render him unworthy, like him. And by bringing his rival to fall into rebellion and disobedience, he might see him damned with him, and see those who were intended to fill up the empty spaces in heaven (made so by the absence of so many millions of fallen angels) be cast out into the same darkness with them.

How he came to know that this new species of creatures was subject to such imperfection is best explained by the Devil's prying, vigilant disposition—judging or leading him to judge by himself (for he was as near being infallible as any of God's creatures had been), and then inclining him to try whether or not it was so.

Modern naturalists, especially some who have not so much benevolence for the fair sex as I have, tell us that as soon as Satan first saw the woman and looked in her face, he evidently saw that she was the best-formed creature to make a fool of, the best to make a hypocrite of that could be made, and therefore the most fit for his purpose.

> He saw by some stubborn lines in her face (legible, perhaps, only to himself) that there was a throne readily prepared for the sin of pride to sit in state upon, especially if it took an early possession. Eve, you may suppose, was a perfect beauty if ever such a thing may be supposed in the human frame. Her figure being so extraordinary was the groundwork of his project. No more was needed than to bring her to be vain of it and to imagine that it either was so, or was infinitely more sublime and beautiful than it really was—and having thus

ARCHANGEL MICHAEL'S VICTORY OVER LUCIFER

tickled her vanity to introduce pride gradually, till at last he might persuade her that she really was angelic, or of heavenly race, and make her want nothing but to eat the forbidden fruit that would make her something even more excellent.

2. Looking further into her frame, and with a nearer view to her imperfections, he saw room to conclude that she

was of a constitution easy to be seduced, and especially by flattering her, raising a commotion in her soul, and causing a disturbance among her passions. And accordingly, he set himself to work to disturb her repose and put dreams of great things into her head together with something of a nameless nature, of which (though some have been ill-natured enough to suggest) I shall not injure the Devil so much as to mention without better evidence.

3. But besides this, upon the very first survey of her outside, he found something so very charming in her demeanor and behavior, so engaging as well as agreeable in the whole texture of her person, and withal such a sprightly wit, such a vivacity of parts, such a fluency of tongue, and, above all, such a winning prevailing whine in her smiles—or at least in her tears—that he had no doubt that if he could but once delude her, she would easily be brought to delude Adam, whom, he found, set not only a great value upon her person but was perfectly captivated by her charms. In a word, he saw plainly, that if he could but ruin her, he should easily make a devil of her to ruin her husband and draw him into any gulf of mischief, were it ever so black and dreadful, that she should first fall into herself. How far some may be wicked enough, from hence, to suggest of the fair sex—that they have been devils to their husbands ever since—I cannot say. I hope they will not be so unmerciful to discover truths of such fatal consequence, though they should come to their knowledge.

Thus, Satan has been subtle and penetrating from the beginning, and upon these discoveries made into the woman's inside, who can wonder that he went immediately to work with her rather than with Adam? Not but that one would think if Adam was fool enough to be deluded by his wife, the Devil might have seen so much of it in his countenance as to have encouraged him to make his attack directly upon him and not go round about, beating the bush and ploughing with the heifer (setting upon the woman first, and then setting her upon her husband, who might as easily have been imposed upon as she).

Other commentators on this critical text suggest to us that Eve was not so pleased with the hopes of being made a goddess, that the pride of a seraphic knowledge did not so much work upon her imagination to bring her to consent as did a certain secret notion, infused into her head by the same wicked instrument, that she should be wiser than Adam and should by the superiority of her understanding necessarily have the government over him—which, at present, she was sensible she had not, he being master of a particular air of gravity and majesty, as well as of strength infinitely superior to her.

This is an ill-natured suggestion, but it must be confessed. The impatient desire of government that (since then) appears in the general behavior of the sex, and particularly of governing husbands, leaves too much room to legitimize the supposition.

The philosophers and expositors who are of this opinion, add to it that this being her original crime, or the particular temptation to that crime, heaven thought fit to show His justice in making her more entire subjection to her husband be a part of the curse so she might read her sin in the punishment, viz., *"He shall rule over thee"* (Gen 3:16).

I only give the general hint of these things as they appear recorded in the annals of Satan's first tyranny, and at the beginning of his government in the world. Those who would be more particularly informed may inquire of him and know further.

I cannot, however, but observe here, with some regret, how it appears by the consequence that the Devil was not mistaken when he made an early judgment of Mrs. Eve, and how Satan really went the right way to work, to judge of her. It is certain the Devil had nothing to do but to look in her face, and upon a near steady view he might easily see there an instrument for his turn.

Nor has he failed to make her a tool ever since by the very methods he at first proposed. To which, perhaps, he has made some additions in corrupting her composition as well as her understanding, qualifying her to be a complete snare to the poor weaker vessel, man—to beguile him with her siren's voice, abuse him with her smiles, delude him with her crocodile tears, and. sometimes cock her head at him and terrify him with the thunder of her treble, and by that making the effeminated male apple-eater tremble at the noise of that very tongue which at first commanded him to sin. For it is yet a debate, which the learned have not decided, whether she persuaded and entreated him, or, like a true she-tyrant, exercised her authority and obliged him to eat the forbidden fruit.

And therefore a certain author, whose name for fear of the sex's resentment I conceal, brings her in, calling to Adam at a great distance in an imperious haughty manner, beckoning to him with her hand, thusly: "Here," says she, "you cowardly faint-hearted wretch, take this branch of heavenly fruit, eat and be a stupid fool no longer. Eat and be wise. Eat and be a god. And know, to your eternal shame, that your wife has been made an enlightened goddess before you."

He tells you Adam hung back a little at first and trembled,

afraid to trespass. "What ails the sot?" says the new termagant.[10] What are you afraid of? Did God forbid you! Yes, and why? That we might not be knowing and wise like himself! What reason can there be that we, who have capacious souls, able to receive knowledge, should have it withheld? Take it, you fool, and eat. Don't you see how I am exalted in soul by it, and am quite another creature? Take it, I say, or, if you don't, I will go and cut down the tree, and you shall never eat any of it at all, and you shall be still a fool, and be governed by your wife forever."

Thus, if this interpretation of the thing is just, she scolded him into it, berated him, and brought him to it by the terror of her voice, a thing that has retained a dreadful influence over him ever since. Nor have the greatest of Adam's successors—however light some husbands make of it in this age—been able to conceal their terror at the very sound ever since that.

With these views, he resolved, it seems, to attack the woman. And if we consider him as a devil and what he aimed it, and consider the fair prospect he had of success, I must confess I do not see who can blame him, or at least, how anything less could be expected from him. But we shall meet with it again by and by.

---

10 Termagant—a violent, turbulent, or brawling woman (Ed.).

5

OF THE STATION SATAN HAD IN HEAVEN BEFORE HE FELL; THE NATURE AND ORIGIN OF HIS CRIME, AND SOME OF MR. MILTON'S MISTAKES ABOUT IT.

Thus far I have gone upon general observation in this great affair of Satan and his empire in this world. I now come to my title and shall enter upon the historical part as the main work before me.

Besides what has been said poetically relating to the fall and wandering condition of the Devil and his host, which poetical part I offer only as an excursion and desire it should be taken so, I shall give you what I think is deduced from good origins on the part of Satan's story in a few words.

He was one of the created angels formed by the same omnipotent hand and glorious power who created the heavens and the earth and all that is therein. This innumerable heavenly host, as we have reason to believe, contained angels of higher and lower stations and of greater and lesser degree expressed in the Scripture by thrones, dominions, and principalities. This, I think, we have as much reason to believe as we have that there are stars in the firmament (or starry heavens) of greater and lesser magnitude.

What particular station among the immortal choir of angels this arch-seraph, this prince of devils, called Satan, was placed in before his expulsion, that, indeed, we cannot receive the knowledge of, at least not with such an authority as may be depended upon. But since from Scripture authority he was placed at the head of all the apostate armies after he had fallen, we cannot think it in the least assuming to say that he might be supposed to be one of the principal agents in the rebellion that happened in heaven and, consequently, that he might be one of the highest in dignity there before that rebellion.

The higher his station, the lower, and with the greater precipitation, was his overthrow. And therefore, those words, though taken in another sense, may very well be applied to him: *"How art thou fallen, O Lucifer, Son of the Morning!"* (Isaiah 14:12).

Having granted the dignity of his person and the high station in which he was placed among the heavenly host, it would necessarily come then to inquire into the nature of his fall and, above all, a little into the reason of it. It is certain he did fall and was guilty of rebellion and disobedience (the just effect of pride)—sins which occurred in that holy place called wonderful.

But what to me is more wonderful and astonishing, which I think will be very ill accounted for, is how it came to be that seeds of crime rose in the angelic nature created in a state of perfect, unspotted holiness? How was it first found in a place where no unclean thing can enter? How did ambition, pride, or envy, come to generate there? Could there be offence where there was no crime? Could untainted purity breed corruption? Could the nature contaminate and infect that which was always partaking nourishment from and taking in principles of perfection?

Happy it is to me that writing the history, not solving the difficulties of Satan's affairs, is my sphere of activity in this work—that I am to relate the fact, not give reasons for it or assign causes. If it were otherwise, I should break off at this difficulty. For I acknowledge I do not see through it; neither do I think that the great Milton, after all his fine images and lofty excursions upon the subject, has left it one jot clearer than he found it. Some are of the opinion, and among them the great Dr. B—s, that crime broke in upon them at some interval when they stopped, but one moment, fixing their eyes and thoughts on the glories of the divine face to admire and adore, which is the full employment of angels. But even this, though it goes as high as imagination can carry us, does not reach it nor, to me, make it one jot more comprehensible than it was before. All I can say to it here is that it was so. The fact is upon record, and the rejected troop are in being (whose circumstances confess the guilt) and still groan under the punishment.

If you will bear with a poetic excursion upon the subject, not to solve but to illustrate the difficulty, take it in a few lines, thusly:

Thou sin of witchcraft! First-born child of crime!
    Produc'd before the bloom of time;
Ambition's maiden sin, in heaven conceiv'd,
    And who could have believed
Defilement could in purity begin,
And bright eternal day be soil'd with sin?
Tell us, sly penetrating crime,
How cam'st thou there, thou fault sublime?
How didst thou pass the adamantine gate,
    And into spirit thyself insinuate?
From what dark state? from what deep place?
From what strange untreated race?

Where was thy ancient habitation found,
Before void chaos heard the forming sound?
Wast thou a substance, or an airy ghost,
    A vapour flying in the fluid waste
    Of unconcocted air?
And how at first didst thou come there?
Sure there was once a time when thou wert not;
By whom wast thou created? and for what?
Art thou a stream from some contagious damp exhal'd?
    How should contagion be entail'd,
    On bright seraphic spirits, and in a place
    Where all's supreme, and glory fills the space?
No noxious vapour there could rise,
    For there no noxious matter lies;
    Nothing that's evil could appear,
Sin never could seraphic glory bear;
The brightness of the eternal face,
    Which fills as well as constitutes the place,
    Would be a fire too hot for crime to bear,
    'Twould calcine sin or melt it into air.
How then did first defilement enter in?
Ambition, thou first vital seed of sin!
Thou life of death! how cam'st thou there?
    In what bright form didst thou appear?
    In what seraphic orb didst thou arise?
Surely that place admits of no disguise;
    Eternal sight must know thee there,
    And being known, thou soon must disappear.
But since the fatal truth we know,
    Without the matter whence or manner how:
Thou high superlative of sin,

Tell us thy nature, where thou didst begin?
The first degree of thy increase,
Debauch'd the regions of eternal peace,
And fill'd the breasts of loyal angels there
With the first treason and infernal war.

Thou art the high extreme of pride,
And dost o'er lesser crimes preside;
Not for the mean attempt of vice design'd,
But to embroil the world and damn mankind.
Transforming mischief, how hast thou procur'd,
That loss that's ne'er to be restor'd,
And made the bright seraphic morning star
In horrid monstrous shapes appear?
Satan, that while he dwelt in glorious light,
Was always then as pure as he was bright,
That in effulgent rays of glory shone,
Excell'd by the eternal light, by Him alone;
Distorted now, and script of innocence,
And banish'd with thee from the high pre-eminence:
How as the splendid seraph chang'd his face,
Transform'd by thee, and like thy monstrous race?
Ugly as is the crime, for which he fell,
Fitted by thee to make a local hell,
For such must be the place where either of you dwell.

Thus, as I told you, I only moralize upon the subject, but as to the difficulty, I must leave it as I find it unless, as I hinted at first, I could prevail with Satan to set pen to paper and write this part of his own history. No question but he could let us into the secret. But to be plain, I doubt I shall tell so many plain truths of the Devil in this history and discover so many of his secrets that are not for his interest to have discovered. And before I finish, the Devil and I may not be such good friends as some may suppose we are, at least not friends enough to obtain such a favor of him, though it be for public good. So we must be content till we come 'tother side the blue-blanket,[11] and then we shall know the whole story.

But now, though, as I said, I will not attempt to solve the difficulty. I may, I hope, venture to tell you that there is not so much difficulty in it as at first sight it appears, and especially not so much as some people would make us believe. Let us see how others are mistaken about it. Perhaps that may help us a little in the enquiry; for to know what it is not, is one help toward knowing what it is.

Mr. Milton indeed told us a great many merry things of the Devil in a most formal, solemn manner, till, in short, he made a good play of heaven and hell. And no doubt if he had lived in our times, he might have had it acted with our Pluto and Proserpine. He made fine speeches both for God and the Devil, and a little addition might have turned it, *a la modern,* into a *Harlequin Dieu et Diable.*

I confess, I do not well know how far the dominion of poetry extends itself. It seems the butts and bounds of Parnassus are not yet ascertained, so that, for aught I know, by virtue of their ancient privileges, called *licentia poetarum* [license of poets], there can be no blasphemy in verse, as some of our divines say there can be no treason in the pulpit. But they who will venture to write that way ought to be better satisfied about that point than I am.

Upon this foot, Mr. Milton, to grace his poem and give

11 Blue Blanket is a reference to the Scottish banner (blue for the background color of the Scottish flag), called "The Banner of the Holy Ghost" taken up by Scottish Christians and reputedly dates back as far as the First Crusade (1096-1099). (Ed.).

room for his towering fancy, went a length beyond all that ever went before him—since Ovid in his *Metamorphoses.* He indeed complimented God Almighty with a flux of lofty words and great sounds and made a very fine story of the Devil, but he made a mere *je ne scat quoi* of Jesus Christ. In one line he has Him riding on a cherub, and in another, sitting on a throne, both in the very same moment of action. In another place he has Him making a speech to His saints, when it is evident he had none there. For we all know man was not created till a long while after. And nobody can be so dull as to say the angels may be called saints without the greatest absurdity in nature. Besides, he makes Christ himself distinguish them as in two separate bands, and of differing persons and species, as to be sure they are.

> Stand still in bright array, ye saints______.
> ______Here stand,
> Ye angels. ______
> *Par. Lost,* lib. vi.

So that Christ here is pictured as drawing up His army before the last battle and making a speech to them, to tell them they shall only stand by in warlike order, but that they shall have no occasion to fight, for he alone will engage the rebels. Then, in embattling his legions, he places the saints here, and the angels there, as if one were the main battle of infantry, and the other the wings of cavalry. But who are those saints? They are indeed all of Milton's own making; for it is certain there were no saints at all in heaven or earth at that time. God and his angels filled up the place, and till some of the angels fell, and men were created, had lived, and were dead, there could have been no saints there. Saint Abel was certainly the proto-saint of all that ever were seen in heaven, as well as the proto-martyr of all that have been upon earth.

Just such another mistake—not to call it a blunder—he makes about hell, is that he not only makes it local but presents it as existing before the fall of the angels and pictures it as opening its mouth to receive them. This is so contrary to the nature of the thing, and so great an absurdity, that no poetic license can account for it. For though the art of poetry may form stories as idea, and fancy may furnish materials, yet that art must not break in upon chronology and make things that in time were to exist act before they existed.

Thus, a painter may make a fine piece of work; the artistry may be good, the strokes masterly, and the beauty of the workmanship inimitably curious and fine and yet it may have some unpardonable improprieties that mar the whole work. So the famous painter of Toledo painted the story of the three wise men of the East coming to worship and bring their presents to our Lord upon his birth at Bethlehem, where he represents them as three Arabian or Indian kings. Two of them are white, and one black. But unhappily, when he drew the latter part of them kneeling, which to be sure was done after their faces, with their legs being necessarily a little intermixed, he made three black feet for the black king, and but three white feet for the two white kings, and yet never discovered the mistake till the piece was presented to the king and hung up in the great church.

As this is an unpardonable error in sculpture or limning, it must be much more so in poetry, where the images must have no improprieties, much less inconsistencies.

In a word, Mr. Milton indeed made a fine poem, but it is the devil of a history. I can easily allow Mr. Milton to make hills and dales, flowery meadows and plains, and the like, in heaven, and places of retreat and contemplation in hell—though, I must add, it can be allowed to no poet on earth but Mr. Milton. Indeed, I will allow Mr. Milton, if you please, to set the angels a dancing in heaven, lib. v., and the devils a singing in hell, lib. i., though they are, in short, especially the last, most horrid absurdities. But I cannot allow him to make their music in hell to be harmonious and charming as he does. Such images are incongruous and indeed shocking to nature. Neither can I think we should allow things to be placed out of time in poetry any more than in history. It is a confusion of images that is allowed to be disallowed by all the critics of whatsoever tribe or species exist in the world and is indeed unpardonable. But we shall find so many more of these things in Mr. Milton that really taking notice of them all would carry me quite out of my way, being I at this time am not writing the history of Mr. Milton, but of the Devil. Besides, Mr. Milton is such a celebrated man, that who but he who can write the history of the Devil dare meddle with him.

But to come back to the business. As I had cautioned you against running to Scripture for shelter in cases of difficulty (Scripture weighing very little among the people I am directing my speech to), so indeed, Scripture gives but very little light into anything of the Devil's story before his fall, and but very little of it for some time after.

Nor did Mr. Milton say one word to solve the main difficulty, viz., how the Devil came to fall, how sin came into heaven, how the spotless seraphic nature could receive infection, whence the contagion proceeded, what noxious matter could emit corruption, and how and whence any vapor to poison the angelic frame could rise up or how it increased and grew up to crime. But all this he passes over, and hurrying up that part in two or three words, he only tells us:

—his pride
Had cast him out from heaven, with all his host
Of rebel angels, by whose aid aspiring
To set himself in glory above his peers,
He trusted to have equall'd the Most High.—Lib. i.

"His pride!" but how came Satan, while an archangel, to be proud? How did it happen that pride and perfect holiness should meet in the same person? Here we must bid Mr. Milton good night. For, in plain terms, he is in the dark about it, and so are we all. And the most that can be said is that we know the fact is so, but nothing of the nature or reason of it.

But to come to the history, the angels fell, they sinned (amazing!) in heaven, and God cast them out. What their sin was is not explicit, but in general it is called a rebellion against God. All sin must be so.

Mr. Milton here takes it upon himself to give the history of it as particularly as if he had been born there and came down hither on purpose to give us an account of it (I hope he is better informed by this time). But this he does in such a manner as jostles with religion and shocks our faith in so many points necessary to be believed, that we must forbear to give up to Milton, or must set aside part of the sacred text in such a manner as will assist some people to set it all aside (I mean by this: his invented scheme of the Son's being declared in heaven to be begotten then, and then to be declared generalissimo of all the armies of heaven, and of the Father's summoning all the angels of the heavenly host to submit to him and pay him homage).

I must admit, the invention, indeed, is very fine, the images exceeding magnificent, the thought rich and bright, and in some respect, truly sublime. But the authorities fail most wretchedly, and the mistiming of it is insufferably gross, as is noted in the introduction to this work. For Christ was not declared the Son of God but on earth. It is true, it was spoken from heaven, but then it was spoken as perfected on earth.[12] If it was at all to be assigned to heaven, it was from eternity, and there, indeed, his eternal generation is allowed; but not to take upon us to say that on a day, a certain day! For so our poet assumes:

Lib. v.:
____When on a day,
____On such day
As heaven's great year brings forth, th' empyreal host
Of angels, by imperial summons called,
Forthwith from all the ends of heaven appear's.

This is, indeed, too gross. At this meeting he makes God declare the Son to be *that day begotten* as before. Had he made Him not begotten that day but declared it in general that day, it would be reconcilable with Scripture and with sense. For either the begetting is meant of ordaining to an office, or else the eternal generation falls to the ground, and if it was to the office (mediator), then Mr. Milton is out in ascribing another fixed day to the work; see lib. x.. But then the declaring of him *that day*

12 "Not made the Son of God, as He was said before to be *made the seed of David,* (v. 3); but declared, or demonstrated, to be the Son of God. In Scripture the resurrection of the dead, is put for resurrection from the dead (1 Cor. 15:42; Heb. 6:2); and hereby is meant the resurrection of Christ himself. He rose again from the dead, and thereby declared or manifested himself to be the Son of God with power."—*Pool's Scripture Annotations.*

is wrong chronologically too; for Christ is declared *"the Son of God with power"* by the resurrection of the dead, and this is both a declaration in heaven and in earth, (Rom. 1:4).[13] And Milton can have no authority to tell us there was any declaration of it in heaven before this, except it be that dull authority called poetic license, which will not pass in so solemn an affair as that.

But the thing was necessary to Milton, who wanted to assign some cause or origin of the Devil's rebellion. And so, as I said above, the design is well laid; it only lacks two trifles called truth and history. So I leave it to struggle for itself.

This ground plot being laid, he has a fair field for the Devil to play the rebel in, for he immediately brings him in not satisfied with the exaltation of the Son of God. The case must be thus: Satan, being an eminent archangel, and perhaps the highest of all the angelic train, hearing this sovereign declaration—that the Son of God was declared to be head or generalissimo of all the heavenly host—took it ill to see another put into the high station over his head, as the soldiers call it. He perhaps being the senior officer and disdaining to submit to any but to his former immediate Sovereign, he, in short threw up his commission and, in order not to be compelled to obey, revolted and broke out in open rebellion.

All this part is a decoration noble and great, nor is there any objection to be made against the invention because of a deduction of probable events. But the plot is laid wrong, as is observed above, because it is contradicted by the Scripture account according to

---

13 "*Declared to be the Son of God.* Or, Determined (definitus). Paul is saying that the power of the resurrection represented the decree by which Christ was declared to be the Son of God: *This day I have begotten thee.* Begetting here refers to that which was being made known...Christ was declared to be the Son of God by the open exercise of a truly heavenly power, i.e. the power of the Spirit, when He rose from the dead."—John Calvin, *Commentary on the New Testament.* (Ed.)

which, Christ was declared in heaven, not then, but from eternity, and not declared with power but on earth, viz., in his victory over sin and death by the resurrection from the dead. So Mr. Milton is not orthodox in this part, but lays an avowed foundation for the corrupt doctrine of Arius, which says there was a time when Christ was not the Son of God.

But to leave Mr. Milton to his flights, I agree with him in this part, viz., that the wicked or sinning angels, with the great archangel at the head of them, revolted from their obedience, even in heaven itself; that Satan began the wicked defection, and being a chief among the heavenly host, consequently carried over a great party with him, who altogether rebelled against God; and that upon this rebellion they were sentenced by the righteous judgment of God to be expelled from the holy habitation. Of this, besides the authority of Scripture, we have visible testimonies from the devils themselves—their influences and operations among us every day, of which mankind are witnesses to all the vile things they do in his name and under his protection in almost every scene of life they pass through, whether we talk of things done openly or in masquerade, things done in or out of it, or things done in earnest or in jest.

But then, what comes of the long and bloody war that Mr. Milton gives such a full and particular account of, and the terrible battles in heaven between Michael with the royal army of angels on one hand, and Satan with his rebel host on the other, in which he supposes the numbers and strength to be pretty near equal? But how is it at length that he brings in the Devil's army, and upon doubling their rage and bringing new engines of war into the field, it puts Michael and all the faithful army to the worst and, in a word, defeats them? For though they were not put to a plain flight, in which case he must at least have given an account of two or three thousand millions of angels cut in pieces and wounded, yet he allows them to give over the fight and make a kind of retreat, and so making way for the complete victory of the Son of God. Now this is all invention, or at least a borrowed thought from the old poets and the fight of the giants against Jupiter so nobly designed by Ovid almost two thousand years ago. And there, it was well enough, but whether or not poetic fancy should be allowed to fable upon heaven, and upon the king of heaven too, that 1 leave to the sages.

By this expulsion of the devils, it is allowed by most authors that they are, *ipso, facto,* stripped of the rectitude and holiness of their nature, which was their beauty and perfection. And being engulfed in the abyss of irrevocable ruin, it is no matter where (from that very time) they lost their angelic beautiful form and commenced to be ugly frightful monsters and devils and became evil doers as well as evil spirits filled with a horrid malignity and enmity against their Maker armed with a hellish resolution to show and exert it on all occasions, while retaining however their exalted spirit nature and having a vast extensive power of action—all which they can exert in nothing else but doing evil. For they are entirely divested of either power or will to do good. And even in doing evil, they are under restraints and limitations of a superior power, which it is their torment and, perhaps, a great part of their hell that they cannot break through.

6

WHAT BECAME OF THE DEVIL AND HIS HOST OF FALLEN SPIRITS AFTER THEIR BEING EXPELLED FROM HEAVEN, AND HIS WANDERING CONDITION TILL THE CREATION, WITH SOME MORE OF MR. MILTON'S ABSURDITIES ON THAT SUBJECT.

Having thus brought the Devil and his innumerable legions to the edge of the bottomless pit, it remains, before I bring them to action, that some enquiry should be made into the posture of their affairs immediately after their precipitate fall and into the place of their immediate residence. For this will appear to be very necessary to Satan's history and, indeed, without it, all the further account we have to give of him will be inconsistent and imperfect.

And first, I take upon myself to lay down some fundamentals, which I believe I shall be able to make out historically though, perhaps, not so geographically as some have pretended to do.

1. That Satan was not immediately nor is yet locked down into the abyss of a local hell, such as is supposed by some and such as he shall be at last; or that,
2. If he was, he has certain liberties allowed him for excursions into the regions of this air and certain spheres of action, in which he can and does move to do all the mischief he can (like a very devil as he is), and of which we see so many examples both about us and in us. In the enquiry after which I shall take occasion to examine whether the Devil is not in most of us sometimes, if not in all of us one time or other.
3. That Satan has no particular residence in this globe, or earth, where we live; that he rambles about among us, and marches over and over our whole country (he and his devils) in camps *volant* [flying]. And that he pitches his grand army or chief encampment in our adjacencies, or frontiers, which the philosophers call atmosphere and whence he is called the prince of the power of that element or part of the world we call air; and that whence he sends out his spies, his agents, and emissaries to get intelligence and carry his commissions to his trusty and well-beloved cousins and councilors on earth, by which his business is done and his affairs carried on in the world.

Here again, I meet Mr. Milton full in my face, who will have it that the Devil, immediately at his expulsion, rolled down directly into a hell proper and local. Indeed, he measures the very distance, at least gives the length of the journey by the time they were passing or falling, which, he says was nine days—a good poetical flight, but neither founded on Scripture nor philosophy. For he might every jot as well have brought hell up to the walls of heaven, advanced to receive them, or he ought to have considered the space which is to be allowed to any locality, let him take what part of infinite distance between heaven and a created hell he pleases.

But let that be as Mr. Milton's extraordinary genius pleases to place it. The passage, it seems, is just nine days betwixt heaven and hell. Well might Dives then see father Abraham and talk to him too. But then the great gulf that Abraham tells him was fixed between them does not seem to be so large as, according to Sir Isaac Newton, Dr. Halley, Mr. Whiston, and the rest of our men of science, we take it to be.

But suppose the passage to be nine days. According to Mr. Milton, what followed? Why, hell gaped wide, opened its frightful mouth and received them all at once. Millions and thousands of millions as they were, it received them all at a gulp, as we call it. They had no difficulty to go in, no, none at all.

Facilis descensus Averni sed revocare gradum
Hoc opus hic labor est.[14] —Virg.

All this, as poetical, we may receive, but not at all as historical; for then come troubles insurmountable in our way, some of which may be as follows:

Hell is here supposed to be a place, indeed, created for the punishment of angels and men, and likewise created long before those had fallen or these had being. This makes me say Mr. Milton was a good poet, but a bad historian. Tophet was prepared of old, indeed, but it was for the king. That is to say, it was prepared for those whose lot it should be to come there. But this does not at all suppose it was prepared before it was resolved whether or not there should be subjects for it, else we must suppose both men

14 The descent to the Avernus is easy, but to retrace your steps This work is the work

and angels were made by the glorious and upright Maker of all things on purpose for destruction, which would be incongruous and absurd.

But there is worse yet to come. For in the next place he adds that hell, having received them, closed upon them—that is to say, took them in, closed or shut its mouth and, in a word, locked them in. As it was said in another place, they were locked in, and the key is carried up to heaven and kept there; for we know the angel came down from heaven, having the key of the bottomless pit. But first, see Mr. Milton.

> Nine days they fell; confounded Chaos roar'd And felt tenfold confusion in their fall:
> —Hell, at last,
> Yawning, receiv'd them whole, and on them clos'd; Down from the verge of heaven, eternal wrath Burnt after them—
> Unquenchable.

This scheme is certainly deficient, if not absurd, and I think is more so than any other he has laid. It is evident, neither Satan nor his host of devils are (no, not any of them, yet even now) confined in the eternal prison where the Scripture says they shall be reserved in *"chains of darkness"* (2 Peter 2:4; Jude 1:6). They must have mean thoughts of hell as a prison, a local confinement that can suppose the Devil able to break jail, knock off his fetters, and come abroad if he had been once locked in there, as Mr. Milton says he was. Now we know that he is abroad again. He presented himself before God, among his neighbors, when Job's case came to be discoursed of. And more than that, it is plain he was a prisoner at large by his answer to God's question, which was, *"Whence comest thou?"* To which he answered, *"From going to and fro in the earth"* and so forth (Job 1:7; 2:2). This, I say, is plain, and if it be as certain that hell closed upon them, I demand then, how did he get out? And why was there not a proclamation for apprehending him as there usually is after such rogues break out of prison?

In short, the true account of the Devil's circumstances since his fall from heaven is much more likely to be thus, that he is more of a vagrant than a prisoner and a wanderer in the wild unbounded waste, where he and his legions, like the hordes of Tartary, who in the wild countries of Karakathay, the deserts of Barkan, Cassan, and Astracan live up and down where they find proper. So Satan and his innumerable legions rove about, *hic et ubique* [here and everywhere], pitching their camps (being beasts of prey) where they find the most spoil, watching over this world (and all the other worlds, for aught we know, and if there are any such) I say, watching and seeking whom they may devour, that is, whom they may deceive and delude and so destroy, for devour they cannot.

Satan being thus confined to a vagabond, wandering, unsettled condition is without any certain abode. For though he has, in consequence of his angelic nature, a kind of empire in the liquid waste or air, yet this is certainly part of his punishment—that he is continually hovering over this inhabited globe of earth, swelling with the rage of envy at the felicity of his rival, man, and studying all the means possible to injure and ruin him. But extremely limited in power, to his unspeakable mortification, this is his present state without any fixed abode, place, or space allowed him to rest the sole of his foot upon.

From his expulsion, I take his first view of horror to be that of looking back toward the heaven which he had lost, and there to see the chasm or opening made up, out through which, as at a breach in the wall of the holy place, he was thrust headlong by the power that expelled him—I say, to see the breach repaired, the mounds built up, the walls garrisoned with millions of angels, and armed with thunders and, above all, made terrible by that glory from whose presence they were expelled, as is poetically hinted at before.

Upon this sight, it is no wonder (if there was such a place) that they fled till the darkness might cover them, and that they might be out of the view of so hated a sight.

Wherever they found it, you may be sure they pitched their first camp and began, after many a sour reflection upon what was past, to consider and think a little upon what was to come.

If I had as much personal acquaintance with the Devil as the world could permit and could depend upon the truth of what answer he would give me, the first question I would ask him would be what measures they resolved on at their first assembly. And the next should be how they were employed in all that space of time between their fleeing from the face of their almighty Conqueror and the creation of man. As for the length of the time, which according to the learned was twenty thousand years, and according to the more learned not a quarter so much, I would not concern my curiosity much about it. It is most certain there was a considerable time between, but of that immediately, first let me inquire what they were doing all that time.

The Devil and his host being thus, I say, cast out of heaven and not yet confined strictly to hell, it is plain they must be somewhere. Satan and all his legions did not lose their existence, no, nor the existence of devils either. God was so far from annihilating him that he still preserved his being. And this, not Mr. Milton only, but God himself, has made known to us, having left his history so far upon record. Several expressions in Scripture also make it evident, as particularly the story of Job, mentioned before, the like in our Savior's time, and several others.

If hell did not immediately engulf them, as Milton suggests, it is certain, I say, that they fled somewhere from the anger of heaven, from the face of the Avenger. And His absence, and their own guilt, wonder not at it, would make hell enough for them wherever they went.

Nor need we flee to the dreams of our astronomers, who take a great deal of pains to fill up the vast spaces of the starry heavens with innumerable, habitable worlds, allowing as many solar systems as there are fixed stars, and that not only in the known constellations, but even in the galaxy itself, and who, to every such system, allow a certain number of planets, and to every one of those planets so many satellites or moons, and all these planets and moons to be worlds—solid, dark, opaque bodies, habitable and (as they would have us believe) inhabited by the like animals and rational creatures as on this earth, so that they may, at this rate, find room enough for the Devil and all his angels without making a hell on purpose. Indeed they may, for aught I know, find a world for every devil in all the Devil's host, and so every one may be a monarch, or master-devil separately in his own sphere or world and play the devil there by himself.

And even if this were so, it cannot be denied but that one devil in a place would be enough for a whole world and be able, if not restrained, to do mischief enough there too, and even to ruin and overthrow the whole body of people contained in it.

But, I say, we need not flee to these shifts or consult the

astronomers in the decision of this point. For wherever Satan and his defeated host went at their expulsion from heaven, we think we are certain none of all these beautiful worlds, or be they worlds or not, I mean the fixed stars, planets, and so forth, had then any existence; for *the beginning*, as the Scripture calls it, had not yet begun.

But to speak a little by the rules of philosophy, that is to say, so as to be understood by others even when we speak of things we cannot fully understand ourselves, though in the beginning of time all this glorious creation was formed, the earth, the starry heavens, and all the furniture thereof (and there was a time when they were not) yet we cannot say so of the void, or that nameless nowhere as I called it before, which now appears to be a somewhere in which these glorious bodies are placed. That immense space that those take up, and in which they move at this time, must be supposed (before they had being) to be placed there. As God himself was and existed before all being, time, or place, so the Heaven of heavens, or the place where the thrones and dominions of his kingdom then existed, inconceivable and ineffable, also had an existence before the glorious seraphs, the innumerable company of angels that attended about the throne of God, existed. These all had a being long before, as the eternal Creator of them all had existed before them.

Into this void or abyss of nothing, however unmeasurable, infinite, and, even inconceivable to those spirits themselves, they certainly launched from the bright precipice from which they fell and shifted as well as they could.

Here, expanding those wings, which fear and horror at their defeat furnished them as I hinted before, they hurried away to the utmost distance possible from the face of God their conqueror and then most dreaded enemy, formerly their joy and glory.

Be this utmost removed distance where it will, here certainly Satan and all his gang of devils, his numberless though routed armies, retired. Here Milton might with some good ground have formed his Pandemonium and have brought them in, consulting what was next to be done, and whether there was any room left to renew the war or to carry on the rebellion. But had they been cast immediately into hell and closed up there—the bottomless pit locked upon them, and the key carried up to heaven to be kept there, as Mr. Milton himself in part confesses and the Scripture affirms—I say, had this been so, the Devil himself could not have been so ignorant as to think of any future steps to be taken to retrieve his affairs, and therefore a Pandemonium or divan in hell, to consider it, was ridiculous.

All Mr. Milton's schemes of Satan's future conduct, and all the Scripture expressions about the Devil and his numerous attendants and of his actions since that time, make it not reasonable to suggest that the devils were confined to their eternal prison at their expulsion out of heaven; but that they were in a state of liberty to act, though limited in acting, of which I shall also speak in its place.

7

OF THE NUMBER OF SATAN'S HOST, HOW THEY CAME FIRST TO KNOW OF THE NEW CREATED WORLDS NOW IN BEING, AND THEIR MEASURES WITH MANKIND UPON THE DISCOVERY.

Several things have been suggested to set us a calculating the number of this frightful throng of devils who, with Satan, the master-devil, was thus cast out of heaven. I cannot say I am so much a master of political arithmetic as to cast up the number of the beast, no, nor the number of the beasts or devils who make up this throng. They tell us St. Francis or some other saint—they do not say who—asked the Devil once how strong he was (for St. Francis, you must know, was very familiar with him). The Devil, it seems, did not tell him but presently raised a great cloud of dust by the help, I suppose, of a gust of wind, and bid that saint count it. He was, I suppose, a calculator who would be called grave, who, dividing Satan's troops into three lines, cast up the number of the devils of all sorts in each battalion at ten hundred times a hundred thousand millions of the first line, fifty millions of times as many in the second line, and three hundred thousand times as many as both in the third line.

The impertinence of this account would hardly have given it a place here, only to hint that it has always been the opinion that Satan's name may well be called a noun of multitude, and that the Devil and his angels are certainly no inconsiderable number.

It was a smart repartee that a Venetian nobleman made to a priest who railed him upon his refusing to give something to the church, which the priest demanded for delivering him from purgatory. When the priest asked him if he knew what an innumerable number of devils they were to take him, he answered, yes, he knew how many devils there were in all.

"How many?" says the priest, his curiosity, I suppose, being raised by the novelty of the answer.

"Why ten million, five hundred and eleven thousand, six hundred and seventy-five devils and a half," says the nobleman.

"A half!" says the priest, please, what kind of a devil is that?"

"Yourself, says the nobleman, for you are half a devil already, and will be a whole one when you come there, for you are for deluding all you deal with and bringing us soul and body into your hands, that you may be paid for letting us go again."

So much for their number.

Here also it would come in very aptly to consider the state of that long interval between the time of their expulsion from heaven and the creation of the world, and what the posture of the Devil's affairs might have been during that time. The horror of their condition can only be conceived of at a distance, and especially by us, who being embodied creatures cannot fully judge of what is or is not a punishment to seraphs and spirits. But it is just to suppose they suffered all that spirits of a seraphic nature were capable to sustain consistent with their existence, notwithstanding that they still retained the hellishness of their rebellious principle, namely, their hatred and rage against God and their envy at the felicity of His creatures.

As to how long their time might have been, I shall leave the search, no lights being given me that are either probable or rational, and we have so little room to make a judgment of it that we may as well believe father M____ (who supposes it to be a hundred thousand years) as those who judge it one thousand years. It is enough that we are sure it was before the creation. How long before is not material to the Devil's history, unless we had some records of what happened to him or was done by him in the interval.

During the wandering condition the Devil was in at that time, we may suppose he and his whole clan to have been employed in exerting their hatred and rage at the Almighty and at the happiness of the remaining faithful angels, by all the ways they had power to show it.

From this determined, stated enmity of Satan and his host against God and everything that brought glory to his name, Mr. Milton brings in Satan (when he first saw Adam in Paradise and the felicity of his station there) swelling with rage and envy and taking up a dreadful resolution to ruin Adam and all his posterity merely to disappoint his Maker of the glory of His creation. I shall come to speak of that in its place.

How Satan, in his remote situation got intelligence of the place where to find Adam out, or that any such thing as a man was created, is just matter of speculation, and there might be many rational schemes laid for it. Mr. Milton does not undertake to tell us the particulars, nor indeed could he find room for it.

Having, as I have said, a liberty to range over the whole void or abyss (which we want as well a name for as indeed powers to conceive of), perhaps the Devil might have discovered that the almighty Creator had formed a new and glorious work, with infinite beauty and variety, filling up the immense waste of space in which he, the Devil and his angels, had roved for so long a time without finding anything to work on, or to exert their apostate rage in against their Maker.

That at length they found the infinite untrodden space suddenly spread full with glorious bodies, shining in self-existing beauty with a new, and to them unknown luster, called light, they found these luminous bodies, though immense in bulk and infinite in number, yet fixed in their wondrous stations, regular and exact in their motions, confined in their proper orbits, tending to their particular centers, and enjoying every one their peculiar systems, within which were contained innumerable planets with their satellites or moons, in which again a reciprocal influence, motion, and revolution conspired to form the most admirable uniformity of the whole.

Surprised, to be sure, with this sudden and yet glorious work of the Almighty (for the creation was enough with its luster even to surprise the devils), they might reasonably be supposed to spring out of their dark retreat, and with a curiosity not below the seraphic dignity (for these are some of the things which the angels desire to look into), to take a flight through all the amazing systems of the fixed suns or stars, which we see now but at a distance and only make astronomical guesses at.

Here the Devil found not a subject of wonder only, but matter to swell his revolted spirit with more rage and to revive the malignity of his mind against his Maker, and especially against this new increase of glory, which, to his infinite regret, was extended over the whole waste, and which he looked upon, as we say in human affairs, as a *pays conquis* [conquered country], or, if you will have it in the language of devils, as an invasion upon their kingdom.

SATAN JUDGED FOR HIS REBELLION.

Here it naturally occurred to them in their state of envy and rebellion that though they could not assault the impregnable walls of heaven, and could no more pretend to raise war in the place of blessedness and peace, yet perhaps they might find room in this new and, however glorious yet inferior kingdom or creation, to work some despite to their great Creator, or to affront His majesty in the person of some of his new creatures. And upon this they may be justly supposed to have doubled their vigilance in the survey they resolved to take of these new worlds, however great, numberless, and wonderful.

We have not yet had an account of what discoveries they may have made in the other and greater worlds than this earth. Possibly they are conversant with other parts of God's creation besides this little, little globe (which is but as a point in comparison to the rest), and with other of God's creatures besides man, who may, according to the opinion of our philosophers, inhabit those worlds. But as nobody knows that part but the Devil, we shall not trouble ourselves with the enquiry.

But it is very reasonable, and indeed probable, that the devils were more than ordinarily surprised at the nature and reason of all this glorious creation after they had, with the utmost curiosity, viewed all the parts of it—the glories of the several systems; the immense spaces in which the glorious bodies that were created and made part of it were allowed respectively to move; the innumerable fixed stars as so many suns in the center of so many distant solar systems; the (likewise innumerable) dark opaque bodies receiving light and depending upon those suns respectively for such light, and then reflecting that light again upon and for the use of one another—to see the beauty and splendor of their forms, the regularity of their position, the order and exactness, and yet inconceivable velocity of their motions, the certainty of their revolutions, and the variety and virtue of their influences. And then, which was even to the devils themselves most astonishing, was that after all the rest of their observations they should find this whole immense work was adapted for, and made subservient to the use, delight, and blessing only of one poor species, in itself small, and in appearance contemptible—the least of all the kinds supposed to inhabit so many glorious worlds as appeared now to be formed (I mean that moon called Earth, and the creature called Man, that all was made for him, upheld by the wise Creator on his account only, and would necessarily end and cease whenever that species should end and be determined).

That this creature was to be found nowhere but (as above) in one little individual moon, a spot less than almost any of the moons that were in such great numbers to be found attendant upon and prescribed with in every system of the whole created heavens, this was astonishing even to the Devil himself. Indeed, the whole clan of devils could scarcely entertain any just ideas of the thing till, at last, Satan (indefatigable in his search or enquiry into the nature and reason of this new work, and particularly searching into the species of man, whom he found God had thus placed in the little globe, called earth,) soon came to an *éclaircissement* [clarification], or a clear understanding of the whole. For example:

1. He found this creature, called man, however unassuming and small in his appearance, a kind of a seraphic species, was made in the very image of God, endowed with reasonable faculties to know good and evil, and possessed of a certain thing till then unknown and unheard of even in hell itself—that is, in the habitation of devils, let that be where it would, viz.,

2. That God had made him indeed of the lowest and coarsest materials, but that he had breathed into him the breath of life, and that he became a living thing called soul, being a kind of an extraordinary heavenly and divine emanation; and consequently that man, however unassuming and terrestrial his body might be, was yet heaven-born, in his spirit part completely seraphic, and after a space of life here (determined to be a state of probation), he should be translated through the regions of death into a life purely and truly seraphic, and should remain so forever—being capable of knowing and enjoying God his Maker and standing in his presence as the glorified angels do.
3. That he had the most sublime faculties infused into him and was not only capable of knowing and contemplating God, and still more of enjoying him, as above, but also capable (which the Devil now was not) of honoring and glorifying his Maker, who also had condescended to accept honor from him.
4. And, which was still more, that being of an angelic nature, though mixed with and confined for the present in a case of mortal flesh, he was intended to be removed from this earth after a certain time of life here to inhabit that heaven, and enjoy that very glory and felicity, from which Satan and his angels had been expelled.

When he found all this, it presently occurred to him that God had done it all as an act of triumph over him (Satan), and that these creatures were only created to people heaven, which had been depopulated, or stripped of its inhabitants by their expulsion, and that these were all to be made angels in the Devil's stead.

If this thought increased his fury and envy as far as rage of devils can be capable of being made greater, it doubtless set him on work to give a vent to that rage and envy by searching into the nature and constitution of this creature called man, and to find out whether he was invulnerable and could by no means be hurt by the power of hell or deluded by his subtlety, or whether he might be beguiled and deluded, and so, instead of being preserved in holiness and purity, wherein he was certainly created, he might be brought to fall and rebel as he (Satan) had done before him. By which, instead of being transplanted into a glorious state after this life in heaven, as his Maker had designed him to be, to fill up the angelic choir and supply the place whence he (Satan) had fallen, he might be made to fall also like him and, in a word, be made a devil like him.

This convinces us that the Devil has not lost his natural powers by his fall, and our learned commentator, Mr. Pool, is of the same opinion, though he grants that the Devil has lost his moral power, or his power of doing good, which he can never recover. See Mr. Pool, upon Acts 19:17, where we may particularly observe, when the man possessed with an evil spirit flew upon the seven sons of Scæva the Jew (who would have exorcised them in the name of Jesus without the authority of Jesus, or without faith in him), he flew on them and mastered them so that they fled out of the house from the Devil, conquered, naked, and wounded. But of this power of the Devil, it shall speak by itself.

In a word, and to sum up all the Devil's story from his first expulsion, it stands thus: For however many years as were between his fall and the creation of man, though we have no memoirs of his particular affairs, we have reason to believe he was without any manner of employment except a certain tormenting endeavor to be always expressing his rage and enmity against heaven. I call it tormenting, because ever disappointed, every thought about it proving empty, every attempt toward it abortive (leaving them only light enough to see still more and more reason to despair of success) this made his condition still more and more a hell than it was before.

After a space of duration in this misery, of which we have no light given us to measure or judge, he at length discovered the new creation of man, as above, upon which he soon found reason to set himself to work upon and has been busily employed ever since.

And now, indeed, there may be room to suggest a local hell (made corrupt and degenerate by him) and the confinement of souls to it as a place, though he himself, as is still apparent by his actions, is not yet confined to it. Of this hell, its locality, extent, dimensions, continuance, and nature, since it does not belong to Satan's history, I have a good excuse for saying nothing and so put off my meddling with that, with which if I would meddle, I could say nothing to the purpose.

8

OF THE POWER OF THE DEVIL AT THE TIME OF THE CREATION OF THIS WORLD, AND WHETHER IT HAS NOT BEEN FURTHER STRAITENED AND LIMITED SINCE THAT TIME, AND WHAT SHIFTS AND STRATAGEMS HE IS OBLIGED TO MAKE USE OF TO ACHIEVE HIS DESIGNS UPON MANKIND.

Cunning men have fabled, and though it be without either religion, authority, or physical foundation (it may be we may think it never the worse for that) that when God made the stars and all the heavenly luminaries, the Devil, to mimic his Maker and insult his new creation, made comets in imitation of the fixed stars. But that the composition of them being combustible, when they came to wander in the abyss, rolling in an irregular ill-grounded motion, they ignited in their approach to some of those great bodies of flame, the fixed stars. And being thus kindled, like a firework unskillfully set off, they then took wild and eccentric, as also different, motions of their own out of Satan's direction and beyond his power to regulate ever after.

Let this thought stand by itself. It matters not to our purpose whether we believe anything of it or not. It is enough to our case that if Satan had any such power then, he has no such power now, and that leads me to inquire into his more recent limitations.

I am to suppose he and all his accomplices being confounded at the discovery of the new creation, and racking their wits to find out the meaning of it, had at last (no matter how) discovered the whole system and concluded, as I have said, that the creature, called man, was to be their successor in the heavenly mansions, upon which I suggest that the first motion of hell was to destroy this new work and, if possible, to overwhelm it.

But when they came to make the attempt, they found their chains were not long enough, and that they could not reach to the extremes of the system. They had no power either to break the order or stop the motion, dislocate the parts, or confound the situation of things. They no doubt traversed the whole work, visited every star, landed upon every solid, and sailed upon every fluid in the whole scheme to see what mischief they could do.

Upon a long and full survey, they came to this point in their enquiry: that in short they could do nothing by force, that they could not displace any part, annihilate any atom, or destroy any life in the whole creation, but that as Omnipotence had created it, so the same Omnipotence had armed it at all points against the utmost power of hell and had made the smallest creature in it invulnerable, as to Satan. So without the permission of the same power that had made heaven and conquered the Devil, he could do nothing at all as to destroying anything that God had made, no, not the little, diminutive thing called man, who Satan saw so much reason to hate, as being created to succeed him in happiness in heaven.

Satan found him placed out of his power to hurt, or out of his reach to touch. And here, by the way, appears the second conquest of heaven over the Devil, that having placed his rival, as it were, just before his face and shown the hateful sight to him, he saw written upon his image, "Touch him if you dare."

It cannot be doubted but had it not been thus (man is so far from being a match for the Devil), that one of Satan's least imps or angels could destroy all the race of them in the world, ay, world and all in a moment.

As he is prince of the power of the air, taking the air for the elementary world, how easily could he, at one blast, sweep all the surface of the earth into the sea or drive weighty immense surges of the ocean over the whole plane of the earth and deluge the globe at once with a storm? Or how easily could he, who by the situation of the empire must be supposed able to manage the clouds, draw them up in such position as should naturally produce thunders and lightnings, causing those lightnings to blast the earth, dash in pieces all the buildings, burn all the populous towns and cities, and lay waste the world?

At the same time, he might command suited quantities of sublimated air to burst out of the bowels of the earth and overwhelm and swallow up, in the opening chasms, all the inhabitants of the globe.

In a word, Satan left to himself as a devil, and to the power that by virtue of his seraphic original he must be vested with, was able to have made devilish work in the world if by a superior power he was not restrained.

But there is no doubt, at least to me, that with his fall from heaven, just as he lost the rectitude and glory of his angelic nature, I mean his innocence, so he lost the power too that he had before. And when he first commenced being Devil, he received the chains of restraint, too, as the badge of his apostacy, viz., a general prohibition to do anything to the prejudice of this creation, or to do anything by force or violence without special permission.

This prohibition was not sent him by a messenger, or by an order in writing, or proclaimed from heaven by a law, but Satan, by a strange, invisible and unaccountable impression, felt the restraint within him. And at the same time, while his moral capacity was not taken away, his power of exerting that capacity yet felt the restraint and left him unable to do even what he was able to do at the same time.

I question not but the Devil is sensible of this restraint, that is to say, not as it is a restraint only, or as an effect of his expulsion from heaven, but that it prevents his capital design against man, who, for the reason I have given already, he entertains a mortal hatred of, and would destroy with all his heart if he might. Therefore, like a chained mastiff, we find him oftentimes making a horrid hellish clamor and noise, barking and howling, and frightening the people, letting them know that if he were loose he would tear them in pieces. But at the same time, his very fury shakes his chain, which lets them know, to their satisfaction, he can only bark but cannot bite.

Some are of the opinion that the Devil is not restrained so much by the superior power of his Sovereign and Maker, but that all his milder measures with man are the effect of a political scheme and done upon mature deliberation—that it was resolved to act thus in the great Council or P—–t of Devils, called upon this very occasion when they first were informed of the creation of man, and especially when they considered what kind of creature he was and what might probably be a reason of making him, viz., to fill up the vacancies in heaven. I say, that then the devils resolved that it was not for their interest to fall upon him with fury and rage, and so destroy the species, for that would be no benefit at all to them and would only cause another original man to be created. For they knew God could, by the same Omnipotence, form as many new species of creatures as He pleased, and, if He thought fit, create them in heaven too, out of the reach of devils or evil spirits. So therefore, to destroy man would in no way answer their end.

On the other hand, examining strictly the mold of this newly made creature and of what materials he was formed, how he was mixed up of a nature convertible and pervertible, capable indeed of infinite excellence, and consequently of eternal felicity, but yet subject likewise to corruption and degeneracy and consequently to eternal misery, that instead of being fit to supply the places of Satan and his rejected tribe (the expelled angels) in heaven and filling up the thrones or stalls in the celestial choir, the Devil saw they might, if they could but be brought into crime, become a race of rebels and traitors like the rest—and so come at last to keep them company as well in the place of eternal misery (as in the merit of it, and in a word, become like devils instead of angels).

Upon this discovery, I say, they found it infinitely more for the interest of Satan's infernal kingdom to go another way to work with mankind and see if it were possible by the strength of all their infernal wit and counsels to lay some snare for him and by some stratagem to bring him to eternal ruin and misery.

This being then approved as their only method (and the Devil showed he was no fool in the choice), he next resolved that there was no time to be lost, that it was to be set about immediately before the race was multiplied and, by that means, the work be not made greater only, but perhaps the more difficult too. Accordingly, the diligent Devil went instantly about it agreeably to all the story of Eve and the serpent, as before, the belief of which, whether historically or allegorically, is not at all obstructed by this hypothesis.

I do not affirm that this was the case at first, because being not present in that black Divan, at least not that I know of, who knows where he was or was not in his pre-existent state? I cannot be positive in the resolve that passed there. But except for some very little apparent contradiction, which we find in the sacred writings, I should, I confess, incline to believe it historically. And I shall speak of those things that I call contradictions to it more largely hereafter.

In the meantime, be it one way or other, that is to say, either Satan had no power to have proceeded with man by violence and to have destroyed him as soon as he was made, or he had the power but chose rather to proceed by other methods to deceive and debauch him. I say, be it which you please, I am still of the opinion that it really was not the Devil's business to destroy the species. It would have been nothing to the purpose and no advantage at all to him if he had done it. For, as above, God could immediately have created another species to the same end, whom He either could have made invulnerable and not subject to the Devil's power or removed him out of Satan's reach, placing him out of the Devil's view, in heaven or some other place where the Devil could not come to hurt him. And therefore it is infinitely more to his advantage, and more suited to his real design of defeating the end of man's creation, to debauch him and make a devil of him so he may be rejected like him and increase the infernal kingdom and company in the lake of misery *in æternum* [forever].

It may be true, for ought I know, that Satan has not the power of destruction put into his hand, and that he cannot take away the life of a man. And it seems probable to be so from the story of Satan and Job, when Satan appeared among the sons of God, as the text says (Job 1:6). Now when God gave such a character of Job to him and asked him if he had considered his servant Job (v. 8), why did not the Devil go immediately and exert his malice against the good man at once to let his Maker see what would become of his servant Job in his distress? On the contrary, we see he only answers by showing the reason of Job's good behavior—that it was but common gratitude for the blessing and protection he enjoyed (v. 10)—and by pleading that if his estate were taken away and he was exposed as he (Satan) was, to be a beggar and a vagabond going to and fro in the earth, and walking up and down therein, he should be a very devil too, like him, and curse God to his face.

Upon this, the text says that God answered, *"Behold all that he hath is in thy power"* (v.12). Now 'tis plain here, that God gave up Job's wealth and estate, indeed his family, and the lives of his children and servants into the Devil's power. And accordingly, like a true merciless Devil, as he is, he destroyed them all. He moved the Sabeans to fall upon the oxen and the asses and carry them off. He moved the Chaldeans to fall upon the camels and the servants to carry off the first and murder the last. He made lightning flash upon the poor sheep and kill them all. And he blew his house down upon his poor children and buried them all in the ruins.

Now here is a specimen of Satan's good will to mankind

and what havoc the Devil would make in the world if he might. And here is a testimony, too, that he could not do this without permission. So I cannot but be of the opinion he has some limitations, some bounds set to his natural fury, and a certain number of links in his chain, which he cannot exceed, or in a Word, that he cannot go a foot beyond his tether.

We have the same kind of evidence in the gospel (Matt. 8:31), where Satan could not so much as possess the filthiest and basest of all creatures, the swine, till he had asked permission. And still, to show his good will, as soon as he had gotten permission, he hurried them all into the sea and drowned them. These, I say, are some of the reasons why I am not willing to say the Devil is not restrained in power. But on the other side, we are told of so many mischievous things the Devil has done in the world by virtue of his dominion over the elements, and by other testimonies of his power, that I don't know what to think of it. Though upon the whole, the first is the safest opinion. For if we should believe the last, we might, for ought I know, be brought like the American Indians to worship him at last, that he may do us no harm.

And now that I have named those people in America, I confess it would go a great way in favor of Satan's generosity, as well as in testimony of his power, if we might believe all the accounts that indeed authors are pretty well agreed in the truth of, namely, the mischiefs the Devil does in those countries where his dominion seems to be established, how he uses them when they deny him the homage he claims of them as his due, what havoc and combustion he makes among them, and how beneficent he is (or at least negative in his mischiefs) when they appease him by their hellish sacrifices.

Likewise, we see a test of his wicked subtlety in his management of those dark nations when he was more immediately worshiped by them, namely, by making them believe that all their good weather, rains, dews, and kind influences upon the earth to make it fruitful was from him. Whereas, they really were the common blessings of a higher hand and came not from him, the Devil, but from Him who made the Devil, and made him a devil or fallen angel by his curse.

But to go back to the method the Devil took with the first of mankind, it is plain the policy of hell was right, though the execution of the resolves they took did not fully answer their end either. For Satan fastening upon poor, proud, ridiculous Mother Eve, as I have said before, he made presently a true judgment of her capacities and of her temper, took her by the right hand, and soothing her vanity (which is to this day the softest place in the head of all the sex), beguiled her out of her senses by praising her beauty and promising to make her a goddess.

The foolish woman yielded presently, and that we are told is the reason why the same method so strangely succeeds with all her posterity, viz., that you are sure to prevail with them if you can but once persuade them that you believe they are witty and handsome. For the Devil, you may observe, never quits any hold he gets, and having once found a way into the heart always takes care to keep the door open so any of his agents may enter after him without any more difficulty.

Hence the same argument, especially the last, has so bewitching an influence on the sex that they rarely deny you anything after they are but weak enough and vain enough to accept the praises you offer them on that mind. On the other hand, you are sure they never forgive you the unpardonable crime of saying they are ugly or disagreeable.

It is suggested that the first method the Devil took to insinuate all those fine things into Eve's giddy head was by creeping close to her one night when she was asleep and laying his mouth to her ear, whispering all the fine things to her that he knew would set her fancy a tip-toe, and so made her receive them involuntarily into her mind—knowing well enough that when she had formed such ideas in her soul, however they came there, she would never be quiet till she had worked them up to some extraordinary thing or other.

It was evident what the Devil aimed at, namely, that she should break in upon the command of God and so, having corrupted herself, bring the curse upon herself and all her race, as God had threatened. But why should the pride of Eve be so easily tickled by the motion of her exquisite beauty when there then was no prospect of the use or need of those charms? That indeed makes a kind of difficulty here that the learned have not determined. For:

1. If she had been as ugly as the Devil, she had no body to rival her, so she need not fear Adam should leave her and get another mistress.
2. If she had been bright and beautiful as an angel, she had no other admirer but poor Adam, and he could have no room to be jealous of her, or afraid she should be unfaithful to him. So in short, Eve had no such occasion for her beauty, nor could she make any use of it either to a bad purpose or to a good. Therefore I believe the Devil, who is too cunning to do anything that signifies nothing, rather tempted her by the hope of increasing her wit, than her beauty.

But to come back to the method of Satan's tempting her, viz. by whispering to her in her sleep, it was a cunning trick; that's the truth of it. And by that means he certainly set her head in a frenzy after deism, and to be made a goddess, and then backed it by the subtle talk he had with her afterward.

I am the more particular upon this part, because, however the Devil may have been the first that ever practiced it, yet I can assure him the experiment has been tried upon many a woman since, to the beguiling her out of her modesty as well as her simplicity. And the cunning men tell us still, that if you can come at a woman when she is in a deep sleep and whisper to her close to her ear, she will certainly dream of the thing you say to her, and so too will a man.

Well, be this so to her race or not, it seems it was so to her; for she woke up with her head filled with pleasing ideas and, as some will have it, unlawful desires such as to be sure she never had entertained before. These are supposed to have been fatally infused in her dream and suggested to her waking soul, when the organ ear that conveyed them was dozed and insensible, the strange fate of sleeping in paradise! From that we have notice but of two sleeps there, that in one a woman should go out from him, and in the other, the Devil should come into her.

Certainly, when Satan first made the attempt upon Eve, he did not think he should have so easily conquered her or brought his business about so soon. The Devil himself could not have imagined she should have been so soon brought to forget the command given, or at least who gave it, and have ventured to transgress against Him and made her forget that God had told her it should be Death to her to touch it, and above all, that she should aspire to be as wise as Him when she was so ignorant before as to believe it was for fear of her being like Him that He had forbid it her.

Well might she be said to be the weaker vessel, though Adam himself had little enough to say for his being the stronger of the two when he was over-persuaded (if it were done by persuasion) by his wife to do the same thing.

And mark how wise they were after they had eaten, and what fools they both acted like, even to one another. Indeed, even all the knowledge they attained by it was, for ought I see, only to know that they were fools and to be sensible both of sin and shame. And see how simply they acted, I say, upon their having committed the crime and being detected in it.

View them today conversing with their God,
His Image both enjoy'd and understood,
Tomorrow skulking with a sordid flight,
Among the bushes from the infinite,
As if that power was blind, which gave them sight;
With senseless labour tagging fig-leaf vests,
To hide their bodies from the sight of beasts.
Hark! How the fool pleads faint, for forfeit life,
First he reproaches Heaven, and then his wife;
The woman which thou gavest as if the gift
Could rob him of the little reason left,
A weak pretense to shift his early crime,
As if accusing her would excuse him;
But thus encroaching crime dethrones the sense,
And intercepts the heavenly influence,
Debauches reason, makes the man a fool,
And turns his active light to ridicule.

It must be confessed that it was unaccountable degeneracy, even of their common reasoning, that Adam and Eve both fell into upon first committing the offence of taking the forbidden fruit. If that was their being made as gods, it made but a poor appearance in its first coming for them to hide their nakedness when there was no body to see them and cover themselves among the bushes from their Maker. But thus it was, and this the Devil had brought them to, and well might he and all the clan of hell, as Mr. Milton presents them, laugh and triumph over the man after the blow was given, as having so egregiously abused and deluded them both.

But here, to be sure, began the Devil's new kingdom. As he had now seduced the two first creatures, he was pretty sure of success upon all the race and, therefore, prepared to attack them also as soon as they came on. Nor was their increasing multitude any discouragement to his attempt, but just the contrary. For he had agents enough to employ if every man and woman that should be born were to desire a devil to wait upon them, separately and singly, to seduce them. Whereas some whole nations have been such willing subjects to him, one of his seraphic imps may, for ought we know, have been enough to guide a whole country—the people being entirely subjected to his government for many ages, as in America for example, where some will have it that he conveyed the first inhabitants. (At least if he did not, we don't well know who did, or how they got thither).

And how came all the communication to be so entirely cut off between the nations of Europe and Africa, whence America must certainly have been populated? The Devil must have done it indeed. I say, how could the communication be so entirely cut off between them that, except the time whenever it was that people first reached from one to the other, none ever came back to give their friends any account of their success or invite them to follow? Nor did they hear of one another afterward, as we have reason to think. Did Satan intervene and keep them thus asunder, lest news from heaven should reach them, and so they should be recovered out of his government? We cannot tell how to give any other rational account of it, that a nation, indeed a quarter of the world, or as some will have it be, half the globe, should be populated from Europe or Africa, or both, and nobody ever go after them, or come back from them in over three thousand years after.

Indeed, that those countries should be populated when there was no navigation in use in these parts of the world, no ships made that could carry provisions enough to support the people that failed in them, but that they must have been starved to death before they could reach the shore of America; the Ferry from Europe or Africa, in any part (which we have known navigation to be practiced in) being at least 1,000 miles, and in most places much more.

But as to the Americans, let the Devil and them alone to account for their coming there. This we are certain of, that we knew nothing of them for many hundred years, and when we did, when the discovery was made, they who went there from here found Satan in a full and quiet possession of them, ruling them with an arbitrary government, particular to him. He had led them into a blind subjection to him (indeed, I might call it devotion to him), for it was of the only religion that was to be found among them—worshipping horrible idols in his name, to whom he directed human sacrifices continually to be made till he deluged the country with blood and ripened them up for the destruction that followed, from the invasion of the Spaniards, who he knew would hurry them all out of the world as fast as he (the Devil) himself could desire of them.

But to go back a little to the origin of things, it is evident that Satan has made a much better market of mankind by thus subtly attacking them and bringing them to break with their Maker, as he had done before them, than he could have done by fulminating upon them at first and sending them all out of the world at once. For now, he has peopled his own dominions with them, though a remnant is snatched as it were out of his clutches by the agency of invincible grace. Yet this may be said of the Devil without offence: that he has in some sense carried his point and, as it were, forced his Maker to be satisfied with a part of mankind (and the least part too) instead of the great glory He would have brought to himself by keeping them all in His service.

Mr. Milton, as I have noted above, brings in the Devil and all hell with him, making a *Feu de Joye* for the victory Satan obtained over one silly woman. Indeed, it was a piece of success greater in its consequence than in the immediate appearance. Nor was the conquest so complete as Satan himself imagined making, since the promise of a redemption out of God's hands, which was immediately made to the man on behalf of himself and his believing posterity, was a great disappointment to Satan and, as it were, snatched the best part of his victory out of his hands.

It is certain the devils knew what the meaning of that promise was, and who was to be the Seed of the woman, namely, the incarnate Son of God. And that was a second blow to the whole infernal body. But as if they had resolved to let that alone, Satan went on with his business. And as he had introduced crime into the common parent of mankind, and thereby secured the contamination of blood and the descent or propagation of the corrupt seed, he had nothing to do but assist nature in time to come to carry on its own rebellion and act itself in the breasts of Eve's tainted posterity. And that indeed has been the Devil's business ever since his first victory upon the kind to this day.

His success in this part has been such, that we see upon innumerable occasions a general defection has followed, a kind of a taint upon nature (call it what you will), a blast upon the race of mankind. And were it not for one thing, he would have ruined the whole family. I say, were it not for one thing, namely, a selected company or number, which his Maker has resolved he shall not be able to corrupt (or if he does, sending the promised Seed shall recover them back again from him by the power of irresistible grace), which number thus selected or elected, call it which we will, are still to supply the vacancies in heaven, which Satan's defection left open. And what was before filled up with created seraphs is now to be restored by recovered saints, by whom infinite Glory is to accrue to the Kingdom of the Redeemer.

This glorious establishment has robbed Satan of all the joy of his victory and left him just where he was, defeated and disappointed. Nor does the possession of all the myriads of the sons of perdition (who yet some are of the opinion will be snatched from him too at last), I say, the possession of all those, make amends to him. For he is such a devil in his nature that his envy of those he cannot seduce eats out all the satisfaction of the mischief he has done in seducing all the rest. But I must not preach, so I return to things as much needful to know, though less solemn.

ANGEL TALKS WITH ADAM AND EVE

9

OF THE PROGRESS OF SATAN IN CARRYING OUT HIS CONQUEST OVER MANKIND FROM THE FALL OF EVE TO THE DELUGE.

I doubt if the Devil were asked the question plainly after he had conquered Eve by his own wicked contrivance (and then by her assistance had brought Adam too, like a fool as he was, into the same gulf of misery), that he would confess he thought he had done his work, compassed the whole race (that they were now his own), and put an end to the grand design of their creation, namely, of populating heaven with a new angelic race of souls, who when glorified, should make up the defection of the host of hell who had been expunged of their crime—in a word, that he had gotten a better conquest than if he had destroyed them all.

But in the midst of his conquest, he found a check put to the advantages he expected to reap from his victory by the immediate promise of grace to a part of the posterity of Adam, who, notwithstanding the fall, were to be purchased by the Messiah and snatched out of his (Satan's) hands, and over whom he could make no final conquest. So his power met with a new limitation, and such that indeed fully disappointed him in the main thing he aimed at, viz., preventing the beatitudes of mankind, which were thus secured. (And what if the numbers of mankind were upon this account increased in such a manner that the selected number should, by length of time, amount to just as many as the whole race, had they not fallen?). And thus, indeed, the world may be said to be upheld and continued for the sake of those few, since till their number can be completed the creation cannot fall any more than that without them, or but for them, it would not have stood.

But leaving this speculation and not having enquired of Satan what he has to say on that subject, let us go back to the Antediluvian world. The Devil, to be sure, gained his point upon Eve, and through her upon all her race. He drew her into sin and got her turned out of Paradise, the man with her. The next thing was to go to work with her posterity, and particularly with her two sons Cain and Abel.

Notwithstanding his fall, and having repented very sincerely of his sin, Adam received the promise of redemption and pardon with an humble but believing heart. Charity bids us suppose that he led a very religious and sober life ever after and, especially in the first part of his time, that he brought up his children very soberly and gave them all the necessary advantages of a religious education and a good introduction into the world that he was capable of, and that Eve likewise assisted with both in her place and degree.

I suppose their two eldest sons, Cain and Abel, the one heir apparent to the patriarchal empire and the other heir presumptive, also lived very sober and religious lives. And since the principles of natural religion dictated an homage and subjection due to the Almighty Maker as an acknowledgment of his mercies and a recognition of their obedience, and with the received usage of religion dictating at that time that this homage was to be paid by a sacrifice, both of them brought a free-will-offering to be dedicated to God respectively for themselves and families.

How it was, and for what reason God had respect to the offering of Abel, which the learned say was a lamb of the firstlings of the flock, and did not give any testimony of the like respect to Cain and his offering, which was of the first fruits of the earth (the offerings being equally suited to the respective employment of the men), that is not my present business. But this we find made heart-burnings and raised envy and jealousy in the mind of Cain. And at that door the Devil immediately entered; for he, who from the beginning was very diligent in his way, never skipped any opportunity, or missed any advantages that the circumstances of mankind offered him to do mischief.

What shape or appearance the Devil took up to enter into a conversation with Cain upon the subject, that authors do not take upon them to determine. But 'tis generally supposed he impersonated or used some of Cain's sons or grandsons to begin the discourse, who attacked their father, or perhaps grandfather, upon this occasion, in the following manner, or to that purpose.

Devil. Sir, I perceive your majesty (for the first race were certainly all monarchs as great as kings to their immediate posterity) to be greatly disturbed of late. Your countenance is changed. Your noble cheerfulness (the glories of your face) are strangely sunk and gone, and you are not the man you used to be. Please your majesty to communicate your griefs to us your children. You may be sure that, if it be possible, we would procure you relief and restore your delights, the loss of which, if thus you go on to subject yourself to too much melancholy, will be very hurtful to you and in the end destroy you.

Cain. It is very kind, my dear children, to show your respect thus to your true progenitor and to offer your assistance. I confess, as you say, my mind is oppressed and displeased. But though 'tis very heavy, yet I know not which way to look for relief, for the distemper is above our reach; no cure can be found for it on earth.

D. Do not say so, sir. There can be no disease sure on earth but may be cured on earth. If it be a mental evil, we have heard that your great ancestor, the first father of us all, who lives still on the great western plains toward the sea, is the oracle to which all his children fly for direction in such cases when they are out of the reach of the ordinary understanding of mankind. If it please you to allow, we will take a journey to him and, representing your case to him, we will hear his advice and bring it to you with all speed for the ease of your mind.

Cain. I know not whether he can reach my case or not.

D. Doubtless he may, and if not, the labor of our journey is nothing when placed in competition with the ease of your mind. 'Tis but a few days travel lost, and you will not be the worse if we fail of the desired success.

Cain. The offer is filial, and I accept your affectionate concern for me with a just sense of an obliged parent. Go then, and my blessing be upon you. But alas! Why do I bless? Can he whom God has not blessed bless others?

D. Oh! Sir, do not say so, has not God blessed you? Are

you not the second sovereign of the earth? And does He not converse with you face to face? Are not you the oracle to all your growing posterity, and next after his sovereign imperial majesty lord Adam, patriarch of the world?

Cain. But has not God rejected me and refused to converse any more with me while He daily favors and countenances my younger brother Abel as if He resolved to set him up to rule over me?

D. No, sir, that cannot be. You cannot be disturbed at such a thing. Is not the right of sovereignty yours by primogeniture? Can God himself take that away when 'tis once given? Are not you lord Adam's eldest son? Are you not the firstborn glory of the creation? And does not the government descend to you by the divine right of birth and blood?

Cain. But what does all that signify to me while God appears to favor and caress my younger brother and to shine upon him, while a black dejection and token of displeasure surrounds me every day, and He does not appear to me as He used to do?

D. And what need your majesty be concerned at that if it be so? If He does not appear pleased, you have the whole world to enjoy yourself, and all your numerous and rising posterity adore and honor you. What need those remote things be any disturbance to you?

Cain. How! My children, cannot the favor of God be valued? Yes, yes, in his favor is life; what can all the world avail without the smiles and countenance of Him who made it?

D. Doubtless, sir, He who made the world and placed you at the head of it all to govern and direct has made it agreeable, and it is able to give you a full satisfaction and enjoyment if you please to consider it well, though you were never to converse with Him all the while you live in it.

Cain. You are quite wrong there, my children, quite wrong.

D. But do you not, great Sir, see all your children as well as us rejoicing in the plenty of all things, and are they not completely happy while yet they know little of this great God? He seldom converses among us. We hear of Him indeed by your sage advices, and we bring our offerings to you for Him as you direct, and when that's done, we enjoy whatever our hearts desire. And so doubtless may you in an abundant manner, if you please.

Cain. But your felicity is wrongly placed then, or you suppose that God is pleased and satisfied that your offerings are brought to me. But what would you say if you knew that God is displeased? That He does not accept your offerings? That when I sacrificed to him on behalf of you all, He rejected my offerings, though I brought a princely gift, being of the finest of the wheat, the choicest and earliest fruits, and the sweetest of the oil, an offering suited to the Giver of them all?

D. But if you offered them, Sir, how are you sure they were not accepted?

Cain. Yes, yes, I am sure. Did not my brother Abel offer at the same time a lamb of his flock? For he, you know, delights in cattle, and covers the mountains with his herds. Over him, all the while he was sacrificing, a bright emanation shone cheering and enlivening. A pledge of favor and light ambient flames played, hovering in the lower air, as if attending his sacrifice. And when ready prepared, it immediately descended and burnt up the flesh as a sweet odoriferous savor ascended to Him who thus testified His acceptance. Whereas, over my head a black cloud, misty and distilling vapor, hung dripping upon the humble altar I had raised. And wetting the finest and choicest things I had prepared, it spoiled and defaced them. The wood unapt to burn by the moisture which fell, scarce received the fire I brought to kindle it, and even then, it rather smothered and choked than kindled into a flame. In a word, it went quite out without consuming what was brought to be offered up.

D. Let not our truly reverenced lord and father be disquieted at all this. If He accepts not what you bring, you are discharged of the debt and need bring no more, nor have the trouble of such labored collections of rarities anymore. When He thinks fit to require it again, you will have notice, no question. And then being called for, it will be accepted or else why should it be required?

Cain. That may indeed be the case, nor do I think of attempting any more to bring an offering, for I rather take it that I am forbidden for the present. But then, what is it that my younger brother triumphs in? And how am I insulted in that he and his house are all joy and triumph, as if they had some great advantage over me in that their offering was accepted when mine was not?

D. Does he triumph over your majesty, our lord and sovereign? Give us but your order and we will go and pull him and all his generation in pieces. For to triumph over you who are his elder brother is a horrid rebellion and treason, and he ought to be expelled from the society of mankind.

Cain. I think so too, indeed. However, my dear children and faithful subjects, though I accept your offer of duty and service, yet I will consider very well before I take up arms against my brother. Besides, with our sovereign father and patriarchal lord, Adam, being yet alive, it is not in my right to act offensively without his command.

D. We are ready therefore to carry your petition to him, and doubt not to obtain his license and commission too, to empower you to do yourself justice upon your younger brother, who being your vassal, or at least inferior since he is junior in birth, insults you upon the fancied opinion of having a larger share in the divine favor and receiving a blessing on his sacrifices on pretense of the same favor being denied you.

Cain. I am content, go then, and give a just account of the state of our affairs.

D. We shall soon return with the agreeable answer. Let not our lord and father continue sad and dejected, but depend on a speedy relief by the assistance of your numerous issue, all devoted to your interest and felicity.

Cain. My blessing be with you in your way and give you a favorable reception at the venerable tent of our universal lord and father.

Note here that with the cursed race being fully given up to the direction of the evil-spirit, which so early possessed them, and with them swelling with rage at the innocent Abel and his whole family, they resolved to form a most wicked and detestable lie to bring about the advice they had already given their father Cain a touch of—to pretend that Adam, being justly provoked at the undutiful behavior of Abel, had given Cain a commission to chastise him and by force cut him off and all his family as guilty of rebellion and pride.

Filled with this mischievous and bloody resolution, they came back to their father Cain after staying away a few days, such as were sufficient to make Cain believe they had been at the spacious plains where Adam dwelt—the same which are now called the blessed valleys, or the Plains of Mecca in Arabia Fælix, near the banks of the Red-Sea.

Note here also, that Cain, having received a wicked hint from these men, his children, and subjects, as before, intimated that Abel had broken the laws of primogeniture in his behavior toward him (Cain) and that he might be justly punished for it. Satan, that cunning manager of all our wayward passions, fanned the fire of envy and jealousy with his utmost skill all the while his other agents were absent. And by the time they came back, he had blown it up into such a heat of fury and rage that it lacked nothing but air to make it burn out, as it soon afterward did in a furious flame of wrath and revenge, even to blood and destruction.

Just in the very critical moment, while things stood thus with Cain, Satan brought in his wicked instruments as if they just arrived with the return of his message from Adam, at whose court they had been for orders. And thus they, that is the Devil assuming to speak by them, approached their father with an air of solemn but cheerful satisfaction at the success of their embassy.

D. Hail sovereign, reverend, patriarchal lord! We come with joy to render you an account of the success of our message.

Cain. Have you then seen the venerable tents where dwell the heaven-born, the angelic pair, to whom all human reverence is highly due and ought always to be humbly paid?

D. We have.

Cain. Did you, together with my grand request, a just, an humble homage for me pay to the great sire and mother of mankind?

D. We did.

Cain. Did you in humble language represent the griefs and anguish which oppress my soul?

D. We did, and bring back to you their blessing.

Cain. I hope with humblest signs of filial duty you took it for me on your bending knees.

D. We did and had our share. The patriarch lifting his hands to heaven expressed his joy to see his spreading race and blessed us all.

Cain. Did you my solemn message deliver, too, my injuries impartially lay down, and due assistance and direction crave?

D. We did.

Cain. What said the Oracle? He's God to me. What just command did you bring; what's to be done? Am I to bear the insulting junior's rage and meekly suffer what unjustly he, affronting primogeniture and laws of God and man, imposes by his pride insufferable? Am I to be crushed and be no more the firstborn son on earth, but bow and kneel to him?

D. Heaven forbid it! As Adam too forbids, who, with a justice godlike and peculiar to injured parents, Abel's pride resents and gives his high command to you to punish.

Cain. To punish! say you? Did he use the word, the very word? Am I commissioned then to punish Abel?

D. Not Abel only, but his rebel race, as in crime they are alike. They alike are joined in punishment.

Cain. The race indeed has shared the merit with him. How did they all insult and with a shout of triumph mock my sorrow when they saw me come from my sacrifice dejected, as if my disappointment was their joy?

D. This too the venerable prince resents, and to preserve the race in bounds of laws subordinate and limited to duty, commands that this first breach be not passed by, lest the precedent upon record stand to future times to encourage like rebellion.

Cain. And is it then my sovereign parent's will?

D. It is his will, that you his eldest son, his image, his beloved, should be maintained in all the rights of sovereignty derived to you from him and not be left exposed to injury and power usurped, but should do yourself justice on the rebel race.

Cain. And so I will. Abel shall quickly know what 'tis to trample on his elder brother and know that he's thus sentenced by his father and I'm commissioned but to execute his high command, his sentence, which is God's, and that he falls by the hand of heavenly justice.

So now Satan had done his work. He had deluded the mother to a breach against the first and only command. He had drawn Adam to the same snare. And now he brings in Cain prompted by his own rage and deluded by his (Satan's) craft to commit murder, indeed, a fratricide, an aggravated murder.

Upon this he sent out Cain while the bloody rage was in its ferment, and wickedly at the same time brought Abel, innocent and fearing no ill, just in his way, he suggested to his thoughts such words as these:

"Look you Cain, see how divine justice concurs with your father's righteous sentence. See there's your brother Abel directed by heaven to fall into your hands unarmed and unguarded so you may do yourself justice upon him without fear. See, you may kill him, and if you have a mind to conceal it, no eyes can see. Nor will the world ever know it, so that no resentment or revenge upon you or your posterity can be apprehended, but it may be said some wild beast had rent him. Nor will anyone suggest that you, his brother and superior, could possibly be the person."

Cain, prepared for the fact by his former avowed rage and resolution of revenge, was so much the less prepared to avoid the snare thus artfully contrived by the master of all subtlety, the Devil. So he immediately ran upon his brother, Abel, and after a little unarmed resistance, the innocent poor man, expecting no such mischief, was conquered and murdered, after which, as is to be supposed, the exasperated crew of Cain's outrageous race, overran all his family and household, killing man, woman, and child.

It is objected here that we have no authority in Scripture to prove this part of the story, but I answer, 'tis not likely but that Abel as well as Cain, being at man's estate long before this, had several children by their own sisters, for they were the only men in the world who were allowed to marry their own sisters, there being no other women then in the world. And as we never read of any of Abel's posterity, 'tis likewise as probable they were all murdered. For if they should have killed Abel only, whose sons might immediately fall upon Cain for the blood of their father, the world would have been involved in a civil war as soon as there were two families in it.

But be it so or not, 'tis no doubt the Devil wrought with Cain in the horrid murder, or he had never done it. Whether it was directly or by agents is not material, nor is the latter unlikely. And if the latter, then there is no improbability in the story; for why might not he who made use of the serpent to tempt Eve be as well supposed to make a tool of some of Cain's sons or grandsons to prompt him in the wicked attempt of murdering his brother? And why must we be obliged to bring in a miracle or an apparition into the story to make it probable that the Devil had any hand in it when 'twas so natural to a degenerate race to act in such a manner?

However it was, and by whatever tool the Devil wrought, 'tis certain that this was the consequence: Poor Abel was butchered, and thus the Devil made a second conquest in God's creation. For Adam was now, as may be said, really childless; for his two sons were thus far lost, Abel was killed, and Cain was cursed and driven out from the presence of the Lord, and his race blasted with him.

It would be a useful enquiry here, and worthy our giving an account of could we come to a certainty in it, namely, what was the mark that God set upon Cain by which he was kept from being fallen upon by Abel's friends or relations? But as this does not belong to the Devil's history, and it was God's mark, not the Devil's, I have nothing to do with it here.

The Devil had now gained his point—the Kingdom of Grace, so newly erected, would have been, as it were, extinct without a new Creation. And had not Adam and Eve been alive, and had not Eve, though now 130 years of age, been a breeding young lady (for we must suppose the woman in that state of longevity bare children till they were seven or eight hundred years old). This abounding of Eve populated not the world so much as it restored the blessed race; for though Abel was killed, Cain had numerous offspring presently. And had Seth (Adam's third son) never been born, they would soon have replenished the world with people such as they were—the seed of a murderer cursed of God, branded with a mark of infamy, and who afterward fell all together in the universal ruin of the race by the Deluge.

But after the murder of Abel, Adam had another son born, namely, Seth, the father of Enos, and indeed the father of the holy race. For during his time and his Son Enos, the text says that men began to call on the name of the Lord. That is to say, they began to look back upon Cain and his wicked race, and being convinced of the wickedness they had committed and led their whole posterity into, they began to sue heaven for pardon of what was past, and lead a new sort of life.

But the Devil had met with too much success in his first attempts not to go on with his general resolution of debauching the minds of men and bringing them off from God. And therefore, as he kept his hold upon Cain's cursed race (embroiled already in blood and murder), so he proceeded with his degenerate offspring till, in a word, he brought both the holy seed and the degenerate race to join in one universal consent of crime and go on in it with such aggravating circumstances that it repented the Lord that He had made man, and He resolved to overwhelm them with a general destruction, and clear the world of them.

The succession of blood in the royal original line of Adam is preserved in the sacred histories and brought down as low as Noah and his three sons for a continued series of 1,450 years, say some, and 1,640 say others, in which time sin spread itself so generally through the whole race that the "sons of God," or so the scripture calls the men of the righteous seed (the progeny of Seth) came in unto the daughters of men—that is, joined themselves to the cursed race of Cain and married promiscuously with them, according to their fancies (the women it seems being beautiful and tempting). And though the Devil could not make the women handsome or ugly in one or other families, yet he might work up the gust of wicked inclination on either side so as to make both the men and women tempting and agreeable to one another, when they ought not to have been so, and perhaps, as it is often seen to this day, to make them more tempting by being under legal restraint.

It is objected here, that we do not find in the Scripture that the men and women of either race were at that time forbidden to intermarry with one another, and it is true that literally it is not forbidden. But if we did not search rather to make doubts than to explain them, we might suppose it was forbidden by some particular command at that time. Seeing we may reasonably allow everything to be forbidden for which they are taxed with a crime for committing, and since the sons of God taking wives as they thought fit to choose from among the daughters of the cursed race is there charged upon them as a general depravity, and a great crime, and for which, 'tis said, God even repented that he had made them, we need go no further to satisfy ourselves that it was certainly forbidden.

Satan no doubt had a hand in this wickedness too; for as it was his business to prompt men to do everything that God had prohibited, so the reason given why the men of those days did this thing was, they saw the daughters of men (that is of the wicked race or forbidden sort) were fair. He tempted them by the lust of the eye. In a word, the ladies were beautiful and agreeable, and the Devil knew how to make use of the allurement. The men liked and took them by the mere direction of their fancy and appetite without regarding the supreme prohibition. They took them wives of all they chose, or such as they liked to choose.

But the text adds that this promiscuous generation went farther than the mere outward crime of it; for it showed that the wickedness of the heart of man was great before God, and that He resented it. In short, God perceived a degeneracy or defect of virtue had seized upon the whole race, that there was a general corruption of manners, a depravity of nature upon them, that even the holy seed was tainted with it, that the Devil had broken in upon them and prevailed to a great degree, that not only the practice of the age was corrupt (for that, God could easily have restrained himself), but the very heart of man was debauched, his desires wholly vitiated, and his senses engaged in it.

So in a word, it became necessary to show the divine displeasure, not in the ordinary manner by judgment and reproofs of such kind as usually reclaim men, but by a general destruction to sweep them away, clear the earth of them, and put an end to the wickedness at once, removing the offence and the offenders all together. This is signified at large in Genesis 6:5. *"And God saw that the wickedness of man was great in the earth, and that every imagination of the thoughts of his heart was only evil continually."* And again in ver. 11 and 12, *"The earth also was corrupt before God; and the earth was filled with violence. And God looked upon the earth and behold it was corrupt; for all flesh had corrupted his way upon the earth."*

It must be confessed, it was a strange conquest the Devil had made in the antediluvian world that he had, as I may say, brought the whole race of mankind into a general revolt from God. Noah was indeed a preacher of righteousness, and he had preached about 500 years to as little purpose as most of the good ministers ever did. For we do not read there was one man converted by him, or at least not one of them left, for at the Deluge there was either none of them alive or none spared but Noah and his three sons and their wives.

And ('tis evident) even they are recorded not so much to be saved for their own goodness but because they were his sons. Indeed, without breach of charity we may conclude that at least one went to the Devil even of those three, namely, Ham, or *Cham*, for triumphing in a brutal manner over his father's drunkenness. For we find the special curse reached to him and his posterity for many ages. And whether it went no farther than the present state of life with them, we cannot tell.

We will suppose now that through this whole 1,500 years the Devil, having so effectually debauched mankind, had advanced his infernal kingdom to a prodigious height; for the text says, the whole earth was *filled with violence.* In a word, blood, murder, rape, robbery, oppression and injustice prevailed everywhere, and man, like the wild bear in the forest, lived by prey, biting and devouring one another.

At this time Noah began to preach a new doctrine to them,

for as he had before been a preacher of righteousness, now he became a preacher of vengeance. First, he told them they shall be all overwhelmed with a deluge—that for their sins God repented they were made, and that he would destroy them all, adding, that to prevent the ruin of himself and family, he resolved [upon God's instruction and design] to build himself a ship to have recourse to when the water should come over the rest of the world.

What jesting, what scorn, what contempt did this work expose the good old man to for above a 100 Years? (For so long the work was building, as ancient authors say.) Let us represent to ourselves, in the most lively manner, how the witty world at that time behaved to poor old Noah, how they took their evening walks to see what he was doing and passed their judgment upon it and upon the progress of it. I say, to represent this to ourselves, we need go no farther than to our own witticisms about religion and about the most solemn mysteries of divine worship, how we damn the serious for enthusiasts, think the grave mad, and the sober melancholy, call religion itself Flatus and Hyppo, make the devout ignorant, the divine mercenary, and the whole scheme of divinity a frame of priestcraft. And thus, no doubt, the building of an ark to float over the mountains and dance over the plains—what could it be but a religious frenzy, and the man who so busied himself with it, a lunatic? And all this in an age when divine things came by immediate revelation into the minds of men! The Devil must therefore have made a strange conquest upon mankind to obliterate all the reverence, which but a little before was so strangely impressed upon them concerning their Maker.

This was certainly the height of the Devil's kingdom, and we shall never find him arriving to such a pitch again. He was then truly and literally the universal monarch and, indeed, *"the god of this world"* (2 Cor. 4:4). As all tyrants do, he governed them with an arbitrary absolute sway. And had not God thought fit to give him a writ of ejectment and afterward drown him out of possession, I know not but what would have been the case that he might have kept his hold (for ought I know) till the Seed of the Woman came to bruise his head—that is to say, to cripple his government, dethrone him and depose his power, as has been fulfilled in the Messiah.

But as he was, I say, drowned out of the world, his kingdom for the present was at an end. At least if he had a dominion he had no subjects. And as the creation was in a manner renewed, so the Devil had all his work to do over again. Unhappy man! Now whether he retired in the meantime, and how he got footing again after Noah and his family had landed upon the new surface, that we come next to enquire.

10

OF THE DEVIL'S SECOND KINGDOM AND HOW HE GOT FOOTING IN THE RENEWED WORLD BY HIS VICTORY OVER NOAH AND HIS RACE.

The story of Noah, his building the ark, his embarking himself and all nature's stock for a new world on board it, the long voyage they took, and the bad weather they met with—though it would embellish this work very well and come in very much to the purpose in this place, yet as it does not belong to the Devil's story (for I cannot prove what some suggest, viz., that he was in the ark among the rest), I say, for that reason I must omit it.

And now having mentioned Satan's being in the ark, as I say, I cannot prove it, so there are, I think, some good reasons to believe he was not there.

First, I know no business he had there. Secondly, we read of no mischief done there, and these joined together make me conclude he was absent. The last, I chiefly insist upon (that we read of no mischief done there). If he had been in the ark, that would certainly have happened. And therefore I suppose, rather, that when he saw his kingdom dissolved and his subjects all engulfed in an inevitable ruin and desolation (a sight suitable enough to him except as it might un-king him for a time), I say, when he saw this, he took care to speed himself away as well as he could and make his retreat to a place of safety. And where that was is no more difficult to us than it was to him.

It is suggested that, since he is prince of the power of the air, he retired only into that region. It is most rational to suppose he went no farther on many accounts, of which I shall speak by and by. There he stayed, hovering in the earth's atmosphere, as he has often done since, and perhaps now does. Or if the atmosphere of this globe was affected by the indraft of the absorption, as some think, then he kept himself upon the watch to see what the event of the new phenomenon would be. And this watch, wherever it was, I doubt not it was as near the earth as he could place himself, perhaps in the atmosphere of the moon or, in a word, the next place of retreat he could find.

Therefore, I took upon myself to insist that Satan has no more a certain knowledge of events than we. I say, he has no more certain knowledge that he may use to be able to make stronger conjectures and more rational conclusions from all that he sees. I will not, though, deny that in which he most outdoes us—that he sees more to conclude from it than we can. But I am satisfied he knows nothing of futurity more than we can see by observation and inference. Nor, for example, did he know whether God would repopulate the world any more or not.

I must therefore concede that he only waited to see what would be the event of this strange eruption of water and what God proposed to do with the ark and all that was in it.

Besides what I hinted above, some philosophers tell us the Devil could have had no retreat in the earth's atmosphere; for the air being wholly condensed into water and having continually poured down its streams to deluge the earth, that body had become so small and had suffered such convulsions, that there was but just enough air left to surround the water (or as might serve by its pressure to preserve the natural position of things) and supply the creatures in the ark with a part to breathe in.

The atmosphere indeed might have suffered some strange and unnatural motions at that time, but (I believe) not to that degree. However, I will not affirm that there could be room in it as is now for the Devil, much less for all the numberless legions of Satan's host. But there was, and now certainly is, sufficient space to receive him and a sufficient body of his troops for the business he had for them at that time, and that's enough to the purpose. And if the earth's atmosphere did suffer any particular convulsion on that occasion, he might have made his retreat to the atmosphere of the moon, or of Mars, or of Venus, or of any of the other planets, or to any other place. For he who is prince of the air could not in such a case lack retreats from where he might watch for the issue of things. Certainly he did not go far, because his business lay here, and he never goes where he cannot do mischief.

In particular, his more than ordinary concern was to see what would become of the ark. He was doubtless wise enough to see that God, who had directed its making (indeed, even the very structure of it), would certainly take care of it, preserve it upon the water, and bring it to some place or other of safety, though where it should be, the Devil with all his cunning could not resolve, whether on the same surface of the waters that were drawing off, or in any other created or to be created place. And this state of uncertainty being evidently his case, and which proves his ignorance of futurity, it was his business, I say, to watch with the utmost vigilance for the event.

If the ark was (as Mr. Burnet thinks) guided by two angels, they not only held it from foundering or being swallowed up in the water but also certainly kept the waters calm about it, especially when the Lord brought a strong wind to blow over the whole globe, which, by the way was the first and, I suppose, the only universal storm that ever blew. For to be sure, it blew over earth's whole surface at once. I say, if it was thus guided, to be sure, the Devil saw it, and that with envy and regret that he could do it no injury. For doubtless had it been in the Devil's power, as God had drowned the whole race of man except what was in the ark, he would have taken care to have dispatched them [the eight souls in the ark] too, and so make an end of the creation at once. But either he was not empowered to go to the ark, or it was so well guarded by angels that when he came near to it he could do no harm. So, it rested at length, the waters abating, on the mountains of Ararat in Armenia, where they say a piece of the keel remains to this day.

The ark having safely landed, 'tis reasonable to believe Noah prepared to go on shore, as the seamen call it, as soon as the dry land began to appear. And here you must allow me to suppose Satan, though himself clothed with a cloud so as not to be seen, came immediately and, perching on the roof, saw all the heaven-kept household safely landed and all the host of living creatures dispersing themselves down the sides of the mountain, as the search of their food or other proper occasions directed them.

This sight was enough! Satan was at no loss to conclude that hence the design of God was to repopulate the world by the way of ordinary generation, from the posterity of these eight persons, without creating any new species.

"Very well," says the Devil. "Then my advantage over them,

by the snare I laid for poor Eve, is still good. And I am now just where I was after Adam's expulsion from the garden, and when I had Cain and his race to go to work with. For here is still the old expunged corrupted race. As Cain was the object then, so Noah is my man now, and if I do not master him one way or another, I am mistaken in my mark."

Pardon me for making a speech for the Devil.

Noah, big with a sense of his late condition, while the wonders of the Deluge were fresh in his mind, spent his first days in the ecstasies of his soul, giving thanks, and praising the Power that had been his protection in and through the flood of waters, and which had in so miraculous a manner safely landed him on the surface of the newly discovered land. The text tells us one of the first things he was employed in. He built an altar unto the Lord and offered burnt offerings upon the altar (Gen. 8:20).

While Noah was thus employed, he was safe, and the Devil himself could nowhere break in upon him, And so we may suppose very reasonably, as he found the old father invulnerable, he left him for some years, watching notwithstanding all possible advantages against his sons and their children. For the family began to increase, and Noah's sons had several children. Whether he himself had any more children after the Flood or not, that we have not arrived to any certainty about.

Among his sons, the Devil found Japhet and Shem good, pious, religious, and very devout persons serving God daily after the example of their good old father, Noah. And he could make nothing of them or of any of their posterity. But Ham, the second, or according to some the younger son of Noah, had a son who was named Canaan. A loose young profligate fellow, his education was probably but cursory and superficial. His father, Ham, not being nearly so religious and serious a man as his brothers Shem and Japheth were, and as Canaan's education was defective, he proved (as untaught youth generally do) to be a wild and, in short, very wicked fellow, and consequently a fit tool for the Devil to go to work with.

Noah, a diligent, industrious man, being with all his family thus planted in the rich fruitful plains of Armenia near the mountains of Caucasus or Ararat, went immediately to work cultivating and improving the soil, increasing his cattle and pastures, sowing corn, and among other things, planting trees for food. And among the fruit trees he planted vines. Of the grapes thereof he made no doubt most excellent wine, rich, luscious, strong, and pleasant, as they in the same country still make.

I cannot come into the notion of our critics, who to excuse Noah from the guilt of what followed, or at least from the censure, tell us he knew not the strength or the nature of wine, but that gathering the heavy clusters of the grapes (their own weight crushing out their balmy juices into his hand), he tasted the tempting liquor, and with the Devil assisting it, he was charmed with the delicious fragrance. And tasting again and again, pressing it out into a bowl or dish so he might take a larger quantity, at length the heady froth ascended, and it seizing his brain, he became intoxicated and drunk, not in the least imagining there was any such strength in the juice of that excellent fruit.

But to make out this story, which is indeed very favorable for Noah but in itself extremely ridiculous, you must necessarily fall into some absurdities and beg the question most egregiously in some particular cases, which way of arguing will by no means suppose what is suggested. At first you must support that there was no such thing as wine made before the Deluge, and that nobody had ever been made drunk with the juice of the grape before

Noah, which, I say, is begging the question in the grossest manner.

If the contrary is true (as I see no reason to question that it was true that there was wine drank, and that men were or had been drunk with it before), they cannot then but suppose that Noah, who was a wise, a great, and a good man, and a preacher of righteousness, both knew of it, and without doubt had in his preaching against their crimes preached against this among the rest, upbraided them with it, reproved them for it, and exhorted them against it.

Again, 'tis highly probable they had grapes growing and consequently wines made from them in the antediluvian world. How else did Noah come by the vines that he planted? For we are to suppose he could plant no trees or shrubs but such as he found the roots of in the earth, and which no doubt had been there before in their highest perfection and had consequently grown up and brought forth the same luscious fruit before.

Besides, as he found the roots of the vines, so he understood what they were and what fruit they bore, or else it may be supposed also that he would not have planted them. For he planted them for their fruit and did it in the provision he was making for his subsistence and the subsistence of his family. And if he did not know what they were, he would not have set them, for he was not planting for diversion but for profit.

Upon the whole, it seems plain to me he knew what he did when he planted the vines as well as when he pressed out the grapes. And, also, when he drank the juice, he knew it was wine, was strong, and would make him drunk if he took enough of it. He knew that other men had been drunk with such liquor before the Flood and that he had reprehended them for it. And therefore, it was not his ignorance but the Devil taking him at some advantage when his appetite was eager, or he was thirsty, and the liquor was cooling and pleasant. In short, as Eve said, the serpent beguiled her and she did eat, so the Devil beguiled Noah and he did drink. The temptation was too strong for Noah, not the wine. He knew well enough what he did, but as the drunkards say to this day, it was so good he could not forbear it, and so he got drunk before he was aware. Or as our ordinary speech expresses it, he was overtaken with drink. And Mr. Pool and other expositors are partly of the same mind.

No sooner was the poor old man conquered and had the wine lightened his head, but it may be supposed he fell off from the chair or bench where he sat. And tumbling backward, his clothes (which in those hot countries were only loose, open robes, like the vests that the Armenians wear to this day) flying open, or the Devil so assisting on purpose to expose him, he lay there in a naked, indecent posture not fit to be seen.

In this juncture, who should come by but young Canaan, say some. Or as others think, this young fellow, first attacking him by way of kindness and pretended affection, prompted his grandfather to drink on the pretense of wine being good for him and proper for the support of his old age. And subtly set upon him, he also drank with him, and so (his head being too strong for the old man's) drank him down. Then, Devil-like, he triumphed over him, boasted of his conquest, insulted the body as it were dead, uncovered him on purpose to expose him and, leaving him in that indecent posture, went and made sport with it to his father Ham, who in that part, wicked like himself, did the same to his brethren Japheth and Shem. But they, like modest and good men, far from carrying on the wicked insult on their parent, went and covered him as the Scripture expresses it, and as may be supposed, informed him how and by whom he had been abused.

Why else should Noah, when he came to himself, show his resentment so much against Canaan his grandson, rather than against Ham his father, and who 'tis supposed in the story the guilt chiefly lay upon? We see the curse is (as it were) laid wholly upon Canaan the grandson, and not a word of the father is mentioned: *"Cursed be Canaan; a servant of servants shall he be,"* and so forth (Gen. 9:25).

That Ham was guilty, that's certain from the history of fact, but I cannot but suppose his grandson was the occasion of it. And in this case the Devil seems to have made Canaan the instrument or tool to delude Noah and draw him into drunkenness as he made the serpent the tool to beguile Eve and draw her into disobedience.

Possibly Canaan might do it without design at first but might be brought into ridicule and make a jest of the old patriarch afterward, as is too frequent since then in the practice of our days. But I rather believe he did it really with a wicked design and on purpose to expose and insult his reverend old parent. And this seems more likely too because of the great bitterness with which Noah resented it, after he came to be informed of it.

But be that as it will, the Devil certainly made a great conquest here, and as to outward appearance no less than that which he gained before over Adam. Nor did the Devil's victory consist barely in his having drawn in the only righteous man of the whole antediluvian world and so beginning or initiating the new young progeny with a crime. Here the great oracle, the preacher of righteousness, for such no doubt he would have been to the new world as he was to the old, was silenced at once. I say, the preacher was turned out of office, or his mouth stopped, which was worse. Indeed, it was a stopping of his mouth in the worst kind, far worse than stopping his breath; for had he died, the office would have descended to his sons Shem and Japheth. But he was dead to the office of an instructor, though alive as to his being. For of what force could the preaching be of him who had thus fallen himself into the most shameful and beastly excess?

Then as for his two sons modestly and decently covering their father, Scripture tells us that represents Shem and Japheth applying themselves in an humble and dutiful manner to their father. Could it be that they did so in consideration of his ancient glory, his own pious exhortations to the late drowned world, the offence that he gave by his evil courses to God, and the scandal to his whole family. Also, once they effectually prevailed upon him, Noah then cursed the wickedness of Ham's degenerate race, in testimony of his sincere repentance after the fact. (Genesis 9:18-27).

The story is not so very unlikely though it is certain that it is not to be proved, and therefore we had better take it as we find it, viz., for one single act. But supposing it was so, 'tis still certain that Noah's preaching was sadly interrupted, the energy of his words flattered, and the force of his persuasions enervated and abated by this shameful fall. He was effectually silenced for an instructor ever after, and this was as much as the Devil had occasion for. And therefore, indeed, we read little more about him, except that he lived three hundred and fifty years after the flood Also, we do not so much as read that he had any more children, And nor indeed could Noah have any more children except by his old and perhaps superannuated wife (who he had very likely had four or five hundred years), unless you will suppose he was allowed to marry some of his own progeny, daughters or grand-daughters, which we do not suppose was allowed, no not to Adam himself.

This was certainly a masterpiece of the Devil's policy, and a fatal instance of his unhappy diligence, viz., that the door of the ark was no sooner open, and the face of the world hardly dry from the universal destruction of mankind, but he was at work among them. And that was not only to form a general defection among the race, upon the foot of the original taint of nature. But like a bold Devil he strikes at the very root, flies at the next general representative of mankind, and attacks the head of the family, that in his miscarriage the rise and progress of a reformation of the new world should receive an early check and should be at once prevented. I say, like a bold Devil, he strikes at the root, and alas! Poor unhappy Noah proved too weak for him. Satan prevailed in his very first attempt and got the victory over him at once.

Noah thus overcome and Satan's conquest carried on to the utmost of his own wishes, the Devil had little more to do in the world for some ages than to carry on an universal degeneracy among mankind, and to finish it by a like diligent application in deluding the generality of the race and them as they came on gradually into life. This he found less difficult because of the first defection that spread like a contagion upon the earth immediately after.

The first evidence we have of his success in this mischievous design was in the building of that great, stupendous staircase, for such it seems it was intended, called Babel, which if the whole world had not been drunk, or otherwise infatuated, they would never have undertaken. Even Satan himself could never have prevailed with them to undertake such a preposterous piece of work, for it had neither end or means, possibility, or probability in it.

I must confess I am sometimes apt to vindicate our old ancestors in my thoughts from the charge itself, as we generally understand it, namely, that they really designed to build a tower that should reach up to heaven, or that it should secure them in case of another flood. And Father Casaubon is of my opinion. (Whether I am of his or not is a question by itself.) His opinion is that the confusion was nothing but a breach among the undertakers and directors of the work, and that the building was designed chiefly as a storehouse for provisions in case of a second Deluge. As to their notion of it reaching up to heaven, he takes the expression to be allegorical rather than literal, and only to mean that it should be exceedingly high.

Perhaps they might not be astronomers enough to measure the distance of space between the earth and heaven, as we pretend to do now, but as Noah was then alive, and as we believe all his three sons were so too, they were able to have informed them how absurd it was to suppose either the one or the other, viz., (1.) that they could build up to heaven, or (2.) that supposing such another flood should happen, they could build firmly enough to resist, or high enough to overtop the waters. I would rather think it was only that they intended to build a most glorious and magnificent city where they might all inhabit together, and that this tower was to be built for ornament and also for strength or, as above, for a storehouse to lay up vast magazines of provisions in case of extraordinary floods or other events (the city being built in a great plain, namely, the plains of Shinar near the river Euphrates).

But the story, as it is recorded, suits better with Satan's measures at that time. And as from the beginning he was prompting them to everything that was contrary to the happiness of man, so the more preposterous it was, and the more inconsistent with common sense, the more it was to his purpose. And it showed all the more what a complete conquest he had gained over the reason as well as the religion of mankind at that time.

Again, 'tis evident in this case they were not only acting contrary to the nature of things but also contrary to the design and to the command of heaven. For God's command was that they should replenish the earth. That is, they should spread their habitations over it and populate the whole globe; whereas they were pitching in one place as if they were not to multiply sufficient to populate anymore.

But what cared the Devil for that or, to put it a little handsomer, that was what Satan aimed at. For it was enough to him to bring mankind to act just contrary to what heaven had directed or commanded them in anything and, if possible, in everything.

But God himself put a stop to this foolish piece of work, and it was time indeed to do so, for a madder thing the Devil himself never proposed to them. I say, God himself put a stop to this new undertaking and disappointed the Devil. And how was it done? Not in judgment and anger, as perhaps the Devil expected and hoped for. But as pitying the simplicity of that dreaming creature man, He confused their speech so as not to understand one another. Or He put a new shibboleth upon their tongues, thereby separating them into tribes or families. For by this, every family found themselves under a necessity of keeping together, and this naturally increased that differing jargons of language, for at first it might be no more.

What a confusion this was to them we all know by their being obliged to leave off their building and immediately separate one from another. But it remains to be considered what a surprise it was to the old serpent, for indeed it belongs to his history.

Satan had never met with any disappointment in all his wicked attempts till then. For first, he succeeded even to triumph upon Eve. He did the like upon Cain, and in short upon the whole world, one man (Noah) excepted, when, for so the Word is understood, he blended the sons of God and the daughters of hell together in promiscuous, voluptuous living as well as generation.

As to the Deluge, authors are not agreed whether it was a disappointment to the Devil or not. It might have been indeed a surprise to him. For though Noah had preached of it for a hundred years together, yet as he (Satan) daily prompted the people not to heed or believe what that old fellow, Noah, said to them and to ridicule his whimsical building a monstrous tub to swim or float in when the said Deluge should come, I am of the opinion he did not believe it himself and am positive he could not foresee it by any insight into futurity that he was master of.

'Tis true, the astronomers tell us there was a very terrible comet seen in the air, that it appeared for 180 days before the flood continually, and that as it approached nearer and nearer every day all the while, it at last burst and fell down in a continual spout or stream of water. Being of a watery substance, and the quantity so great, it was forty days a falling; so that this comet not only foretold the Deluge or drowning of the earth, but actually performed it and drowned it from itself.

But to leave this tale to them who told it, let us consider the Devil, surprised, and a little amazed at the absorption or inundation, or whatever we are to call it, of the earth in the Deluge. Not, I say, that he was much concerned at it, perhaps just the contrary. And if God would drown it again, and as often as he thought fit, I do not see by anything I meet with in Satan's history or in the nature of him that he would be at all disturbed at it. All that I can see in it that could give Satan any concern would be that all his favorites were gone, and he had his work to do over again, to lay a foundation for a new conquest in the generation that was to come.

But in this, his prospect was fair enough. For why should he be discouraged when he had now eight people to work upon considering he met with such success when he had but two? And why should he question breaking in now where nature was already vitiated and corrupted when he had before conquered the same nature, when in its primitive rectitude and purity it had just come out of the hands of its maker fortified with the awe of God's high and solemn command just given them and the threatening of death also annexed to it, if broken?

But I go back to the affair of Babel. This confusion of language was the first disappointment that I find the Devil met with in all his attempts and practices upon mankind, or upon the new creature, which I mentioned above. For he foresaw what would follow, namely, that the people would separate and spread themselves over the whole surface of the earth, and a thousand new scenes of actions would appear, in which he therefore prepared himself to behave as he should see occasion.

How the Devil learned to speak all the languages that were now to be used, and how many languages they were, the several ancient writers of the Devil's story have not yet determined. Some tell us they were divided only into fifteen, some into seventy-two, others into one hundred and eighty, and others again into several thousand.

It also remains a doubt with me, and I suppose it will be so with others also, whether or not Satan has yet found out a method to converse with mankind without the help of language and words, seeing man has no other medium of conversing, no not with himself. This, I have no time to enter upon here.

However, this seems plain to me, viz., that the Devil soon learned to make mankind understand him whatever language he spoke, and no doubt but he found ways and means to understand them whatever language they spoke.

After the confusion of languages, the people necessarily sorted themselves into families and tribes, every family understanding their own particular speech and that only. Those families multiplied and grew into nations. And those nations, lacking room and seeking out habitations, wandered some this way, and some that, till they found out countries respectively proper for their settling. And there they became a kingdom, spreading and possessing still more and more land as their people increased till at last the whole earth was scarcely big enough for them.

This presented Satan with an opportunity to break in upon their morals at another door, viz., their pride; for men being naturally proud and envious, nations and tribes began to jostle with one another for room. Either one nation enjoyed better accommodations or had a better soil or a more favorable climate than another. And these, being numerous and strong, thrust the other out and encroached upon their land. The other liking their situation, prepared for their defense, and so began oppression, invasion, war, battle and blood, with Satan all the while beating the drums and his attendants clapping their hands as men do when they set dogs on one another.

The bringing of mankind thus to war and confusion—as it was the first game the Devil played after the confounding of languages and divisions at Babel, so it was a conquest upon mankind, purely devilish, born from hell, and so exactly tinctured with Satan's original sin of ambition that it really transformed men into mere Devils. For when is man transformed into the very image of Satan himself, and when is he turned into a mere Devil if it is not when he is fighting with his fellow creatures and dipping his hands in the blood of his own kind?

Let his picture be considered. The fire of hell flames or sparkles in his eyes. A voracious grin sits upon his countenance. Rage and fury distort the muscles of his face. His passions agitate his whole body. And he is metamorphosed from a comely, beauteous angelic creature into a fury, a satyr, a terrible and frightful monster, indeed, into a devil. For Satan himself is described by the same word that on his very account is changed into a substantive, and the devils are called Furies.

This sowing the seeds of strife in the world and bringing nations to fight and make war upon one another would take up a great part of the Devil's History. And abundance of extraordinary things would occur in relating the particulars. For there have been very great conflagrations kindled in the world by the artifice of hell under this leading, viz., of making war (in which it has been the Devil's masterpiece), and he has indeed shown himself a workman in it. He has beguiled mankind into strange unnatural notions of things in order to propagate and support the fighting principle in the world—such as laws of war, fair fighting, behaving like men of honor, fighting at the last drop, and the like, by which killing and murdering is understood to be justifiable.

Virtue and a true greatness in spirit is rated now by rules that God never appointed, and the standard of honor is quite different from that of reason and of nature. Bravery is denominated not from a fearless, undaunted spirit in the just defense of life and liberty but from a daring defiance of God and man, fighting, killing and treading under foot his fellow creatures at the ordinary command of the officer—whether it be right or wrong, and whether it be in a just defense of life, and our country's life, that is liberty, or whether it be for the support of injury and oppression.

A prudent avoidance of causeless quarrels is called cowardice, and to take an affront is baseness and meanness of spirit. To refuse fighting and casting oneself upon the point of a sword, a practice forbade by the laws of God and of all good government, is yet called cowardice. And a man is bound to die dueling or live and be laughed at.

This trumping up of these imaginary things called bravery and gallantry, naming them virtue and honor, is all from the Devil's new management and his subtle influencing of the minds of men to fly in the face of God and nature and act against his senses. Nor but for his artifice in the management could it be possible that such inconsistencies could go down with mankind or that they could pass such absurd things among them for reasoning.

For example, A is found in bed with B's wife. B is the person injured and therefore offended. And B coming into the chamber with his sword in his hand, A exclaims loudly, "Why sir, you won't murder me, will you? As you are a man of honor, let me rise and take my sword."

A very good story indeed! Fit for nobody but the Devil to put into any man's head.

But so it is, B being put in mind, in truth, that he is *a man of honor,* starts back and must act the honorable part. So he lets A get up, put on his clothes, and take his sword. Then they fight, and B is killed for his honor. Whereas had the laws of God, of nature, and of reason taken place, the adulterer and the adulteress should have been taken prisoners and carried before the judge. And being taken in the fact, they should have been immediately sentenced, he to the block and she to the stake, and the innocent abused husband had no reason to have run any risk of his life for being made a cuckold.[15]

But thus has Satan abused the reason of man. And if a man does me the greatest injury in the world, I must provide him justice by venturing my life upon an equal standing with him and fight him upon equal hazard, in which the injured person is as often killed as the person offering the injury.

Suppose now it be in the same case as above. A man abuses my wife, and then to give me satisfaction tells me he will fight me, which the French call *doing me reason.*

"No sir," say I, "let me lie with your wife too, and then if you desire it, I may fight you. Then I am upon even terms with you." But this indeed is the reasoning that the Devil has brought mankind to at this day.

But to go back to the subject, viz., the Devil bringing the nations to fall out and to quarrel for room in the world, and so to fight in order to dispossess one another of their settlements, this began at a time when certainly there were places enough in the world for everyone to choose, and therefore the Devil, not the lack of elbow-room, must be the occasion of it. And 'tis carried on ever since, as apparently from the same interest, and by the same origin.

But we shall meet with this part again very often in the Devil's story. And as we bring him further into the management of mankind, I therefore lay it by for the present and come to the next steps the Devil took with mankind after the confusion of languages, and this was in the affair of worship. It does not appear yet that the Devil was ever so bold, as either,

15 Cuckold—a man whose wife commits adultery (Ed.).

1. To set himself up to be worshiped as a god, or which was still worse,
2. To persuade man to believe there was no god at all to worship.

Both of these were introduced since the Deluge—one indeed by the Devil, who soon found the means to set himself up for a god in many parts of the world, and holds it to this day. But the last was brought in by the invention of man, in which it must be confessed that man has out-sinned the Devil. For to do Satan justice, he never thought it could ever pass upon mankind, or that anything so gross would go down with them. So, in short, these modern rationalists in the reach of our days have, I say, out-sinned the Devil.

Since then both of these are modern inventions, Satan went on gradually, and being to work upon human nature by stratagem, not by force, it would have been too gross to have set himself up as an object of worship at first, it was to be done step-by-step. For example:

1. It was sufficient to bring mankind to a neglect of God, to worship him by halves, give little or no regard to his laws, and so grow loose and immoral in direct contradiction to his commands. Yet, this would not go down with them at first, so the Devil went on gradually.
2. From a negligence in worshiping the true God, he by degrees introduced the worship of false gods. And to introduce this, he began with the sun, moon, and stars, called in the holy text the host of heaven. These had greater majesty upon them and seemed fitter to command the homage of mankind. So, when they had once forgotten the true God, it was not the hardest thing in the world to bring men to embrace the worship of

such gods as those.

3. Having thus debauched their principles in worship and led them from the true and only object of worship to a false one, it was the easier to carry them on. So in a few gradations more he brought them to downright idolatry, and even in that idolatry he proceeded gradually too, for he began with awful names such as were venerable in the thoughts of men, as Baal or Bell, which in Chaldaick and Hebrew signifies Lord or Sovereign, or Mighty and Magnificent. And this was therefore a name ascribed at first to the true God. But afterward they descended to make images and figures to represent Him, and then they were called by the same name, as Baal, Balaam, and afterward Bell, from which, by a hellish degeneracy, Satan brought mankind to adore every block of their own hewing and to worshipping stocks, stones, monsters, hobgoblins, and every sordid frightful thing—and at last the Devil himself.

What notions some people may entertain of the forwardness of the first ages of the world to run into idolatry, I do not enquire here. I know they tell us strange things of its being the product of mere nature, one step removed from its primitive state. But I, who pretend to have so critically enquired into Satan's history, can assure you, and that from very good authority, that the Devil did not find it so easy a task to obliterate the knowledge of the true God in the minds and consciences of men as those people suggest.

It is true he carried things a great length under the patriarchal government of the first ages, but still, he was sixteen hundred years bringing it to pass. And though we have reason to believe the old world before the Flood had arrived to a very great height of wickedness, yet we do not read that Satan had ever come to such a length as to bring them into idolatry. Indeed, we do read of wars carried on among them, whether it was one nation against another, or only personal, we cannot tell. But the world seemed to be swallowed up in a life of wickedness, that is to say, of luxury and lewdness, raping and violence, and there were giants among them, and *"men of renown"* (Gen. 6:4), that is to say, men famed for their mighty valor, great actions of war, we may suppose, and their strength, who personally opposed others.

We read of no considerable wars indeed, but 'tis not to be doubted but there were such wars, or else it is to be understood that they lived (in common) a life somewhat like the brutes, the strong devouring the weak. For the Scripture text says, *"the earth was filled with violence"* (Gen. 6:13), hunting and tearing one another in pieces. And either for dominion or for wealth, either for ambition or for avarice, we know not well which.

Thus far the old antediluvian world went, and very wicked they were, there is no doubt of that. But we have reason to believe there was no idolatry. The Devil had not brought them to that length yet. Perhaps it would soon have followed, but the Deluge intervened.

After the Deluge, as I have said, he had all his work to do over again, and he went on by the same steps. First, he brought them to violence and war, then to oppression and tyranny, then to the neglect of true worship, then to false worship, and then to idolatry by the mere natural consequence of the thing. Who were the first nation or people that fell from the worship of the true God is something hard to determine. The Devil, who certainly of all God's creatures is best able to inform us, left us nothing upon record on that subject, but we have reason to believe it was thus introduced.

Nimrod was the grandson of Ham, Noah's second son, the same whose son was cursed by his father for exposing him in his drunkenness. This Nimrod was the first who it seems Satan picked out for a hero. Here he inspired him with ambitious thoughts, dreams of empire, and having the government over all the rest, that is to say, universal monarchy—the very same bait with which he has played upon the frailty of princes and ensnared the greatest of them ever since, even from his most August Imperial Majesty King Nimrod the First to his most Christian Majesty Louis the XIV, and many a mighty monarch between.

When these mighty monarchs and men of fame went off the stage, the world had their memories in esteem many ages after. And as their great actions were not otherwise recorded than by oral tradition and the tongues and memories of fallible men, and with time and the custom of magnifying the past actions of kings men soon fabled up their histories (with Satan assisting) into miracle and wonder. Hence their names were held in veneration more and more. Statues and busts representing their persons and great actions were set up in public places till from heroes and champions they made gods of them, and thus (Satan prompting) the world was quickly filled with idols.

This Nimrod is he who according to the received opinion, though I do not find Satan's history exactly concurring with it, was first called Belus, then Baal, and worshiped in most of the eastern countries under those names, sometimes with additions of surnames, according to the several countries, or people, or towns where he was particularly set up, as Baal Peor, Baal Zephon, Baal Phegor, and in other places plain Baal, as Jupiter in later times had like additions such as Jupiter Ammon, Jupiter Capitolinus, Jupiter Pistor, Jupiter Feretrius, and about ten or twelve Jupiters more.

I must acknowledge, that I think it was a masterpiece of hell to bring the world to idolatry so soon after they had had such an eminent example of the infinite power of the true God, as was seen in the Deluge and particularly in the escape of Noah in the ark—that is, to bring them (even before Noah or his sons were dead) to forget whose hand it was that delivered Noah and give the homage of the world to a name (and that a name of a mortal man dead and rotten) of one who was famous for nothing when he was alive but blood and war. I say, to bring the world to set up this nothing, this mere name, indeed the very image and picture of him for a god was first a mark of most prodigious stupidity in the whole race of men, a monstrous degeneracy from nature, and even from common sense. And next, 'twas a token of an inexpressible craft and subtlety in the Devil, who had now gotten the people into so full and complete a management that, in short, he could have brought them, by the same rule, to have worshiped *anything*. And in a little while more, he did bring many of them to worship him, plain Devil as he was, and knowing him to be such.

As to the antiquity of this horrible defection of mankind, though we do not find the beginning of it particularly recorded, yet we are certain it was not long after the confusion of Babel. For Nimrod, as is said, was no more than Noah's great grandson. And Noah himself, I suppose, might have been alive some years after Nimrod was born. And Nimrod was not long dead before they forgot that he was a tyrant and a murderer and made him a Baal (that is a lord or idol of him). I say, he was not long dead, for Nimrod was born in the year of the world 1847 and built Babylon the year 1879. And we find Terah, the father of Abraham, who lived from the year 1879 was an idolater, as was doubtless Bethuel, who was Terah's grandson. For we find Laban, who was Bethuel's son, was so. And all this was during the life of the first postdiluvian family, for Terah was born within one hundred ninety-three years after the Flood and one hundred fifty seven years before Noah was dead. And even Abram himself was eight and fifty years old before Noah died, and yet idolatry had been then, in all probability, above an hundred years practiced in the world.[16]

How long the whole world may be said to have been thus overwhelmed in ignorance and idolatry, we may make some tolerable guess at by the history of Abraham. For it was not till God called him from his father's house that any such thing as a church was established in the world. Nor was it even then except in his own family and successors for almost four hundred years after that call. And till God brought the Israelites back out of Egypt, nearly the whole world may be said to have been involved in idolatry and Devil worship.

So absolute a conquest had the Devil made over mankind immediately after the Flood (and all taking its rise and beginning at the fatal defeat of Noah), had Noah lived untainted and invulnerable, as he had done for six hundred years before, that would have gone a great way to have stemmed the torrent of wickedness that broke in upon mankind. Therefore the Devil, I say, was very cunning and very much rightly took it upon himself

16 N.B. It is worth remark here, what a terrible advantage the Devil gained by the debauching poor Noah and drawing him into the sin of drunkenness. For by this, as I said, he silenced and stopped the mouth of the great preacher of righteousness, that father and patriarch of the whole world, who not being able for the shame of his own foul miscarriage, to pretend to instruct or reprove the world any more, the Devil took hold of them immediately, and for lack of a prophet to warn and admonish, ran that little of religion which there might be left in Shem and Japhet, quite out of the world, and deluged them all in idolatry. (Defoe).

(as he is a mere devil) to attack Noah personally and give him a blow so soon.

It is true, the Devil did not immediately remove the notion of religion and of God from the minds of men, nor could he easily suppress the principle of worship and homage to be paid to a Sovereign Being, the author of nature and guide of the world. The Devil saw this clearly in the first ages of the new world, and therefore, as I have said, he proceeded politically and by degrees. That it was so is evident from the story of Job and his three friends, which, if we may take it for a history, not a fable, we may judge the time of it by the length of Job's life, and by the family of Eliphaz the Temanite (who it is manifest was at least grandson or great-grandson to Esau, Isaac's eldest son) and by the language of Abimilech king of Gerar to Abraham, and of Laban to Jacob, both Abimilech and Laban being at the same time idolaters. I say, if we may judge it by all these, there were still very sound notions of religion in the minds of men. Nor could Satan with all his cunning and policy deface those ideas and root them out of the minds of the people.

And this moved him to take new measures to keep up his interest and preserve the hold he got upon mankind. And his method was like himself, subtle and politick to the last degree, as his whole history makes apparent. For seeing he found they could not but believe the being of a god, and that they would need to worship something, it is evident he had no game left him to play but this: namely, to set up wrong notions of worship and bring them to a false worship instead of a true, supposing the object worshiped to be still the same.

To finish this stratagem, he first insinuated that the true God was a terrible, dreadful, unapproachable being, that to see Him was so frightful that it would be immediate death, that to worship Him immediately was a presumption that would provoke his wrath, and that since He was a consuming fire himself, so He would burn up those in his anger who dared to offer up any sacrifice to Him but by the interposition of some mediator who might receive their adorations in His name.

Hence it occurred presently that subordinate gods were to be sought and set up to whom the people might pay the homage due to the supreme God, and whom they might worship in His name. This I take from the most ancient account of idolatry in the world. Nor indeed could the Devil himself find out any other reason why men should canonize or rather deify their princes and men of fame and worship them after they were dead as if they could save them from death and calamity when they were not able to save them when they were alive. Much less could Satan bring men to swallow so gross, so absurd a thing as the bowing of the knee to a stock or a stone, a calf, an ox, a lion, indeed, the image or figure of a calf such as the Israelites made at Mount Sinai, and say, *"These be thy gods, O Israel, which brought thee up out of the land of Egypt"* (Exod. 32:4).

Having thus, I say, brought them to satisfy themselves that they worshiped the true God and no other under the figures and appearances that they made to represent him, it was easy after that to worship anything for the true God. And thus in a few ages they worshiped nothing but idols, even throughout the whole world. Nor has the Devil lost this hold in some parts of the world—indeed, not in most parts of the world to this day.

He still holds all the eastern parts of Asia, the southern parts of Africa, and the northern parts of Europe, and in them, the vast countries of China and Tartary, Persia and India, Guinea,

Ethiopia, Zanquebar, Congo, Angola, Monomotapa, and so forth. In all of them, except Ethiopia, we find there were no vestiges of any other worship but that of idols, monsters, and even the Devil himself till after the very coming of our Savior (and even then, if it be true that the gospel was preached in the Indies and China by St. Thomas, and in other remote countries by other of the Apostles).

We see that whatever ground Satan lost, he seems to have recovered it again, and all Asia and Africa is at present overrun with Paganism or Mohammedanism, which I think of the two is rather the worst. This is besides all of America, a part of the world, as some say, equal in bigness to all the other in which the Devil's kingdom was never interrupted from its first being inhabited, whenever it was, to the first discovery of it by the European nations in the sixteenth century.

In a word, the Devil got what we may call an entire victory over mankind and drove the worship of the true God in a manner quite out of the world, forcing, as it were, his maker in a new kind of creation—the old one proving thus ineffectual to recover a certain number by force and mere Omnipotence to cause them to return to their duty, serve him, and worship him—but more of that hereafter.

11

OF GOD'S CALLING A CHURCH OUT OF THE MIDST OF A DEGENERATE WORLD, AND OF SATAN'S NEW MEASURES UPON THAT INCIDENT. HOW HE ATTACKED THEM IMMEDIATELY, AND HIS SUCCESS IN THOSE ATTACKS.

Satan having, as I have said in the preceding chapter, made, as it were, a full conquest of mankind, debauched them into idolatry, and brought them at least to worshiping the true God by the wretched intercession of corrupt and idolatrous representations. God seemed to have no true servants or worshippers left in the world. But if I may be allowed to speak so, He was obliged, in order to restore the world to their senses again, to call a select number out from among the rest, who He himself undertook should own His Godhead or supreme authority and worship Him as he required to be worshiped. This, I say, God was obliged to do, because 'tis evident it has not been done so much by the choice and council of men; for Satan would have over-ruled that part, as by the power and energy of some irresistible and invincible operation. And this our divines give high names to. But be it what they will, it is referring to the second defeat or disappointment that the Devil met with in his progress in the world. The first I have spoken of already.

It is true, Satan very well understood what he was threatened with in the original promise to the woman immediately after the fall, namely, *"thou shalt bruise His heal"* and so forth (Gen 3:15). But he did not expect it so suddenly but thought himself sure of mankind till the fullness of time when the Messiah should come. Therefore, it was a great surprise to him to see that Abraham being called was so immediately received and established, though he did not so immediately follow the voice that directed him. Yet in him, in his loins, was all God's Church at that time contained.

In the calling of Abraham, it is easy to see that there was no other way (as the world was then stated) for God to form a church, that is to say, to single out a people to himself but by immediate revelation and a voice from heaven. All mankind were gone over to the enemy, overwhelmed in idolatry, and in a word, engaged to the Devil. God Almighty, or as the Scripture distinguishes Him, the Lord, the true God, was out of the question. Mankind knew little or nothing of Him, much less did they know anything of His worship, or that there was such a being in the world.

Well might it be said that the Lord appeared to Abraham (Gen. 17:1). For if God had not appeared himself, He must have sent a messenger from heaven, and perhaps it was so too, for he had not one true servant or worshiper that we know of then on earth to send on that errand—no prophet, and no preacher of righteousness.[17] Noah was dead, and had been so above seventeen

17 The Scriptures do refer to one, Melchizedek, King of Salem (Jerusalem), who was *the priest of God Most High,* who ministered to Abram (Abraham),

years. And if he had not been gone, his preaching (as I observed after his great miscarriage) would have had but little effect. We are indeed told that Noah left behind himself certain rules and orders for the true worship of God, which were called the Precepts of Noah, and they remained in the world for a long time, though how written when neither any letters much less writing were known in the world is a difficulty that remains to be solved. And this makes me look upon those laws called the Precepts of Noah to be a modern invention, as I do also the Alphabetum Noachi [The Alphabet of Noah], which Bochart pretends to give an account of.

But to leave that fiction and come back to Abraham, God called him, and whether at first by voice without any vision, whether in a dream or night vision (which was very significant in those days), or whether by some awful appearance, we know not. The second time, 'tis indeed said that God expressly appeared to him. Be it which way it will, God himself called him, showed him the land of Canaan, gave him the promise of it for his posterity, and withal gave him such a faith that the Devil soon found there was no room for him to meddle with Abraham. This is certain, as we do not read that the Devil ever so much as tempted Abraham at all.

Some will suggest that the command to Abraham to go and offer up his son Isaac was a temptation of the Devil, if possible to defeat the glorious work of God's calling a holy seed into the world. For first, if Abraham had disobeyed that call, the new favorite would have been overcome and made a rebel of, or secondly, if he had obeyed, then the promised Seed would have been cut off and Abraham defeated. But as the text is express that God himself proposed it to Abraham, I shall not start the

---

and Abram gave him a tithe (Gen. 14:18-20; Heb. 7:1-3). (Ed.).

suggestions of such critics in contradiction of the sacred oracle.

Be it one way or other, Abraham showed a hero-like faith and courage, and if the Devil had been the author of it, he had seen himself disappointed in both his views:

1. By Abraham's ready and bold compliance, as believing it to be God's command.
2. By the divine countermand of the execution [of his son, Isaac] just as the fatal knife was lifted up.

But if the Devil left Abraham and made no attack upon him, seeing him invulnerable, he made himself amends upon the other branch of his family, viz., his poor nephew, Lot, who was so immediately under the particular care of heaven that the angel who was sent to destroy Sodom could do nothing till he was out of it, and who left Zoar and retired into a cave to dwell. Yet the subtle Devil found him out, deluded his two daughters, took an advantage of the fright they had been in about Sodom and Gomorrah, and made them believe the whole world was burnt too as well as those cities, and that, in short, they could never have any husbands, and so forth. And so in their abundant concern to repopulate the world, and so the race of mankind might not be destroyed, they went and lay with their own father, the Devil telling them doubtless how to do it, by intoxicating his head with wine. In all the story, whether they were not as drunk as their father seems to be a question, or else they could not have supposed all the men in the earth were consumed when they knew that the little city Zoar had been preserved for their sakes.

This now was the third conquest Satan obtained by the gust of human appetite, that is to say, once by eating and twice by drinking or drunkenness. And still, the last was the worst and

THE FLIGHT OF LOT.

most shameful. For Lot, however his daughters managed him, could not pretend he did not understand what the strength of wine was. And one would have thought after so terrible a judgment as that of Sodom, which was, as we may say, executed before his face, his thoughts should have been too solemnly engaged in praising God for sparing his life to be made drunk, and that two nights together.

But the Devil played his game surely. He set his two daughters to work, and as the Devil's instruments seldom fail, so he secured his by that hellish stratagem of deluding the daughters to think all the world was consumed but they two and their father. To be sure, the old man could not suspect that his daughters' design was so wicked as indeed it was, or that they intended to debauch him with wine and make him drink till he knew not what he did.

Now the Devil having carried his game here, gained a great point. For as there were but two religious families in the world before, whence a twofold generation might be supposed to rise religious and righteous like their parents, viz., that of Abraham and this of Lot, this crime ruined the hopes of one of them. It could no more be said that just Lot, who vexed his righteous soul from day to day with the wicked behavior of the people of Sodom still existed. Righteous Lot was degenerated into drunken incestuous Lot and fallen from what he was to become a wicked and unrighteous man—no pattern of virtue, no reprover of the age, but a poor fallen, degenerate patriarch who could now no more reprove or exhort but look down and be ashamed with nothing to do but repent.

And see the poor, mean excuses of all the three:

- Eve says, *The serpent beguiled me, and I did eat* (Gen. 3:13).
- Noah says, "My grandson beguiled me, or the wine beguiled me, and I did drink." (Gen. 9:24)
- Lot says, "My Daughters beguiled me, and I also did drink." (Gen. 19:30-36)

It is observable that, as I said above, Noah was silenced, and his preaching was at an end after that one action. So the like may be said of Lot, and in short, you never hear one word more of either of them after it (this sin). As for mankind, both were useless to them. And as to themselves, we never read of any of their repentance, nor have we much reason to believe they did repent.

From this attack of the Devil upon Lot, we hear no more of the Devil being so busily employed as he had been before in the world. He had indeed but little to do, for all the rest of the world was his own, lulled asleep under the witchcraft of idolatry, and are so still.

But it could not be long that the Devil lay idle. As soon as God called to himself a people, the Devil could not be at rest till he attacked them.

Wherever God sets up a house of prayer, the Devil always builds a chapel there.

Abraham indeed went off the stage free, and so did Isaac. They were a kind of first-rate saints. We do not so much as read of any failings they had, or of anything the Devil ever had the gall to offer to them,—no, or with Jacob either if you will excuse him for beguiling his brother Esau out of both his birthright and his blessing. But he (the Devil) was busy enough with all his children. For example,

He sent Judah to his sheep-shearing and placed a whore (Tamar) in his way in the posture of temptation, so he made him commit incest and whoredom both together. (Gen. 38).

He sent incestuous Reuben to lie with his father's concubine, Bilhah. (Gen. 35:22).

He sent Dinah to the ball to dance with the Shechemite ladies and play the whore with their master. (Gen. 34).

He enraged Simeon and Levi at the supposed injury, and then prompted them to revenge, for which their father heartily cursed them.

He set them all together to fall upon poor Joseph, first to murder him intentionally, and then actually sell him to the Midianites. (Gen. 37).

He made Joseph's brothers show the many-colored coat and tell a lie to their father to make the poor old man believe Joseph was killed by a lion, and so forth.

He sent Potiphar's wife to attack Joseph's chastity and filled her with rage at the disappointment. (Gen. 39).

He taught Joseph to swear by the life of Pharaoh.

In a word, he debauched the whole family of brothers, except Benjamin, and never man had such a set of sons so wicked and so notorious after so good an introduction into the world as they all of them had, to be sure. For Jacob, no doubt, gave them as good instruction as the circumstances of his wandering condition would allow him to do.

We must now consider the Devil and his affairs in a quite different situation. When the world first appeared populated by the creative power of God, he had only Adam and Eve to take care of, and I think he played his time with them to purpose enough. After the Deluge he had only Noah to pitch upon, and he quickly conquered him by the instigation of his grandson.

At the building of Babel he guided them by their acting all in a body as one man so that, in short, he managed them with ease, taking them as a body politic. And we find they came into his snare as one man. But now, the children of Israel multiplying in the land of their bondage, and God seeming to show a particular concern for them, the Devil was obliged to new measures, stand at a distance, and look on for some time.

The Egyptians were plagued even without his help, though the cunning artist, as I said, stood and looked on. Yet he durst not meddle; nor could he make a few lice, the least and basest of the armies of insects raised, to afflict the Egyptians.

However, when he perceived that God resolved to bring the Israelites out, he prepared to attend them, to watch them, and be at hand upon all the wicked occasions that might be offered (as if he had been fully satisfied such occasions would be offered, and that he should not fail to have an opportunity to draw them into some snare or another). And therefore, it was his business not to be out of the way but to be ready (as we say) to make his market of them in the best manner he could. How many ways he attempted them, indeed, how many times he conquered them in their journey, we shall see presently.

First, he put them in a fright at Baal-Zephon, where he thought he had drawn them into a noose, and where he sent Pharaoh and his army to block them up between the mountains of Piahiroth and the Red Sea. But there indeed, Satan was outwitted by Moses so far as it appeared to be a human action. For he little thought of their going dry footed through the sea but depended upon having them all cut in pieces the next morning by the Egyptians, which is an eminent proof, by the way, that the Devil has no knowledge of events or any insight into futurity—indeed, that he has not so much as a second sight or knows today what his Maker intends to do tomorrow. For had Satan known that God intended to ford them over the sea, if he had not been able to have prevented the miracle, he would certainly have prevented the escape by sending out Pharaoh and his army in time to have taken the strand before them, and so had driven them to the necessity of travelling on foot round the north point of that sea by the wilderness of Etan, where he would have pursued and harassed them with his cavalry and in all probability have destroyed them.

But the blind, short-sighted Devil, being perfectly in the dark and unacquainted with futurity, knowing nothing of the matter and as much deceived as Pharaoh himself, stood still flattering himself with the hopes of his booty and the revenge he should take upon them the next morning till he saw the frightening waves in an uproar and, to his utter astonishment and confusion, saw the passage laid open and Moses leading his vast army in full march over the dry space. Indeed, even then 'tis very probable Satan did not know that if the Egyptians followed them the sea would return upon and overwhelm them. For I can hardly think so hard of the Devil himself that if he had, he would have suffered, much less prompted Pharaoh to follow the chase at such an expense and show that either he must be an ignorant unforeseeing Devil or a very ungrateful false Devil to his friends the Egyptians.

I am inclined also to the more charitable opinion of Satan too, because the escape of the Israelites was really a triumph over him. For the war was certainly his, or at least he was auxiliary to Pharaoh. It was a victory over hell and Egypt together, and he would never have suffered the disgrace if he had known it beforehand. That is to say, though he could not have prevented the escape of Israel or the dividing of the water, yet he might have warned the Egyptians and cautioned them not to venture in after them.

But we shall see a great many weak steps taken by the Devil in the affairs of this very people and their forty years wandering in the wilderness. And though he was in some things successful, and beguiled them into many foolish and miserable murmurings and wranglings against God, and mutinies against poor Moses, yet the Devil was oftentimes baulked and disappointed. And 'tis for this reason that I choose to finish the first part of his history with the particular relation of his behavior among the Jews, because, also, we do not find any extraordinary things happening anywhere else in the world for above one thousand five hundred years—no variety, no revolutions. All the rest of mankind, lying still under his yoke, quietly submitted to his government and did just as he bade them, worshiping every idol he set up. And in a word, he had no difficulty with anybody but the Jews. For this reason, I say, this part of his story will be the more useful and instructing.

To return therefore to Moses and his dividing of the Red Sea, that the people went over or through it, we have the sacred history for that. But how the Devil behaved, that you must come to me for, or I know not where you will find a true account of it, at least not in print.

It was in the night that they marched through. Whether the Devil saw it in the dark or not, that's not my business.

But when he had daylight for it and viewed the next day's work, I make no question but all hell felt the surprise, the prey being thus snatched out of their hands unexpectedly. 'Tis true the Egyptian host was sent to him in their place, but that was not what he aimed at. For he was sure enough of them his own way, and if it was not just at that time, yet he knew what and who they were, as he had devoured the whole Israelitish host in his imagination to the tune of at least a million and a half of souls, men, women and children. It was, no doubt, a great disappointment to the Devil to miss his prey and see them all triumphing on the other side in safety.

It is true that Satan's annals do not mention this defeat, for historians are generally backward to register their own misfortunes. But as we have an account of the fact from other hands, so as we cannot question the truth of it, the nature of the thing will tell us it was a disappointment to the Devil, and a very great one too.

I cannot but observe here that I think this part of the Devil's story very entertaining because of the great variety of incidents that appear in every part of it. Sometimes he is like a hunted fox, curvetting and counter-running to avoid being pursued and found out, while at the same time he is carrying on his secret designs to draw the people he pretends to manage into some snare or other to their hurt. At another time, though the comparison is a little too low for his dignity, he is like a monkey that has done mischief and who making his own escape sits and chatters at a distance as if he had triumphed in what he had done. So when he had drawn them in to worship a calf, to offer strange fire, to set up a schism, and the like, and so to bring the divine vengeance upon them, leaving them in their distress, Satan kept at a distance as if he looked on with satisfaction to see them burnt, swallowed up, swept away, and the like, as the several stories relate.

His indefatigable vigilance is, on the other hand, a useful caveat as well as an improving view to us. No sooner is he routed and exposed, defeated, and disappointed in one enterprise but he begins another, and like a cunning gladiator he warily defends himself and boldly attacks his enemy at the same time. Thus, we see him up and down, conquering and conquered through this whole part of his story till at last he receives a total defeat, of which you shall hear in its place. In the meantime, let us take up his story again at the Red Sea, where he received a great blow instead of what he expected to be a complete victory. For doubtless the Devil, and the king of Egypt too, thought of nothing but conquest at Piahiroth.

However, though the triumph of the Israelites over the Egyptians must needs have been a great mortification to the Devil, and exasperated him very much, yet the consequence was only this: viz., that Satan, like an enemy who is baulked and defeated but not overcome, redoubles his rage and reinforces his army, and what the Egyptians could not do for him, he resolved to do for himself. In order then to take his opportunity for what mischief might offer, being defeated and provoked, I say, at the slur that was put upon him, he resolved to follow them into the wilderness, and many a vile prank he played on them there. As first, he hampered them for water and made them murmur against God, and against Moses, within a very few days, indeed, hours of their great deliverance.

Nor was this all, but in less than one year more, we find them (at his instigation too) setting up a golden calf and making all the people dance about it at Mount Sinai, even when God himself had but just before appeared to them in the terrors of a burning fire upon the top of the mountain. And what was the pretense? Truly, nothing but that they had lost Moses, who used to be their guide. He hid himself in the mount and had not been seen in forty days, so they could not tell what had become of him. This put them all into confusion, a poor pretense indeed to turn them all back to idolatry! But the watchful Devil took the hint, pushed the advantage, insinuated that they should never see Moses again (that he was certainly devoured by venturing too near the flashes of fire in the mount), and presumed upon the liberty he had taken before, in a word, that God had destroyed Moses, or he had starved to death for lack of food, having been forty days and forty nights absent.

All these were, it's true, in themselves most foolish suggestions considering Moses was admitted to the vision of God and that God had been pleased to appear to him in the most intimate manner. And as they might depend that God would not destroy His faithful servant, so they might have concluded He was able to support his being without food as long as He thought fit. But to a people so easy to believe anything, what could be too gross for the Devil to persuade them of?

A people who could dance round a calf and call it their God might do anything. That they could say to one another the calf was the Great Jehovah who brought them out of the land of Egypt, and do that within so few days after God's miraculous appearance to them and for them, I say, that such a people were really fit to be imposed upon. Nothing could be too gross for them.

This was indeed his first considerable experiment upon them as a people, or as a body. And the truth is, his affairs required it. For Satan, who had been a successful Devil in most of his attempts upon mankind, could hardly doubt having success in anything after he had carried his point at Mount Sinai—to bring them to idolatry in the very face of their deliverer, and just after their deliverance! It was more astonishing on the whole than even their passing the Red Sea. In a word, the Devil's whole history does not furnish us with a story equally surprising.

And how was poor Aaron bewildered in it too? He who was Moses's partner in all the great things that Moses did in Pharaoh's sight, and who was appointed to be his assistant and oracle, or rather, orator, upon all public occasions—that he, above all the rest, should come into this absurd and ridiculous proposal, and that he who was singled out for the sacred priesthood, for him to defile his holy hands with a polluted abominable sacrifice and with making the idol for them too, (for 'tis plain that he made it), how monstrous it was!

And see what an answer he gives to his brother, Moses; how weak! How simple! I did so and so, indeed. I bade them bring the earrings, and so forth, and I cast the gold into the fire, and it came out this calf. Ridiculous! As if the calf came out by mere fortuitous adventure without a mold to cast it in. That could not be supposed. And if it had not come out so without a mold, Moses would certainly have known of it.

Had Aaron been innocent, he would have answered after quite another manner and told Moses honestly that the whole body of the people came to him in a fright, that they forced him to make them an idol, which he did by making first a proper mold to cast it in, and then by taking the proper metal to cast it from, that indeed he had sinned in so doing but was mobbed into it, and the people terrified him, perhaps they threatened to kill him. And if he had added that the Devil prompting his fear beguiled him, he had said nothing but what was certainly true. For if it were in Satan's power to make the people insolent and outrageous enough to threaten and bully the old venerable prophet (for he was not yet a priest), who was the brother of their oracle Moses and had been partner with him in so many of his commissions, I say, if he could bring up the passions of the people to a height to be rude and unmannerly to him (Aaron) and perhaps to threaten and insult him, he may be easily supposed to be able to intimidate Aaron and terrify him into a compliance.

See this cunning agent, when he has man's destruction in his view, how securely he acts! He never lacks a handle. The best of men have one weak place or other, and he always finds it out, takes the advantage of it, and conquers them by one artifice or another. Only take it with you as you go, 'tis always by stratagem, never by force, a proof that he is not empowered to use violence. He may tempt, and he does prevail. But 'tis all sleight of hand, 'tis all craft and artifice. He is still Διαβολή [slander], the calumniator and deceiver, that is, the misrepresenter. He misrepresents man to God and misrepresents God to man. Also, he misrepresents things. He puts false colors and then manages the eye to see them with an imperfect view, raising clouds and fogs to intercept our sight. In short, he deceives all our senses and imposes upon us in things which otherwise would be the easiest to discern and judge of.

This indeed is in part the benefit of the Devil's history, to let us see that he has used the same methods all along, and that ever since he has had anything to do with mankind, he has practiced upon them with stratagem and cunning. Also 'tis observable that he has carried his point better that way than he would have done by fury and violence if he had been allowed to make use of it. For by his power he indeed might have laid the world desolate and made a heap of rubbish of it long ago. But as I have observed before, that would not have answered his ends half so well. For by destroying men he would have made martyrs and sent an abundance of good men to heaven, who would much rather have died than yielded to serve him and, as he aimed to have it, fall down and worship him. I say, he would have made martyrs, and that not a few. But this was none of Satan's business. His design lies quite another way. His business is to make men sin, not to make them suffer, to make devils of them, not saints, to delude them and draw them away from their maker, not send them away to him. And therefore, he works by stratagem, not by force.

We are now come to his story as it relates to the Jewish church in the wilderness and to the children of Israel in their travelling circumstances. And this was the first scene of public management that the Devil had upon his hands in the world. For as I have said, till now he dealt with mankind either in their separate condition, one by one, or else carried all before him engrossing whole nations in his systems of idolatry and overwhelming them in an ignorant destruction.

But having now a whole people, as it were, snatched away from him, taken out of his government, and, which was still worse, having a view of a kingdom being set up independent of him and superior to his authority, it is not to be wondered at if he endeavored to overthrow them in the infancy of their constitution and tried all possible arts to bring them back into his own hands again.

He found them carried away from the country where they were even in his clutches, surrounded with idols, and where we have reason to believe the greatest part of them were polluted with the idolatry of the Egyptians. For we do not read of any stated worship that they had of their own, or if they did worship the true God, we scarcely know in what manner they did it. They had no law given them, nothing but the covenant of circumcision. And even Moses himself had not strictly observed that till he was frightened into it. We read of no sacrifices among them, no feasts were ordained, and no solemn worship appointed. And how or in what manner they performed their homage, we know not. The Passover was not ordained till just at their coming away. So there was not much religion among them, at least that we have any account of, and we may suppose the Devil was pretty easy with them all the while they were in the house of their bondage.

But now, to have a million people fetched out of his hands as it were, all at once, to have the immediate power of heaven engaged in it, and Satan seeing that evidently God had singled them out in a miraculous manner to favor them and call them his own, this alarmed him at once. And therefore he resolved to follow them, lay close siege to them, and take all the measures possible to bring them to rebel against and disobey God so He might be provoked to destroy them. And how near he came to bring it to pass, we shall see presently.

This making a calf and paying an idolatrous worship to it (for they acted the heathens and idolaters not only in the setting up the calf but also in the manner of their worshiping, viz., dancing and music, things they had not been acquainted with in the worship of the true God), I mention here to observe how the Devil not only imposed upon their principles but also upon their senses too. As if the awesome Majesty of Heaven, whose glory they had seen in Mount Sinai, where they stood, and whose pillar of cloud and fire was their guide and protection, would be worshiped by dancing round a calf! (And that, not a living creature or a real calf but the mere image of a calf cast in gold, or as some think, in brass gilded over.)

But this was the Devil's way with mankind, namely, to impose upon their senses and bring them into the grossest follies and absurdities. And then, having first made them fools, it was much the easier to make them offenders.

In this very manner, he acted with them through all the course of their wilderness travels. For they were led by the hand like children, defended by omnipotence, fed by miracles, instructed immediately from heaven, and in all things had Moses for their guide. They had no room to miscarry, but by acting the greatest absurdities and committing the greatest follies in nature, the Devil brought them to be guilty of even what follows in a surprising manner.

As God himself relieved them in every exigence and supplied them in every want, one would think 'twas impossible they should ever be brought to question either his willingness or his ability. And yet they really objected against both, which was indeed very provoking. And I doubt not that when the Devil had brought them to act in such a preposterous manner, he really hoped and believed God would be provoked effectually. The testimonies of His care of them and ability to supply them were miraculous and undeniable. He gave them water from the rock, bread from the air, sent the fowls to feed them with flesh, and supported them all the way by miracles. Their health was preserved. None were sick among them. Their clothes did not wear out. Nor did their shoes grow old upon their feet. Could anything be more absurd than to doubt whether he could provide for them who had never let them lack for so many years?

But the Devil managed them in sight of miracles. Nor did he ever give them over till he had brought six hundred thousand of them to provoke God so highly that he would not suffer above two of them to go into the Land of Promise. So in short, Satan gained his point as to that generation, for all their carcasses fell in the wilderness. Let us take but a short view to what a height he brought them, and in what a rude, absurd manner they acted, how he set them to murmuring upon every occasion, now for water, then for bread. Indeed, they murmured at their bread when they had it, "Our soul loathes this light bread."

He sowed the seeds of church-rebellion in the sons of Aaron and made Nadab and Abihu offer strange fire till they were strangely consumed by fire for doing it.

He set them a complaining at Taberah and a lusting for flesh at the first three days journey from Mount Sinai.

He planted envy in the hearts of Miriam and Aaron against the authority of Moses, to pretend God spoke by them as well as by him, till he humbled the father and made a leper of the daughter.

He debauched ten of the spies, frightened them with sham appearances of things when they went out to search the land, and made them frighten the whole people out of their understanding as well as duty, for which six hundred thousand of them fell in the wilderness.

He raised the rebellion of Korah and the two hundred and fifty princes till he brought them to be swallowed up alive.

He put Moses into a passion at Meribah and ruffled the temper of the meekest man upon earth, through which he made both him and Aaron forfeit their share of the promise and be shut out from the Holy Land.

He raised a mutiny among them when they travelled from Mount Hor till they brought fiery serpents among them to destroy them.

He tried to make Baalam the prophet curse them, but there the Devil was disappointed. However, he brought the Midianites to debauch them with women as in the case of Zimri and Cosbi.

He tempted Achan with the wedge of gold and the Babylonish garment, that he might take of the accursed thing and be destroyed.

He tempted the whole people to not effectually drive out the cursed inhabitants of the Land of Promise, that they might remain and be goads in their sides, till at last they often oppressed them for their idolatry and, which was worse, debauched them *to* idolatry.

He prompted the Benjaminites to refuse satisfaction to the people in the case of the wickedness of the men of Gibeah, to the destruction of the whole tribe, four hundred men excepted, in the rock Rimmon.

At last, he tempted them to reject the theocracy of their Maker and call upon Samuel to make them a king, and he made most of those kings plagues and sorrows to them in their time, as you shall hear in their order.

Thus, he plagued the whole body of the people continually, making them sin against God and bringing judgments upon them to the consuming of some millions of them, first and last, by the vengeance of their Maker.

As he did with the whole congregation, so he did with their rulers and several of the judges, who were made instruments to deliver the people yet were drawn into snares by this subtle serpent to ruin them or the people they had delivered.

He tempted Gideon to make an ephod, contrary to the Law of the Tabernacle, and made the children of Israel go a whoring (that is, a worshiping) after it.

He tempted Samson to debauch himself with a harlot and betray his own happy secret to a whore at the expense of both his eyes, and at last his life.

He tempted Eli's sons to lie with the women in the very doors of the Tabernacle when they came to bring their offerings to the priest, and he tempted poor Eli to connive with them, or not sufficiently reprove them.

He tempted the people to carry the Ark of God into the camp that it might fall into the hands of the Philistines.

He tempted Uzzah to reach out his hand to hold up the Ark as if He who had preserved it in the house of Dagon, the idol of the Philistines, could not keep it from falling out of the cart.

When the people had gotten a king, he immediately set to work in diverse ways to bring that king to load them with many plagues and calamities.

He tempted Saul to spare the king of Amalek, contrary to God's express command.

He not only tempted Saul but also possessed him with an evil spirit, by which he was left to wayward dispositions and was forced to have it fiddled out of him with a minstrel.

He tempted Saul with a spirit of discontent and with a spirit of envy at poor David, to hunt him like a partridge upon the mountains.

He tempted Saul with a spirit of divination and sent him to a witch to enquire of Samuel for him, as if God, who had forsaken him when he was alive would help him when he was dead.

After that, he tempted him to kill himself on a pretense that he might not fall into the hands of the uncircumcised, as if self-murder was not half so bad as either sin against God or disgrace among men (as being taken prisoner by a Philistine)! That was a piece of madness none but the Devil could have brought mankind to submit to, though he made it a fashion among the Romans some ages after that.

After Saul was dead and David came to the throne, by how much he was a man chosen and particularly savored by heaven, the Devil fell upon him with more vigor, attacked him in so many ways, and conquered him so very often that just as no man was so good a king, so hardly any good king was ever a worse man. In many cases one would have almost thought the Devil had made sport with David to show how easily he could overthrow the best man God could choose of the whole congregation.

He made him distrust his benefactor so much as to feign himself mad before the king of Gath when he had fled to him for shelter.

He made him march with his four hundred cut-throats to cut off poor Nabal and all his household only because he would not send him the good cheer he had provided for his honest sheep-shearers.

He made him, for his word's sake, give Ziba half his master's estate for his treachery after he knew he had been the traitor and betrayed poor Mephibosheth for the sake of it.

Then he tempted him to the ridiculous project of numbering the people against God's express command, a thing Joab himself was not wicked enough to do till David and the Devil forced him to it.

And to make him completely wicked, he carried him to the top of his house and showed him a naked lady (Bathsheba) bathing herself in her garden, in which it appeared that the Devil knew David too well and what was the particular sin of his inclination. And so he took him by the right hand, drawing him at once into the sins of murder and adultery.

Then, that he might not quite give him over (though David's repentance for the last sin kept the Devil off for a while), when he could attack him no further personally, he fell upon him in his family and made him as miserable as he could desire him to be through his children, three of whom he brought to destruction before his face, and another after his death.

First, he tempted Amnon to ravish his sister Tamar, so there was an end of her (poor girl!) as to this world, for we never hear anymore of her.

Then he tempted Absalom to murder his brother Amnon in revenge for Tamar's Maidenhood.

Then he made Joab run Absalom through the body, contrary to David's command.

And after David's death, he brought Adonijah (weak man!) to the block for usurping King Solomon's throne.

As to Absalom, he tempted him to rebellion and raising war against his father, to the turning of him shamefully out of Jerusalem and almost out of the kingdom.

He tempted him, for David's further mortification, to lie with his father's wives in the face of the whole city. And had Athithophel's honest council been followed, he had certainly sent him to sleep with his fathers long before his time. But there, Satan and Athithophel were both out-witted together.

Through all the reigns of the several successors of David, the Devil took care to carry on his own game to continually insult the measures that God himself had taken for establishing His people in the world, and especially as a Church, till at last he effectually debauched them to idolatry—that crime that, of all others, was most provoking to God since it was carrying the people away from their allegiance and transposing the homage they owed God their maker to a contemptible block of wood or an image of a brute beast. And as sordid and brutish as it was in itself, yet his artifice so prevailed among them that, first or last, he brought them all into it, the ten tribes as well as the two tribes, till at last God himself was provoked to unchurch them and give them up to their enemies. And the few who were left of them after incredible slaughters and desolation were hurried away, some into Tartary,[18] and others into Babylon, whence very few (of that few who were carried away) ever found their way home again. And some, when they might have come, would not accept it but continued there to the very coming of the Messiah. See the epistles of St. James and of St. Peter, at the beginning.

But to look a little back upon this part (for it cannot be omitted since it makes so considerable a part of the *Devil*'s history), I mean his drawing God's people, kings and all, into all the sins and mischiefs that gradually contributed to their destruction:

First (for he began immediately with the very best and wisest of the race), he drew in King Solomon in the midst of all his zeal for the building of God's house and for the making the most glorious and magnificent appearance for God's worship that ever the world saw. I say, in the middle of all this, he drew him into such immoderate and insatiable an appetite for women as to set up the first, and perhaps the greatest, seraglio of whores that ever any prince in the world had or pretended to before. Indeed, and to bring whoring so much into reputation, as the text says, seven hundred of them were princesses, that is to say, ladies of quality. This was not as the grand seigniors and great moguls (other princes of the Eastern world) have since practiced, namely, to pick up their most beautiful slaves, but these, it seems, were women of rank, king's daughters, as Pharaoh's daughter, and the daughters of the princes and prime men among the Moabites, Ammonites, Zidonians, Hittites, and so forth (1 Kings 11:1).

Nor was this all; but as he drew him into the love of these forbidden women (for such they were, as to their nation, as well as number), so he ensnared him by those women to a familiarity

18 Tartary: A vast historical region in Asia and eastern Europe roughly extending from the Sea of Japan (East Sea) to the Dnieper River. (Ed.).

with their worship and by degrees brought that famous prince (famous for his wisdom) to be the greatest and most-imposed-upon old fool in the world, bowing down to those idols by the enticing of his whores (idols whom he had abhorred and detested in his youth as dishonoring God, for whom, and for whose worship, he had finished and dedicated the most magnificent building and temple in the world. Nothing but the invincible subtlety of this *Arch Devil* could ever have brought such a man as Solomon to such a degeneracy of manners, and to such wretchedness (no, not the Devil himself without the assistance of his whores, nor the whores themselves without the Devil to help them).

As to Solomon, Satan had made conquest enough there that we need hear no more of him. The next advance he made was in the person of his son Rehoboam. Had not the Devil prompted his pride and tyrannical temperament, he would never have given the people such an answer as he did. And when he saw a fellow at the head of them, too, whom he knew wanted and waited for an occasion to raise a rebellion, he also ripened up the people's temperament to the occasion. Well might the text call it listening to the council of the young heads, that it was indeed with a vengeance! But those young heads were also acted by an old Devil, who for his craft is called, as I have observed, the old serpent.

Having thus paved the way, Jeroboam revolted. So far God had directed him; for the text says expressly, speaking in the first person of God himself, *"this thing is from me"* (1 Kings 12:24).

But though God might appoint Jeroboam to be king (that is to say, of ten tribes), yet God did not appoint him to set up the two calves in the two extreme parts of the land, viz., in Dan and in Bethel. That was Jeroboam's own doing and done on purpose to keep the people from falling back to Rehoboam and being obliged to go to Jerusalem to the public worship. And the text adds, Jeroboam made Israel to sin. This was indeed a masterpiece of the Devil's policy, and it was effectual to answer the end. Nothing could have been more to the purpose. What reason he had to expect the people would so universally come into it and be so well satisfied with a couple of calves, instead of the true worship of God at Jerusalem! Or what arts and management he (Satan) made use of afterward to bring the people in to join with such a delusion that we find but little of it in all the annals of Satan! 'Tis certain the Devil found a strange kind of propensity to worshiping idols rooted in the temper of that whole people, even from their first breaking away from the Egyptian bondage. So he had nothing to do but to work upon the old stock and propagate the crime that he found was so natural to them. And this is Satan's general way of working, not with them only, but with us also, and with all the world even then and ever since.

When he had thus secured Jeroboam's revolt, we need not trace him among his successors. For the same reason of state that held for the setting up the calves at Bethel and Dan held good for keeping them up to all of Jeroboam's posterity. Nor had they one good king ever after, not even Jehu, who called his friends to come and see his zeal for the Lord, and who fulfilled the threatening of God upon Ahab and his family, and upon Queen Jezebel and her offspring, and knew all the while that he was executing the judgment of the true God upon an idolatrous race. Yet he would not part with his calves but would have thought it to have been parting with his kingdom, and that as the people would have gone up to Jerusalem to worship, so they would at the same time have transferred their civil obedience to the king of Judah, (whose right it really was, as far as they could claim by birth and right lineage). So, by the way, Satan is not any more than other Politicians for the *jus divinum* [divine justice] of lineal succession, or what we call hereditary right, any farther than serves for his purpose.

Thus, Satan ridded his hands of ten of the twelve tribes. Let us now see how he went on with the rest, for his work was now brought into a narrower compass. The Church of God was now reduced to two tribes, except a few religious people who separated from the schism of Jeroboam and came and planted themselves among the tribes of Judah and Benjamin. The first thing the Devil did after that was to foment a war between the two kings while Judah was governed by a boy or youth, Abijah by name (and he not one of the best either). But God's time had not come, and the Devil received a great disappointment when Jeroboam was so entirely overthrown that, if the records of those ages do not mistake, no less than 500,000 men of Israel were killed. It was such a slaughter that one would think the army of Judah, had they known how to improve as well as gain a victory, might have brought all the rest back again and have entirely reduced the house of Jeroboam and the ten tribes that followed him to their obedience. Indeed, they did take a great deal of the country from them and, among the rest, Bethel itself. Yet so cunningly did Satan manage, that the king of Judah, who was himself a wicked king and perhaps an idolater in his heart, did not take down the golden calf that Jeroboam had there, no, nor destroy the idolatry itself. So in short, his victory signified nothing.

From then to the captivity, we find the Devil busy with the kings of Judah, especially the best of them. As for such as Manasseh and those who transgressed by the general tenor of their lives, he had no great trouble with.

But such as Asa, Jehoshaphat, Hezekiah, and Josiah, he hung about them and their courts till he brought every one of them into some mischief or another.

As first, good King Asa, of whom the Scripture says his heart was perfect all his days, yet this subtle spirit that could break in upon him nowhere else tempted him when the king of Israel came out against him to send to hire Benhadad the King of Syria to help him, as if God who had before enabled him to conquer the Ethiopians, with an army of ten hundred thousand men, could not have saved him from the king of the ten tribes.

In the same manner, he tempted Jehoshaphat to join with that wicked King Ahab against the king of Syria, and also to marry his son to Ahab's daughter, which was fatal to Jehoshaphat and to his posterity.

Again, he tempted Hezekiah to show all his riches to the king of Babylon's messengers. And who can doubt but that he (Satan) is to be understood to be the wicked spirit that stood before the Lord (2 Chron. 18:20) and offered his service to entice Ahab, the king of Israel, to come out to battle to his ruin, by being a lying spirit in the mouths of all his prophets, and who for that time had a special commission, as he had another time in the case of Job? And indeed, it was a commission fit for nobody but the Devil: *"Thou shalt entice him, and thou shalt also prevail: go out and do even so"* (v. 21).

Even good Josiah himself, of whom it is recorded that there was no like king before him, neither after him arose there any like him (2 Kings 23:25)—the Devil yet never left him with his machinations till, finding he could not tempt him to anything wicked in his government, he tempted or moved him to a needless war with the king of Egypt, in which he lost his life.

From the death of this good king, the Devil prevailed so with the whole nation of the Jews and brought them to such an incorrigible pitch of wickedness that God gave them up, forsook His habitation of glory, the temple, which He suffered to be spoiled first, then burnt and demolished, destroying the whole nation of the Jews except a small number who were left, and those the enemy carried away into captivity.

Nor was he satisfied with this general destruction of the whole people of Israel, for the ten tribes were gone before. But he followed them even into their captivity. Those who fled away to Egypt, which they tell us were seventy thousand, he first corrupted, and then they were destroyed there upon the overthrow of Egypt by the same king of Babylon.

Also, he went very near to having them rooted out, young and old, man, woman and child, who were in captivity in Babylon, by the ministry of that true agent of hell, Haman the Agagite. But there Satan met with a disappointment too, as in the story of Esther, which was but the fourth that he had met with in all his management since the Creation. I say, there he was disappointed, and his prime minister, Haman, was executed, as he deserved.

Having thus far traced the government and dominion of the Devil from the creation of man to the captivity. I think I may call upon him to set up his standard of universal empire at that period. It seemed just then as if God had really forsaken the earth and given the entire dominion of mankind up to His outrageous enemy, the Devil. For excepting the few Israelites who were left in the territories of the king of Babylon, and they were but a few, I say, except among them, there was not one corner of the world left where the true God was called upon or his dominion so much as acknowledged. All the world was buried in idolatry, and that of so many horrid kinds that one would think the light of reason should have convinced mankind that he who exacted such bloody sacrifices as that of Molech, and such a bloody cutting themselves with knives as the Priests of Baal did, could not be a god, a good and beneficent being, but must be a cruel, voracious and devouring devil, whose end was not what's good but the destruction of his creatures.

But to such a height was the blind, demented world arrived to at that time that in these sordid and corrupt ways, they went on worshiping dumb idols and offering human sacrifices to them, and in a word, committing all the most horrid and absurd abominations that they were capable of or that the Devil could prompt them to till heaven was again put, as it were, to the necessity of bringing about a revolution in favor of His own forsaken people, by miracle and surprise, as He had done before.

We come therefore to the restoration or return of the captivity. Had Satan been able to have acted anything by force, as I have observed before, all the princes and powers of the world having been, as they really were, at his devotion, he might easily have made use of them, armed all the world against the Jews, and prevented the rebuilding of the temple and even the return of the captivity.

But now the Devil's power manifestly received a check, and the hand of God appeared in it. He was resolved to reestablish His people, the Jews, and to have a second temple built. The Devil, who knew the extent of his own power too well, and what limitations were laid upon him, stood still, as it were, looking on, not daring to oppose the return of the captivity, which he very well knew had been prophesied and would come to pass.

He did indeed make some little opposition to the building and to the fortifying of the city. But as it was to no purpose, so he was soon obliged to give it up. And thus the captivity being returned, and the temple rebuilt, the people of the Jews increased and multiplied to an infinite number and strength. And from that time, we may say the power of the Devil rather declined and decreased than went on with success as it had done before.

It is true the Jews fell into sects and errors and divisions of many kinds after the return from the captivity, and no doubt the Devil had a great hand in those divisions, but he could never bring them back to idolatry. And not being able to do that made him turn his hand many ways to plague and oppress them, as particularly by Antiochus the Great, who brought the Abomination of Desolation into the holy place. And there, the Devil triumphed over them for some time. But they were delivered many ways, till at last they came peaceably under the protection rather than the dominion of the Roman Empire. When Herod the Great governed them as a king, he reedified, indeed, almost rebuilt, their temple with so great an expense and magnificence that he made it, as some say, greater and more glorious than that of Solomon's, (though that I take to be a great fable, to say no worse of it).

In this condition, the Jewish church stood when the fullness of time, as 'tis called in Scripture, had come. And the Devil was kept at bay, though he had made some encroachments upon them as above. For there was a glorious remnant of saints among them, such as old Zacharias, the father of John the Baptist, and old Simeon, who waited for the salvation of Israel. I say, in this condition the Jewish church stood when the Messiah came into the world, which was such another mortal stab to the thrones and principalities infernal, as that of which I have spoken already in Genesis 3 at the creation of man.

And therefore, with this I break off the antiquities of the Devil's history, or the ancient part of his kingdom. For hence downward we shall find his empire has declined gradually. And though by his wonderful address, his prodigious application, and the vigilance and fidelity of his instruments (as well human as infernal and diabolical, and of the human as well the ecclesiastic as the secular) he has many times retrieved what he has lost, and sometimes bid fair for recovering the universal empire he once possessed over mankind, yet he has been still defeated again, repulsed and beaten back, and his kingdom has greatly declined in many parts of the world—especially in the northern parts, except Great Britain. And how he has politically maintained his interest and increased his dominion among the wise and righteous generation that we cohabit with and among will be the subject of the modern part of Satan's history of which we are next to give an account.

SATAN CAST OUT FROM HEAVEN TO THE EARTH

PART II

THE HISTORY OF THE DEVIL

1

INTRODUCTION

I have examined the antiquities of Satan's history in the former part of this work and brought his affairs down from the Creation as far as to our blessed Christian times, especially to the coming of the Messiah, when one would think the Devil could have nothing to do among us. I have indeed but touched at some things that might have admitted of a further description of Satan's affairs, and the particulars of which we may all come to a further knowledge of hereafter. Yet, I think I have spoken to the material part of his conduct as it relates to his empire in this world. What has happened to his more sublimated government, and his angelic capacities, I shall have an occasion to touch on in several solid particulars as we go along.

The Messiah was now born. The *fullness of time* had come when the old serpent was to have his head broken. That is to say, his empire or dominion over man, which he gained by the fall of our first father and mother in Paradise, received a downfall or overthrow.

In order to confirm what I have already mentioned of the limitation of Satan's power, it is worth observing that not only his angelic strength seems to have received a further blow upon the coming of the Son of God into the world, but he seems to have had a blow upon his intellect. And instead of his being so cunning a fellow as before, when, as I said, 'tis evident he outwitted all mankind, not only Eve, Cain, Noah, Lot, and all the Patriarchs but even nations of men (and that in their public capacity) and thereby led them into absurd and ridiculous things, such as the building of Babel, and deifying and worshiping their kings (when dead and rotten), and even idolizing beast, stocks, stones, anything, and even nothing (managing mankind just as he pleased), his serpentine craft and devil-like subtlety seems to have been circumscribed and cut short.

Now and from that time forward he appeared a weak, foolish, ignorant Devil compared to what he was before. He was upon almost every occasion resisted, disappointed, baulked, and defeated, especially in all his attempts to thwart or cross the mission and ministry of the Messiah while he was upon earth and sometimes upon other and very ordinary occasions too.

And first, how foolish a project was it, and how below Satan's celebrated artifice in like cases was it, to put Herod upon sending to kill the poor innocent children in Bethlehem in hopes to destroy the infant [Messiah]? For I take it for granted it was the Devil who put into Herod's thoughts that execution, howsoever simple and foolish. Now we must allow him to be very ignorant himself of the Nativity, or else he might easily have guided his friend Herod to the place where the infant [Jesus] was.

This shows that either the Devil is, in general, ignorant as we are of what is to come in the world before it is really come to pass, and consequently can foretell nothing, no not so much as our famous old Merlin or Mother Shipton did, or else that great event was hidden from him by an immediate power superior to his, neither of which I think accurate considering how much he was concerned in it, and how certainly he knew that it was to come to pass.

But be that as it will, 'tis certain the Devil knew nothing where Christ was born, or when. Nor was he able to direct Herod to find him out, and therefore put him upon that foolish, cruel order, to kill all the children, that he might be sure to destroy the Messiah among the rest.

The next simple step that the Devil took, and indeed the most foolish one that he could ever be charged with, unworthy the very dignity of a devil, and below the understanding that he was always allowed to act with, was that of coming to tempt the Messiah in the wilderness. It is certain, and he owned it himself afterward upon many occasions, that the Devil knew our Savior to be the Son of God. And 'tis as certain he knew that, as such, he could have no power or advantage over Him. How foolish then was it of him to attack Him in that manner—*"if thou art the Son of God?"* (Matt. 4:1-11). Why, he knew him to be the Son of God well enough. He said so afterward. *"I know thee who thou art; the holy One of God"* (Luke 4:34). How then could he be so weak a devil as to say, if thou art, then do so and so?

The case is plain, the Devil, though he knew Him to be the Son of God, did not fully know the mystery of the Incarnation. Nor did he know how far the inanition[19] of Christ extended, and whether, as man, he was not subject to falling as Adam was, though His reserved Godhead might be still immaculate and pure. And upon this foot, as he would leave no method untried, he attempted him three times, one immediately after another. But then, finding himself disappointed, he fled.

This evidently proves that the Devil was ignorant of the great

19 Inanition—the exhausted condition that results from lack of food and water (Ed.).

mystery of godliness as the Scripture text describes it: *"God was manifest in the flesh"* (1 Tim 3:16), and therefore made that foolish attempt upon Christ thinking to have conquered His human nature as capable of sin, which it was not. And at this repulse, hell groaned, and the whole army of regimented devils received a wound and felt the shock of it. 'Twas a second overthrow to them, they had had a long chain of success and carried a devilish conquest over the greatest part of the Creation of God. But now they were cut short, the Seed of the Woman had now come to break the Serpent's Head (Gen 3:15), that is to cut short his power, to contract the limits of his kingdom, and, in a word, to dethrone him in the world. No doubt the Devil received a shock; for you find him always afterward crying out in a horrible manner whenever Christ met with him, or else very humble and submissive, as when he begged permission to go into the herd of swine (Matt. 8:31), a thing he has often done since.

Defeated here, the first stratagem I find him concerned in after it, was his entering into Judas [Iscariot] and putting him upon betraying Christ to the chief priest. But here again, he was entirely mistaken, for he did not see, as much a devil as he was, what the event would be. So when he came to know that if Christ was put to death He would become a propitiatory and be the great sacrifice of mankind, so to rescue the fallen race from that death they had incurred the penalty of by the fall, that this was the fulfilling of all Scripture prophecy, and that thus it was that Christ was to be the end of the law—I say, as soon as he perceived this, he strove all he could to prevent it and disturbed Pilate's wife in her sleep in order to set her upon her husband to hinder his delivering Him up to the Jews. For then, and not till then, he knew how Christ was to vanquish hell by the power of His cross.

Thus, the Devil was disappointed and exposed in every step he took, and as he plainly saw his kingdom declining and the temporal Kingdom of Christ rising up upon the ruins of his (Satan's) power, he seemed to retreat into his own region of the air to consult there with his fellow devils what measures he should take next to preserve his dominion among men.

Here it was that he resolved upon that truly hellish thing called persecution, by which, though he proved a foolish Devil in that too, he flattered himself that he should be able to destroy God's Church and root out its professors from the earth even almost as soon as it was established. Whereas on the contrary, though he armed the whole Roman Empire against the Christians, that is to say, the whole world, and they were fallen upon everywhere with all the fury and rage of some of the most flaming tyrants that the world ever saw, of whom Nero was the first, heaven counteracted him there too. In spite of hell, God made all the blood, which the Devil caused to be spilt, to be *semen ecclesiæ* [Seed of the Church], and the Devil had the mortification to see that the number of Christians increased even under the very means he made use of to root them out and destroy them. This was the case through the reign of all the Roman emperors for the first three hundred years after Christ.

Having thus tried all the methods that best suited his inclination, I mean those of blood and death complicated with tortures and all kinds of cruelty, and that for so long a stage of time as above, the Devil all of a sudden (as if glutted with blood and satiated with destruction) sat still and became a peaceable spectator for a good while, as if he either found himself unable, or had no disposition to hinder the progress of Christianity in the first ages of its settlement in the world. In this interval the

Christian Church was established under Constantine. Religion flourished in peace and under the most perfect tranquility.

The Devil seemed to be at a loss over what he should do next, and things began to look as if Satan's kingdom was at an end. But he soon let them see that he was the same indefatigable Devil that ever he was, and the prosperity of the Church gave him a large field of action. For knowing the disposition of mankind to quarrel and dispute the universal passion rooted in nature, especially among the churchmen for precedency and dominion, he fell to work with them immediately. So by turning the tables and reassuming the subtlety and craft that, I say, he seemed to have lost in the former four hundred years, he gained more ground in the next ages of the Church and went farther toward restoring his power and empire in the world—and toward overthrowing the very Church that was so lately established than all he had done by fire and blood before.

His policy now seemed to be edged with resentment for the mistakes he had made as if the Devil, looking back with anger at himself to see what a fool he had been to expect to crush religion by persecution, rejoiced for having discovered that liberty and dominion was the only way to ruin the Church, not fire and firewood. So he had nothing to do but give the zealous people their utmost liberty in religion, only sowing error and variety of opinion among them, and they would bring fire and firewood in fast enough among themselves.

It must be confessed, these were devilish politics. And so sure was the aim, and so certain was the Devil to hit his mark by them, that we find he not only did not fail then, but the same hellish methods have prevailed still, and will do so to the end of the world. Nor had the Devil ever a better game to play than this for the ruin of religion, as we shall have room to show in many examples besides that of the Dissenters in England, who are evidently weakened by the late toleration. Whether the Devil had any hand in baiting his hook with an Act of Parliament or not, history is silent, but 'tis too evident he has caught the fish by it. And if the honest Church of England does not in pity and Christian charity to the Dissenters straighten her hand a little, I cannot but fear the Devil will gain his point, and the Dissenter will be undone by it.

Upon this new foot of politics, the Devil began with the emperors themselves. Arius, the father of the heretics of that age having broached his opinions, and Athanasius, the orthodox Bishop of the East opposing him, the Devil no sooner saw the door open to strife and imposition but he thrust himself in. And raising the quarrel up to a suited degree of rage and spleen, he involved the good Emperor [Constantine] himself in it first, and Athanasius was banished and recalled, and banished and recalled again, several times, as error [Arianism] ran high, and as the Devil either got or lost ground.

After Constantine, the next emperor was a child of his own (Constantine II). Arius and the Court came all into the quarrel, as courts often do, and then the Arians and the Orthodox persecuted one another as furiously as the pagans persecuted them all before. To such a height, the Devil brought his conquest in the very infancy of the question, and so much so that he brought confusion over the true Christianity of the primitive Church.

Flushed with this success, the Devil made a push for restoring paganism and bringing on the old worship of the heathen idols and temples. But like our King James II, he drove too hard, and Julian had so provoked the whole Roman Empire, which had generally at that time become Christian, that had the apostate lived he would not have been able to have held the throne. And as he was cut off in his beginning, paganism expired with him, and the Devil himself might have cried out, as Julian did, and with much more propriety, *Vicisti Galileane* [conquered Galilean]!

Jovian, the next Emperor, being a glorious Christian and a very good and great man, the Devil abdicated for a while and left the Christian armies to re-establish the Orthodox Faith. Nor could he bring the Christians to a breach again among themselves a great while after.

However, time and a diligent Devil did the work at last, and when the emperors concerning themselves did not appear sufficient one way or other to answer his end, he changed hands again and went to work with the clergy. To set the doctors effectually together by the ears, he threw in the new notion of primacy among them for a bone of contention. The bait taken, the priests eagerly swallowed it down, and the Devil, a more cunning fisherman than ever St. Peter was, struck them (as the anglers call it) with a quick hand, and hung them fast upon the hook.

Having them thus in his clutches, and them being now, as we may say, his own, they took their measures afterward from him and most obediently followed his directions. Indeed, I will not say but he may have had pretty much the management of the whole society ever since, of whatsoever profession or party they may have been, with exception only to the reverend and right reverend among us.

The sacred being thus hooked in, as above, and the Devil being at the head of their affairs, matters went on most gloriously his own way. First, the bishops fell to bandying and party-making for the superiority as heartily as ever temporal tyrants did for dominion. And they took as black and devilish methods to carry it on as the worst of those tyrants ever had done before them.

At last Satan declared for the Roman Pontiff, and that upon excellent conditions, in the reign of the Emperor Mauritius. For Boniface, who had long contended for the title of Supreme, fell into a treaty with Phocas, captain of the emperor's guards. Whether the bargain was from hell or not, let anyone judge. The conditions absolutely entitle the Devil to the honor of making the contract, viz., that Phocas, first murdering his master (the emperor) and his sons, Boniface should countenance the treason and declare him emperor. And in return, Phocas should acknowledge the primacy of the Church of Rome and declare Boniface universal Bishop [Pope]. A blessed compact! Which at once set the Devil at the head of affairs in the Christian world, spiritual as well temporal, ecclesiastic, and civil. Since the conquest over Eve in Paradise, by which death and the Devil, hand in hand, established their first empire upon earth, the Devil never gained a more important point than he gained at that time.

He had indeed prospered in his affairs tolerably well for some time before this, and his interest among the clergy gained ground for some ages. But that was indeed a secret management carried on privately and with difficulty, as in sowing discord and faction among the people, perplexing the councils of their princes, and secretly influencing the dignified clergy.

Also, the Devil had raised an abundance of little church-rebellions by setting up heretics of several kinds and raising them favorers among the clergy, such as Ebion, Cerinthius, Pelagius, and others.

He had drawn in the bishops of Rome to set up the ridiculous pageantry of the key. And while he, the Devil, set open the gates of hell to them all, he set them upon locking up the gates of heaven and giving the bishop the key—a fraud which, as gross as it was, the Devil so gilded over it, or so blinded the age to receive it, that like Gideon's Ephod, all the Catholic world went a whoring after the idol. The bishop of Rome sent more fools to the Devil by it than he ever pretended to let into heaven, though he opened the door as wide as his key was able to do.

The story of this key being given to the Bishop of Rome by St. Peter (who, by the way, never had it himself,), and of its being lost by somebody or other (the Devil it seems did not tell them who), and its being found again by a Lombard soldier in the army of King Antharis (who attempting to cut it with his knife was miraculously forced to direct the wound to himself and cut his own throat), that King Antharis and his nobles happened to see the fellow do it and were converted to Christianity by it, and that the king sent the key, with another made like it, to Pope Pelagius, then Bishop of Rome, who thereupon assumed the power of opening and shutting heaven's gates (he afterwards setting a price or toll upon the entrance, as we do here at passing a turnpike), these fine things, I say, were successfully managed for some years before this I am now speaking of. And the Devil got a great deal of ground by it too. But now he triumphed openly, and having set up a murderer upon the temporal throne and a church emperor upon the ecclesiastic throne, and both of his own choosing, the Devil may be said to have begun his new kingdom from this Epocha, and called it the *Restoration.*

Since this time indeed the Devil's affairs went very merrily on, and the clergy brought so many gewgaws [trinkets] into their worship, and such devilish principles were mixed with that which we called the Christian Faith, that in a word, from this time, the Bishop of Rome commenced being the Whore of Babylon in all the most express terms that could be imagined. Tyranny of the worst sort crept into the Pontificate and errors of all sorts into the profession, and they proceeded from one thing to another till the very Popes (for so the Bishop of Rome was now called by way of distinction), I say, the Popes themselves and their spiritual guides professed openly to confederate with the Devil and to carry on a personal and private correspondence with him while at the same time taking upon themselves the title of Christ's *Vicar* and the infallible guide of the consciences of Christians.

This we have sundry instances of in some merry Popes who, if fame lies not, were sorcerers, magicians, had familiar spirits and immediate conversation with the Devil, visibly as well as invisibly, and who by this means became what we call devils incarnate. Upon this account it is that I have left the conversation that passes between devils and men to this place as well, because I believe it differs much now in his modern state from what it was in his ancient state, and therefore that which most concerns us belongs rather to this part of his history—also because, as I am now writing to the present age, I choose to bring the most significant parts of his history, especially as they relate to us, into that part of time that we are most concerned about.

The Devil had once, as I observed before, the universal monarchy or government of mankind in himself, and I doubt not but in that flourishing state of his affairs, he governed them like what he is, viz., an absolute tyrant. During this theocracy of his, for Satan is called, *"the god of this world,"* he did not familiarize himself to mankind so much as he finds occasion to do now.

There was not then so much need of it. He governed then with an absolute sway. He had his oracles where he gave audience to his advocates like a deity. And he had his sub-gods, who under his several dispositions received the homage of mankind in their names. Such were all the rabble of the heathen deities, from Jupiter the Supreme to the lairs or household gods of every family. These, I say, like residents, received the prostrations, but the homage was all Satan's. The Devil had the substance of it all, which was the idolatry.

During this administration of hell there was less witchcraft, less true literal magic than there has been since. There was indeed no need of it. The Devil did not stoop to the mechanism of his more modern operations but ruled as a deity and received the vows and the bows of his subjects in more state, and with more solemnity. Whereas since then, he is content to employ more agents and take more pains himself too. Now he runs up and down hackney [like a hireling] in the world, more like a drudge than a prince, and much more than he did then.

Hence all those things we call apparitions and visions of ghosts, familiar spirits and dealings with the Devil, of which there is so great a variety in the world at this time, were not so much known among the people in those first ages of the Devil's kingdom. In a word, the Devil seems to be put to his shifts and to flee to art and stratagem for carrying on his affairs much more now than he did then.

One reason for this may be that he has been more discovered and exposed in these ages than he was before. Then, he could appear in the world in his own proper shapes and yet not be known. When the Sons of God appeared at the divine summons, Satan came along with them, but now he has played so many scurvy tricks upon men, and they know him so well, that he is obliged to play quite out of sight and act in disguise. Mankind will allow nothing of his doing, and hear nothing of his saying, in his own name. And if you propose anything to be done, and it be but said the Devil is to help in the doing of it, or if you say of any man that he deals with the Devil, or that the Devil has a hand in it, everybody flees from him and shuns him as the most frightful thing in the world.

Indeed, if anything strange and improbable be done or is related to be done, we presently say the Devil was at the doing of it. Thus, the great ditch at Newmarket Heath is called the Devil's Ditch. Similarly, the Devil built Crowland Abbey and the Whispering-Place in Gloucester Cathedral, and, indeed, the Cave at Castleton only because there's no getting to the farther end of it. It is called the Devil's A—— and the like. The poor people of Wiltshire, when you ask them how the great stones at Stonehenge were brought thither, they'll all tell you the Devil brought them. If any extraordinary mischief befalls us, we presently say the Devil was in it, and the Devil would have it so. In a word, the Devil has got an ill name among us, and so he is inclined to act more in *tenebris* [in the dark], more *incog.* than he used to do, play out of sight himself, and work by the sap,[20] as the engineers call it, and not openly and avowedly in his own name and person, as formerly, though perhaps not with less success than he did before.

And this leads me to enquire more narrowly into the manner of the Devil's management of his affairs since the Christian religion began to spread in the world, which manifestly differs from his conduct in more ancient times, in which if we discover some of the most consummate fool's policy, the most profound

20 Sap—the extension of a trench to a point beneath an enemy's fortifications (Ed.).

simple craft, and the most subtle shallow management of things that can by our weak understandings be conceived, we must only resolve it into this: that in short, it is the Devil.

2

OF HELL, AS IT IS REPRESENTED TO US, AND HOW THE DEVIL IS TO BE UNDERSTOOD AS BEING PERSONALLY IN HELL, WHEN AT THE SAME TIME WE FIND HIM AT LIBERTY RANGING OVER THE WORLD.

It is true, as that learned and pleasant author, the inimitable Dr. Brown says, the Devil is his own hell. One of the most constituting parts of his infelicity is that he cannot act upon mankind *brevi manu* [short hand], by his own inherent power as well as rage, and that he cannot unhinge this creation, which, as I have observed in its place, he had the utmost aversion to from its beginning, as it was a stated design in the Creator to replace his place in heaven with a new species of beings called *man* and fill the vacancies occasioned by his degeneracy and rebellion.

This filled him with inexpressible rage and horrible resolutions of revenge. And the impossibility of executing those resolutions torments him with despair. This added to what he was before, makes him a complete devil with a hell in his own breast and a fire unquenchable burning about his heart.

I might enlarge here, and very much to the purpose in describing spherically and mathematically that exquisite quality called a devilish spirit, in which it would naturally occur to give you a whole chapter upon the glorious articles of *malice* and *envy*, and especially upon that luscious, delightful, triumphant passion called revenge—how natural to man, indeed, even to both sexes it is, and how pleasant in the very contemplation—how palatable it is in itself, and how well it relishes when dished up with its proper sauces such as plot, contrivance, scheme, and confederacy, all leading on to execution—how it possesses a human soul in all the most sensible parts, and how it empowers mankind to sin in imagination as effectually to all future intents and purposes (damnation) as if he had actually sinned. How safe a practice it is too, as to punishment in this life, namely, that it empowers us to cut throats, slander virtue, reproach innocence, wound honor, and stab reputation—and in a word, to do all the wicked things in the world out of the reach of the law.

It would also require a few words to describe the secret operations of those nice qualities when they reach the human soul, how effectually they form a hell within us and how imperceptibly they assimilate and transform us into devils, mere human devils, really devils as Satan himself or any of his angels. And therefore 'tis not so much out of the way, as some imagine, to say such a man is an incarnate devil. For as crime made Satan a devil who was before a bright immortal seraph, or angel of light, how much more easily may the same crime make the same devil, though every way meaner and more contemptible, of a man or a woman either? But this is too grave a subject for me at this time.

The Devil being thus, I say, fired with rage and envy in

consequence of his jealousy upon the creation of man, his torment is increased to the highest by the limitation of his power and his being forbidden to act against mankind by force of arms. This, I say as above, is part of his hell that is within him and which he carries within him wherever he goes. Nor is it so difficult to conceive of hell, or of the Devil either, under this just description, as it is by all the usual notions that we are taught to entertain them by (the old women) our instructors. For every man may, by taking but a common view of himself and making a just scrutiny into his own passions on some of their particular excursions, see a hell within himself and see himself as a mere devil as long as the inflammation lasts (and view that as really, and to all intents and purposes, as if he had the angel, Satan, before his face in his locality and personality—that is to say, all devil and monster in his person and an immaterial but intense fire flaming about and from within him at all the pores of his body).

The notions we receive of the Devil as a person being in hell as a place are infinitely absurd and ridiculous. First, we are certain it is not true in fact, because he has a certain liberty (however limited that is not to the purpose), and is daily visible and to be traced in his several attacks upon mankind, and has been so ever since his first appearance in Paradise. As to his corporeal visibility, that is not the present question either. 'Tis enough that we can hunt him by foot, that we can follow him as hounds do a fox upon a hot scent. We can see him as plainly by the effect, by the mischief he does, and more by the mischief he puts us upon doing, I say, as plainly as if we saw him by eye.

It is not to be doubted that the Devil can see us when and where we cannot see him. And as he has a personality, though it be spirit in nature, he and his angels too may be reasonably supposed to both inhabit the world of spirits and have free access from there to the regions of life, and to pass and return in the air, as really, though not perceptible to us, the spirits of men after their release from the body pass to the place that is appointed for them (wherever that is).

If the Devil was confined to a place (hell) as a prison, he could then have no business here. And if we pretend to describe hell as not a prison, but that the Devil has liberty to be there or not be there as he pleases, then he would certainly never be there, or hell is not such a place as we are taught to understand it to be.

Indeed, according to some, hell should be a place of fire and torment to the souls that are cast into it, but not to the devils themselves, who we make little more or less than keepers and turnkeys to hell as a goal, that they are sent about to bring souls thither, lock them in when they come, and then fly away upon the scent to fetch more.

That one sort of devils is made to live in the world among men and be busy continually debauching and deluding mankind, bringing them as it were to the gates of hell, and then others are porters and carriers to fetch them in, is, in short, little more or less than the old story of Pluto, of Cerberus, and of Charon, only that our tale is not half so well told, nor the parts of the fable so well laid together.

In all these notions of hell and Devil, the torments of the first, and the agency of the last tormenting, we meet with not one word of the main and perhaps only accent of horror, which belongs to us to judge of about hell, I mean the *absence of heaven*—expulsion and exclusion from the presence and face of the Chief Ultimate, the only eternal and sufficient Good, and this loss sustained by a sordid neglect of our concern in that excellent part in exchange for the most contemptible and justly condemned trifles (and all this eternal and irrecoverable). These people tell us nothing of the eternal reproaches of conscience, the horror of desperation, and the anguish of a mind hopeless of ever seeing the glory that alone constitutes heaven, and which makes all other places dreadful and even darkness itself.

And this brings me directly to the point in hand, viz, the state of hell that we ought to have in view when we speak of the Devil as being in hell. This is the very hell that is the torment of the Devil, in short, the Devil is in hell, and hell is in the Devil. He is filled with this unquenchable fire. He is expelled from the place of glory and banished from the regions of light. Being absent from the life of all beatitude is his curse. Despair is the reigning passion in his mind, and all the little constituent parts of his torment, such as rage, envy, malice, and jealousy are consolidated in this to make his misery complete, viz., the duration of it all, the eternity of his condition, that he is without hope, without redemption, and without recovery.

If anything can inflame this hell and make it hotter, 'tis this only, and this does add an inexpressible horror to the Devil, namely, seeing man (the only creature he hates) placed in a state of recovery, a glorious establishment of *redemption* formed for him in heaven, and the scheme of it perfected on earth by which this man, though even the Devil by his art may have deluded him and drawn him into crime, is yet in a state of *recovery,* which the Devil is not, and that it is not in his (Satan's) power to prevent it.

Now take the Devil as he is in his own nature, angelic, a bright immortal seraph, heaven-born, and having tasted the eternal beatitude that these are now appointed to enjoy, the loss of that state to himself, and the possession of it granted to his rival though wicked like and as himself. I say, take the Devil as he is. Having a quick sense of his own perdition and a stinging sight of his rival's felicity 'tis *hell enough,* and more than enough even for an angel to support. Nothing we can conceive can be worse.

As to any other fire than this, such and so immaterially intense as to torment a spirit, which is itself fire, also, I will not say it cannot be, because to the Infinite everything is possible, but I must say, I cannot conceive rightly of it.

I will not enter here into the wisdom or reasonableness of representing the torments of hell to be fire, and that fire to be a commixture of flame and sulphur. It has pleased God to let the horror of those eternal agonies about a lost heaven be laid before us by those similitudes or allegories that are most moving to our senses and to our understandings. Nor will I dispute the possibility. Much less will I doubt but that there is to be a consummation of misery to all the objects of misery when the Devil's kingdom in this world ends with the world itself, and that the liberty he has now may be further abridged when he is returned to the same state he was in between the time of his fall and the creation of the world with perhaps some additional vengeance on him (such as at present we cannot describe) for all that treason and those high crimes and misdemeanors that he has been guilty of here in his conversation with mankind.

Since his infelicity will then be consummated and completed, so the infelicity of that part of mankind who are condemned with him may receive a considerable addition from those words in their sentence, to be tormented with *"the devil and his angels"* (Matt. 25:41). For as the absence of the Supreme Good is a complete hell, so the hated company of the deceiver, who was the great cause of his ruin, must be a subject of additional horror.

And he will be always saying, as a Scots gentleman who died of his excesses said to the famous Dr. P——, who came to see him on his deathbed, but who had been too much his companion in his life,

O tu fundamenta jecisti.[21]

I would not treat the very subject itself with any indecency, nor do I think my opinion of that hell, which I say consists of the absence of Him in whom *is* heaven, one jot less solemn than theirs who believe it all fire and brimstone. But I must admit that, to me, nothing can be more ridiculous than the notions that we entertain and fill our heads with about hell and about the Devil being there tormenting souls, broiling them upon gridirons, hanging them up upon hooks, carrying them upon their backs, and the like, with the various pictures of hell represented by a great mouth with horrible teeth, gaping like a cave on the sides of a mountain. Suppose that appropriated to Satan in the peak, which indeed is not much unlike it, with a stream of fire coming out of it, as there is of water, and smaller devils going and coming continually in and out to fetch and carry souls the Lord knows where, and for the Lord knows what.

These things, however intended for terror, are indeed so ridiculous that the Devil himself, to be sure, mocks at them, and a man of sense can hardly refrain doing the same. Only I avoid it, because I would not give offence to weaker heads.

However, I must not compliment the brains of other men at the expense of my own, or talk nonsense because they can understand no other. I think all these notions and representations of hell and of the Devil to be as profane as they are ridiculous, and

21 Translation. Oh you laid the foundations.

I ought no more to talk profanely than merrily of them.

Let us learn to talk of these things then, as we should. And since we really cannot describe them to our reason and understanding, why should we describe them to our senses? We ought, I think much better, not describe them at all, that is to say, not attempt it. The blessed Apostle Paul, was (as he said himself) carried up or caught up into the third heaven, yet when he came down again, he could neither tell what he heard or describe what he saw. All he could say of it was that what he heard was unutterable and what he saw was inconceivable. (2 Cor. 12:2-4).

It is the same thing as to the state of the Devil in those regions that he now possesses, and where he now more particularly inhabits. My present business then is not to enter into those grave things so as to make them ridiculous, as I think most people do that talk of them. But let his residence be where it will since the Devil has evidently free access to come and go, not into this world only (I mean, the region of our atmosphere), but for ought we know, to all the other inhabited worlds that God has made, wherever they are and by whatsoever names they are or may be known or distinguished. For if he is not confined in one place, we have no reason to believe he is excluded from any place (heaven only excepted, from where he was expelled for his treason and rebellion).

His liberty then being thus ascertained, three things seem to be material for us to give an account of in order to form this part of his history:

1. ***What his business is on this globe of earth***, which we commonly call the world, how he acts among us, what affairs mankind and he have together, and how far his conduct here relates to us and ours, or may be influenced by him.

2. ***Where his principal residence is, and whether he has not a particular empire of his own,*** to which he retreats upon proper occasions, where he entertains his friends when they come under his particular administration, and where, when he gets any victory over his enemies, he carries his prisoners of war.
3. ***What may probably be the great business this black emperor has at present upon his hands,*** either in this world or out of it, and by what agents he works.

As these things may perhaps run promiscuously through the course of this whole work and frequently be touched on under other branches of the Devil's history, so I do not propose them as heads of chapters or particular sections (for the order of discourse to be handled apart). For (by the way) as Satan's actions have not been the most regular things in the world, so in our discourse about him it must not be expected that we can always tie ourselves down to order and regularity, either as to time, or place, or persons. For Satan being *hic & ubique* [here and everywhere], a loose ungoverned fellow, we must be content to trace him where we can find him.

It is true, in the foregoing chapter I showed you the Devil entered into the herd ecclesiastic and gave you some account of the first successful step he took with mankind since the Christian Epoch—how having secretly managed both temporal and spiritual power apart, and by themselves, he now united them in point of management and brought the Church usurpation and the army's usurpation together, the Pope to bless the general in deposing and murdering his master, the emperor, and the general to recognize the Pope in dethroning his Master, Christ Jesus.

From this time forward you are to allow the Devil a mystical empire in this world—not an action of moment done without him, not a treason but he has a hand in it, not a tyrant but he prompts him, not a government but he has a say in it, not a fool but he tickles him, and not a knave but he guides him. He has a finger in every fraud, a key to every cabinet from the divan at Constantinople, to the Mississippi in France, and to the South-Sea, cheats at everything from the first attack upon the Christian world, in the person of the Romish Antichrist, down to the Bull *Unigenitus* [only-begotten Son], from the mixture of St. Peter and Confucius in China to the holy office in Spain, and down to the Emlins and Dodwells of the current age.

How he has managed, and does manage, and how in all probability he will manage till his kingdom shall come to a period, and how at last he will probably be managed himself, enquire within, and you shall know further.

3

OF THE MANNER OF SATAN'S ACTIONS AND CARRYING ON HIS AFFAIRS IN THIS WORLD, AND PARTICULARLY OF HIS ORDINARY WORKINGS IN THE DARK BY POSSESSION AND AGITATION.

The Devil being thus reduced to act upon mankind by stratagem only, it remains to enquire how he performs, and which way he directs his attacks. The faculties of man are a kind of a garrison in a strong castle, which as they defend it on the one hand under the command of the reasoning power of man's soul, they are proscribed on the other hand and can't venture out without permission; for the governor of a fort does not permit his soldiers to hold any correspondence with the enemy without special order and direction.

Now the great enquiry before us is: How does the Devil come to a parley with us? How does he converse with our senses and with the understanding? How does he reach us, which way does he come at the affections, and which way does he move the passions? 'Tis a little difficult to discover this treasonable correspondence, and that difficulty is indeed the Devil's advantage and, for ought I see, the chief advantage he has over mankind.

It is also a great enquiry here whether or not the Devil knows our thoughts. If I may give my opinion, I am with the negative. I deny that he knows anything of our thoughts except for those thoughts that he puts us upon thinking. For I will not doubt but he has the art to inject thoughts and to revive dormant thoughts in us.

It is not so wild a scheme that Mr. Milton lays down as some take it to be, to represent the Devil injecting corrupt desires and wandering thoughts into the head of Eve by dreams, and that he brought her to dream whatever he put into her thoughts by whispering to her vocally when she was asleep. And to this end, he imagines the Devil laying himself close to her ear when she was fast asleep. I say, this is not so wild a scheme, seeing, even now, if you can whisper anything close to the ear of a person in a deep sleep, so as to speak distinctly to the person and yet not awaken him, as has been frequently tried, the person sleeping shall dream distinctly of what you say to him—indeed, shall dream the very words you say.

We have then no more to ask but how the Devil can convey himself to the ear of a sleeping person, and it is granted then that he may have power to make us dream what he pleases. But this is not all. For if he can so forcibly, by his invisible application, cause us to dream what he pleases, why can he not with the same facility prompt our thoughts, whether sleeping or awake? To dream is nothing else but to think sleeping. And we have an abundance of deep-headed gentlemen among us who give us ample testimony that they dream awake.

But if the Devil can prompt us to dream, that is to say, to think when yet he does not know our thoughts, how then can he tell whether the whisper had its effect? The answer is plain. The Devil, like the angler, baits the hook. If the fish bite, he lies ready to take the advantage. He whispers to the imagination and then waits to see how it works.

As Naomi said to Ruth, *"Sit still, my daughter, until thou know how the matter will fall: for the man will not be at rest until he have finished the thing this day"* (Ruth 3:18). Thus, when the Devil had whispered to Eve in her sleep, according to Milton, and suggested mischief to her imagination, he only sat still to see how the matter would work. For he knew if it took with her, he should hear more of it. And then by finding her alone the next day without her ordinary guard, her husband, he presently concluded she had swallowed the bait and so attacked her afresh.

A small deal of craft, and less by far than we have reason to believe the Devil is master of, will serve to reveal whether or not such and such thoughts as he knows he has suggested have taken place. The action of the person presently reveals it, at least to him who lies always upon the watch and has open to him every word, every gesture, every step we take subsequent to his operation. It may therefore, for ought we know, be a great mistake, and what most of us are guilty of, to tell our dreams to one another in the morning after we have been disturbed with them in the night. For if the Devil converses with us so insensibly as some are of the opinion he does, that is to say, if he can hear as far as we can see, we may be telling our story to him indeed when we think we are only talking to one another.

This brings me most naturally to the important enquiry, whether or not the Devil can walk about the world invisibly. The truth is, this is no question to me. For as I have taken away his visibility already and have denied him all prescience of futurity too, and have proved he cannot know our thoughts nor put any force upon persons or actions, if we should take away his invisibility, too, we should un-devil him quite to all intents and purposes as to any mischief he could do. Indeed, it would banish him from the world, and he might even go and seek his fortune somewhere else. For if he could neither be visible nor invisible, neither act in public nor in private, he could neither have business nor be in this sphere, nor could we be any way concerned with him.

The Devil, therefore, most certainly has a power and liberty of moving about in this world after some manner or another. This is verified as well by way of allegory as it is by way of history, and in the Scripture itself. And as the first strongly suggests and supposes it to be so, the last positively asserts it. And not to crowd this work with quotations from a book that we have not much to do with in the Devil's story, at least not much to his satisfaction, I only hint his personal appearance to our Savior in the wilderness, where it is said, *"the devil taketh him up to an exceeding high mountain"* (Matt. 4:8), and in another place, the Devil *"departed from him"* (Luke 4:13). What shape or figure he appeared in we do not find mentioned, but I cannot doubt his appearing to him there any more than I can his talking to our Savior by mouth and with the voices of the several persons who were under the terrible affliction of an actual possession.

These things leave us no room to doubt of what is advanced above, namely, that he (the Devil) has a certain residence, or liberty of residing in and moving about upon the surface of this earth as well as in the compass of the atmosphere, commonly called the air, in some manner or other. That is usual. But it remains to inquire into the manner, which I resolve into two kinds:

1. *Ordinary,* which I suppose to be his invisible motions as a spirit, under which consideration I suppose him to have an unconfined, unlimited, unrestrained liberty as to the manner of acting, and this either in persons, by possession, or in things by agitation.
2. *Extraordinary,* which I understand to be his appearances in borrowed shapes and bodies, or shadows rather than bodies, assuming speech, figure, posture, and several powers of which we can give little or no account, in which extraordinary manner of appearances he is either limited by a superior power or limits himself politically as being not the way best for his interest or purpose to act in his business, which is more effectually done in his state of obscurity.

Hence, we must suppose the Devil has it very much in his own choice whether to act in one capacity or in the other, or in both—that is to say, of appearing or not appearing as he determines for his purpose. In this state of invisibility, and under the operation of these powers and liberties, he performs all his functions and offices as Devil, as prince of darkness, as god of this world, as tempter, accuser, deceiver, and all whatsoever other names of office or titles of honor he is known by.

Now taking him in this large, unlimited, or little limited state of action, he is well called "the god of this world" (2 Cor. 4:4). For he has very much of the attribute of omnipresence and may be said, either by himself or his agents, to be everywhere and see everything—that is to say, everything that is visible; for I cannot allow him any share of omniscience at all.

In that he ranges about everywhere, he is with us, and

sometimes in us, sees when he is not seen, hears when he is not heard, comes in without leave, goes out without noise, and is neither to be shut in or shut out. When he runs from us we can't catch him, and when he runs after us we can't escape him. He is seen when he is not known and known when he is not seen. All these things, and more, we have knowledge enough about to convince us of the truth of them. So as I have said above, he is certainly walking to and fro through the earth, and so forth, after some manner or other, and in some figure or other, visible or invisible, as he finds occasion.

Now in order to make our history of him complete, the next question before us is how and in what manner he acts with mankind, how his kingdom is carried on, and by what methods he does his business, for he certainly has a great deal of business to do. He is not an idle spectator, nor is he walking about incognito and clothed in mist and darkness purely in kindness to us so we should not be frightened by him. But 'tis his policy that he may act undiscovered, that he may see and not be seen, play his game in the dark, and not be detected in his roguery—that he may prompt mischief, raise tempests, blow up coals, kindle strife, embroil nations, use instruments, and not be known to have his hand in anything when at the same time he really has a hand in everything.

Some are of opinion, and I among the rest, that if the Devil were personally and visibly present among us, and we conversed with him face to face, we should be so familiar with him in a little time that his ugly figure would not affect us at all, that his terrors would not frighten us, or that we should any more trouble ourselves about him than we did with the last great comet in 1678, which appeared so long and so constantly without any particular known event that at last we took no more notice of it than of the other ordinary stars that had appeared before we or our ancestors were born.

Nor indeed should we have much reason to be frightened by him, or at least none of those silly things could be said of him that we now amuse ourselves with, and by which we set him up like a scarecrow to frighten children and old women, to fill up old stories, make songs and ballads, and in a word, carry on the low-prized buffoonery of the common people. We should either see him in his angelic form, as he was from his origin, or if he has any deformities entailed upon him by the supreme sentence and in justice to the deformity of his crime, they would be of a superior nature and more appropriate for our contempt as well as horror than those weak fancied trifles contrived by our ancient devil-raisers and devil-makers to feed the wayward fancies of old witches and sorcerers, who cheated the ignorant world with a Devil of their own making, set forth in terrorem [to intimidate or terrorize] with bat's wings, horns, cloven foot, long tail, forked tongue, and the like.

In the next place, be his frightful figure what it would, and his legions as numerous as the host of heaven, we should see him still as the prince of devils—though monstrous as a dragon, flaming as a comet, and tall as a mountain, yet, dragging his chain after him equal to the utmost of his supposed strength, always in the custody of his jailors, the angels, with his power over-powered and his rage cowed and abated (or at least awed and under correction), limited, and restrained. In a word, we should see him as a vanquished slave, his spirit broken, his malice though not abated yet hand-cuffed and overpowered, and as not able to work anything against us by force—so that he would be to us but like the lions in the tower, encaged and locked up, unable to do the hurt he wishes to do and that we fear, or indeed any hurt at all.

Hence 'tis evident that 'tis not his business to be public, or to walk up and down in the world visibly and in his own shape. His affairs require a quite different management, as might be made apparent from the nature of things and the manner of our actions as men, either with ourselves or to one another.

Nor could he be serviceable in his generation as a public person as now he is or answer the end of his party who employ him and who, if he were to do their business in public as he does in private, would not be able to employ him at all.

As in our modern meetings for the propagation of impudence and other virtues, there would be no entertainment and no improvement for the good of the age if the people did not all appear masked and concealed from the common observation. So neither could Satan (from whose management those more happy assemblies are taken as copies of a glorious original) perform the usual and necessary business of his profession if he did not appear wholly covert and under needful disguises. How but for the convenience of his clothing could he call himself into so many shapes, act on so many different scenes, and turn so many wheels of state in the world as he has done? As a mere professed devil, he could do nothing.

Had he been obliged always to act the mere devil in his own clothes and with his own shape, appearing uppermost in all cafes and places, he could never have preached in so many pulpits, presided in so many councils, voted in so many committees, sat in so many courts, and influenced so many parties and actions in Church and State as we have reason to believe he has done in our nation, and in our memories too, as well as in other nations and in more ancient times. The share Satan has had in all the weighty confusions of the times ever since the first ages of Christianity in the world has been carried on with so much secrecy, and so much with an air of cabal and intrigue, that nothing can have been managed more subtly and closely. And in the same manner he has acted in our times in order to conceal his interest and the influence he has had in the councils of the world.

Could it have been possible for him to have raised the flames of rebellion and war so often in this nation as he certainly has done? Could he have agitated the parties on both sides and inflamed the spirits of three nations if he had appeared in his own dress, a mere naked devil? It is not the Devil as a *devil* who does the mischief, but the Devil in masquerade, Satan in full disguise, and acting at the head of civil confusion and distraction.

If history may be credited, the French Court at the time of our old confusions was made the scene of Satan's politics and prompted both parties in England and in Scotland also to quarrel. And how was it done? Will any man offer to scandalize the Devil so much as to say, or so much as to suggest, that Satan had no hand in it all? Did not the Devil, by the agency of Cardinal Richelieu, send 400,000 crowns at one time and 600,000 at another to the Scots to raise an army and march boldly into England? And did not the same Devil at the same time, by other agents, remit 800,000 crowns to the other party in order to raise an army to fall upon the Scots? Indeed, did not the Devil with the same subtlety send down the Archbishop's order to impose the service-book upon the people in Scotland, and at the same time raise a mob against it in the great church at St. Giles'? Indeed, did not he actually, in the person of an old woman (his favorite instrument) throw the three-legged stool at the service-book and animate the zealous people to take up arms for religion and turn rebels for God's sake?

All these happy and successful undertakings, though 'tis no more to be doubted they were done by the agency of Satan, and in a very surprising manner, too, were yet all done in secret by what I call possession and injection, and by the agency and contrivance of such instruments, or by the Devil in the disguise of such servants as he found fitting to be employed in his work, and who he took a more effectual care of concealing.

But we shall have occasion to touch all this part over again when we come to discourse about the particular habits and disguises that the Devil has made use of all along in the world to better cover his actions and conceal his being involved in them.

In the meantime, the cunning or artifice the Devil makes use of in all these things is in itself very considerable. 'Tis an old practice of his use, and he has gone on in diverse measures for better concealing himself in it, which measures (though he varies sometimes as his extraordinary affairs require) are yet in all ages much the same and have the same tendency, namely, that he may get all his business carried on by the instrumentality of fools, that he may make mankind agents in their own destruction, and that he may have all his work done in such a manner that he may seem to have had no hand in it. Indeed, he contrives so well that the very name *Devil* is put upon his opposite party, and the scandal of the black agent lies all upon them.

In order then to look a little into his conduct, let us enquire into the common mistakes about him, see what use is made of them to his advantage and how far mankind is imposed upon in those particulars and to what purpose.

4

OF SATAN'S AGENTS OR MISSIONARIES AND THEIR ACTIONS UPON AND IN THE MINDS OF MEN IN HIS NAME.

Infinite advantages attend the Devil in his retired government as they respect the management of his interests and the carrying on of his absolute monarchy in the world, particularly as it gives him room to act by the agency of his inferior ministers and messengers (called on many occasions his angels, of whom he has an innumerable multitude at his command—enough, for ought we know, to spare one to attend every man and woman now alive in the world—and with whom, if we may believe our second-sight Christians, the air is always as full as a beam of the evening sun is of insects, where they are ever ready for business and to go and come as their great governor issues out orders for their directions).

As they are all of the same spirit quality with him and consequently invisible like him (except as above), they are ready upon all occasions to be sent to and into any such person, and for such purposes (superior limitations only excepted) as the grand director of devils (the Devil properly so called) guides them.

And they are ready to be the subject or the object of whatever it be, that is to say, to be the person they are sent to, or into, as above, whoever he is. And they are sufficiently qualified for the business of the messengers to do that. For this is particular to Satan's messengers or agents, they are not like us human devils here in the world, some bred up one way, some another, some of one trade, some of another, and consequently some fit for some business, some for another, some good for something, and some good for nothing. But his messengers are all fit for everything, can find their way everywhere, and are a match for everybody they are sent to. In a word, there are no foolish devils. They are all fully qualified for their employment, fit for anything he sets them about, and very seldom mistake their errand or fail in the business they are sent to do.

Nor is it strange at all that the Devil should have such a numberless train of deputy devils to act under him. For it must be acknowledged that he has a great deal of business upon his hands, a vast deal of work to do, an abundance of public affairs under his direction, and an infinite variety of particular cases always before him.

For example, how many governments in the world are wholly in his administration? How many divans and great councils under his direction? Indeed, I believe, it would be hard to prove that there is or has been one council of state in the world for many hundreds of years past, up to the year 1713 (we don't pretend to come nearer home), where the Devil by himself or his agents in one shape or another has not sat as a member, if not taken the chair.

And though some learned authors may dispute this point with me by giving some examples where the councils of princes have been influenced by a better hand, and where things have been carried against Satan's interest, and even to his great mortification, it amounts to no more than this: Namely, that in such cases, the Devil has been outvoted. It does not argue that he was not present there pushing his interest as far as he could, only that he had not the success he expected. For I don't pretend to say that he has never been disappointed. But those examples are so rare and of so small significance that when I come to the particulars, as I shall do in the sequel of this history, you will find them hardly worth naming.

Considering one time with another, the Devil has met with such a series of successes in all his affairs, and has so seldom been baulked (and where he has met with a little check in his politics he has notwithstanding so soon and so easily recovered himself, regained his lost ground, or replaced himself in another country when he has been supplanted in one) that his empire has been far from being lessened in the world for the last thousand years of the Christian establishment.

Suppose we take an observation from the beginning of Martin Luther, or from the year 1420, and call the Reformation a blow to the Devil's kingdom, which before that was come to such a height in Christendom, that was a question not yet thoroughly decided. Whether that medley of superstition and horrible heresies, that mass of enthusiasm and idols called the Catholic hierarchy was a church of God or a church of the Devil, and whether it was an assembly of saints or a synagogue of Satan, I say, take that time to be the epoch of Satan's declension and of Lucifer's falling from heaven, that is, from the top of his terrestrial glory.

Yet whether or not he gained in the defection of the Greek church as much as he lost in the Reformation of the Roman about that time, and since then, is what authors have not yet agreed on—not reckoning what he has regained since of the ground that he had lost even by the Reformation, viz., the countries of the Duke of Savoy's dominion (where the Reformation is almost eaten out by persecution), the whole Valtoline and some adjacent countries, the whole kingdom of Poland, and almost all of Hungary (for since the last war, the Reformation, as it were, lies gasping for breath and expiring in that country), also several large provinces in Germany (as Austria, Carinthia, and the whole kingdom of Bohemia, where the Reformation once powerfully planted received its death's wound at the Battle of Prague (1627) and languished but a very little while, died, was buried, and good King Popery reigned in its stead.)

To these countries thus regained to Satan's infernal empire, let us add his modern conquests and the encroachments he has made upon the Reformation in the present age, which are, however light we make of them, very considerable, viz., the Electorate of the Rhine and the Palatinate (the one fallen to the House of Bavaria and the other to that of Neuburgh, both popish), the Dutchy of *Deux Ponts* fallen just now to a popish branch, the whole Electorate of Saxony fallen under the power of popish government by the apostasy of their princes. And more likely to follow is the fate of Bohemia whenever the diligent Devil can bring his new project in Poland to bear; as 'tis more than probable he will do so some time or other by the growing zeal as well as power of the house of A______ (that house of bigots).

But to sum up the dull story, we must add in the roll of the Devil's conquests the whole kingdom of France, where we have in one year seen, to the immortal glory of the Devil's politics, that his measures have prevailed to the total extirpation of the

Protestant churches without a war. And that interest, which for 200 years had supported itself in spite of persecutions, massacres, five civil wars, and innumerable battles and slaughters, at last received its mortal wound from its own champion, Henry IV, and sank into utter oblivion by Satan's most exquisite management under the agency of his two prime ministers, Cardinal Richelieu and Louis the XIV, whom he entirely possessed.

Thus far we have a melancholy view of the Devil's new conquests and the ground he has regained through the Reformation, in which his secret management has been so exquisite and his politics so good that could he bring but one thing to pass, which by his own former mistake (for the Devil is not infallible) he has rendered impossible, he would bring the Protestant interest so near its ruin that heaven would be, as it were, put to the necessity of working a miracle to prevent it. This is the case.

Ancient historians tell us, and from good authority, that the Devil found it in his interest to bring his favorite Mohamed upon the stage and spread the victorious half-moon upon the ruin of the cross (with the half-moon raised with great success first by the Saracen empire and then the Turkish to such a height that the name of *Christian* seemed to be extirpated in those two quarters of the world, which were then not the greatest only but by far the most powerful), I mean in Asia and Africa where was totally laid waste all those ancient and flourishing churches of Africa, the labors of St. Cyprian, Tertullian, St. Augustine, and 670 Christian bishops and fathers, who governed there at once, also all the churches of Smyrna, Philadelphia, Ephesus, Sardis, Antioch, Laodicea, and innumerable others in Pontus, Bithynia, and the provinces of the lesser Asia.

The Devil, having, I say, finished these conquests so much to his satisfaction, began to turn his eyes northward. And though he had a considerable interest in the Whore of Babylon and had brought his power by the subjection of the Roman hierarchy to a great height, yet finding the interest of Mohamed most suitable to his devilish purposes (as most adapted to the destruction of mankind and laying waste the world), he resolved to espouse the growing power of the Turk and bring him in upon Europe like a deluge.

In order to do this, and to make way for an easy conquest, he worked underground like a true Devil and sapped the foundation of the Christian power by sowing discord among the reigning princes of Europe so that, envying one another, they might be content to stand still and look on while the Turk devoured them one by one and at last might swallow them up all.

This devilish policy took to his heart's content. The Christian princes stood still, stupid, dozing, and unconcerned till the Turk conquered Thrace, Serbia, Macedonia, Bulgaria, and all the remains of the Grecian empire, and at last the imperial city of Constantinople itself.

Finding this political method so well answering his ends, the Devil, who always improves upon the success of his own experiments, resolved from that time to lay a foundation for making those divisions and jealousies of the Christian princes immortal, whereas they were at first only personal and founded in private quarrels between the princes respectively, such as the emulation of one another's glory, envy at the extraordinary valor or other merit of this or that leader, or revenge of some little affront. For which notwithstanding, the piety of Christian princes in those days was so great that they made no scruple to sacrifice whole armies, indeed, nations, to their resentment and private quarrels (a certain sign whose management they were under).

These being the causes by which the Devil first sowed the seeds of mischief among them, and with the success of it so well answering his design, he could not but wish to have the same advantage always ready at his hand. And therefore he resolved to order it so—that these divisions, however useful to him, were only personal and consequently temporary, like an annual in the garden that must be raised anew every season, might for the future be national and, consequently, durable and immortal.

To this end, it was necessary to lay the foundation of eternal feuding, not in the temperaments and passions of men only, but in the interests of nations. The way to do this was to form and state the dominion of those princes by such a plan drawn in hell and laid out from a scheme truly political, of which the Devil was chief engineer—that the divisions should always remain, being made a natural consequence of the situation of the country, the temper of their people, the nature of their commerce, the climate, the manner of living, or something which should forever render it impossible for them to unite.

This (in which the Devil was as certainly the principal operator to illustrate great things by small) was, I say, a scheme truly infernal as ever John of Leyden was of the High Dutch Rebellion, or Sir John B____t of the late project, called the South-Sea Stock. Nor did this contrivance of the Devil at all dishonor his author or its success appear unworthy of the undertaker. For we see it not only answered the end and made the Turk victorious at the same time, and formidable to Europe ever after, but it works to this day. The foundation of the divisions remains in all the several nations, and that to such a degree that it is impossible they should unite.

This is what I hinted before, in which the Devil was mistaken, and it is another instance to show he knows nothing of what is to come. For this very foundation of immortal jealousy and discord between the several nations of Spain, France, Germany, and others, which the Devil himself with so much policy contrived, and which served his interests so long, is now the only obstruction to his designs and prevents the entire ruin of the Reformation. For though the reformed countries are very powerful, and some of them, as Great Britain and Prussia are particularly more powerful than ever, it can yet not be said that the Protestant interests in general are stronger than formerly, or so strong as they were in 1623 under the victorious Arms of the Swede.

On the other hand, were it possible that the Popish powers, to wit, of France, Spain, Germany, Italy, and Poland, which are entirely Popish, could heartily unite their interests and should join their powers to attack the Protestants, the latter would find it very difficult if not impossible to defend themselves.

But as fatal as such a union of the Popish powers would be, and as useful as it would be to the Devil's cause at this time, the Devil with all his angels are not able to bring it to pass. No, not with all his craft and cunning. He divided them, but he can't unite them. So even just as 'tis with men, so 'tis with devils. They may do in an hour what they can't undo in an age.

This may comfort those faint-hearted Christians among us who cry out about the danger of a religious war in Europe and what terrible things will happen when France, Spain, Germany, Italy, and Poland shall all unite. Let this answer satisfy them:

The Devil himself can never make France and Spain, or

France and the Emperor, unite. Jarring temperaments may be reconciled, but jarring interests never can. They may unite so as to make peace (though that can hardly be long), but never so as to make conquests together. They are too much afraid of one another for one to bear that any addition of strength should come to the other. But this is a digression. We shall find the Devil mistaken and disappointed too on several other occasions as we go along.

I return to Satan's interest in the several governments and nations by virtue of his invisibility, and which interest he carries on by possession. 'Tis by this invisibility that he presides in all the councils of foreign powers (for we never mean our own, that we always premise) even though it is alleged by the critics that he does not preside because there is always a President. I say, if he is not in the President's chair, yet if he be in the President himself, the difference is not much. And if he does not vote as a counsellor, if he votes in the counsellor, 'tis much the same. And here as it was in the story of Ahab the King of Israel, as he was a lying spirit in the mouths of all his prophets, so we find him a spirit of some particular evil quality or other in all the transactions and transactors on that stage of life we call *the State*.

Thus, he was a dissembling spirit in Charles IX, a turbulent spirit in Charles V, a bigoted spirit of fire and a bundle of sticks in our Queen Mary, an apostate spirit in Henry IV, a cruel spirit in Peter of Castile, a revengeful spirit in Ferdinand II, and a phaeton in Louis XIV.

In the great men of the world, even them being a degree lower than the class of crowned heads, he has the same secret influence. Hence, it comes to pass that the greatest heroes and men of the highest character for achievements of glory, either by their virtue or valor, however they have been crowned with victories and elevated by human tongues, whatever the most consummate virtues or good qualities by which they have been known, they yet have always had some devil or other in them to preserve Satan's claim to them uninterrupted and prevent their escape out of his hands. Thus, we have seen a bloody Devil in a D'Alva, a profligate Devil in a Buckingham, a lying, artful, or politic Devil in a Richelieu, a treacherous Devil in a Mazarin, a cruel, merciless Devil in a Cortez, a debauched Devil in a Eugene, a conjuring Devil in a Luxemburg, and a covetous Devil in a M———h. In a word, tell me the man, I tell you the spirit that reigned in him.

Nor does he thus carry on his secret management by possession in men of the first magnitude only, but have you not had evidences of it among ourselves? How has he been a lying spirit in the mouths of our prophets, a factious spirit in the heads of our politicians, a profuse Devil in a B______s, a corrupt Devil in M______, a proud spirit in my Lord Plausible, a bullying spirit in my Lord Bugbear, a talkative spirit in his Grace, the Duke of Rattlehall, a scribbling spirit in my Lord H________, a runaway spirit in my Lord Frightful, and through a long roll of heroes whose exceeding and particular qualifications proclaim loudly what handle the Devil took them by, and how fast he held them. For these were all men of ancient fame; I hope you know that.

From men of figure we descend to the mob, and 'tis there the same thing. Possession, like the plague, is *Morbus Plebæi* [disease of the commons]. There is no a family but he is a spirit of strife and contention among them, not a man but he has a part in him. He is a drunken Devil in one, a whoring Devil in another, a thieving Devil in a third, a lying Devil in the fourth, and so on, to a thousand, and a hundred thousand, *ad infinitum* [to infinity].

Indeed, even the ladies have their share in the possession, and if they have not the Devil in their heads, or in their tails, in their faces, or their tongues, it must be some poor despicable she-devil who Satan did not think it worth his while to meddle with. And the number of those who are below his operation, I think is very small. But that part I have much more to say to in its place.

From degrees of persons to professions and employments, 'tis the same. We find the Devil is a true posture-master. He assumes any dress, appears in any shape, counterfeits every voice, and acts upon every stage. Here he wears a gown, there a long robe; here he wears the Jack-Boots, there the small-sword; is here an enthusiast, there a buffoon; on this side he acts the *Mountebank*, on that side the Merry-Andrew. Nothing comes amiss to him from the Great Mogul to the Scaramouche. The Devil is in them, more or less, and plays his game so well that he makes sure work with them all. He knows where the common foible lies (which is universal passion), what handle to take hold of every man by, and how to cultivate his interest so as not to fail of his end or mistake the means.

How then can it be denied but that his acting thus in *tenebris* [in the dark], and keeping out of the sight of the world, is abundantly his interest, and that he could do nothing, comparatively speaking, by any other method?

What would his public appearance have signified? Who would have entertained him in his own proper shape and person? My Lord Simpleton, also, who Satan has set up for a cunning fool, seems to have it sit much better upon him as he passes for a fool of art than it should have done if the naked Devil had come and challenged him for a fool in nature.

Infinite variety illustrate the Devil's reign among the sons of men, all which he manages with admirable dexterity and a slight particular to himself by the mere advantage of his present concealed situation, and which, had he been obliged to have appeared in public, had been all lost, and he would be capable of just nothing at all (or at least of nothing more than the other ordinary politicians of wickedness could have done without him).

Now authors are much divided as to the manner in which the Devil manages his proper instruments for mischief; for Satan has a great many agents in the dark who neither have the Devil in them nor are much acquainted with him. And yet he serves himself with them, whether of their folly, or of that other frailty called wit. 'Tis all one. He makes them do his work when they think they are doing their own. Indeed, so cunning is he in his guiding the weak part of the world that even when they think they are serving God, they are doing nothing less or more than serving the Devil. 'Tis some of the most deceptive part of his operation, to make them believe they are serving God when they do his work.

Thus those who the Scripture foretold should persecute Christ's Church in the latter days were to think they do God some good service.[22] Thus the Inquisition (for example), it may be at this time, in all the acts of Christian cruelty they are so famous for (if any of them are ignorant enough not to know that they are Devils incarnate), that they may, for ought we know, go on for God's sake and torture, murder, starve to death, mangle, and macerate—all for God and God's Catholic [universal] Church. And 'tis certainly the Devil's masterpiece to bring mankind to such a perfection of devilism as the inquisition. For if the Devil had not been in them, could they christen such a hell-fire judicature as the

22 "They shall put you out of the synagogues: yea, the time cometh, that whosoever killeth you will think that he doeth God service" (John 16:2).

Inquisition by the name of the Holy Office? And so, in paganism, how could so many nations among the poor Indians offer human sacrifices to their idols and murder thousands of men, women, and children to appease this god of the air when he is angry if the Devil did not act in them under the visor of devotion?

But we need not go to America or to the Inquisition, not to paganism or to Popery either, to look for people who are sacrificing to the Devil or who give their peace-offerings to him while they are offered upon God's altar. Are not our churches (indeed, and meeting-houses too, as much as they pretend to be more sanctified than their neighbors) full of devil worshipers? Where do his devotees hail one another with joy and congratulate him more than at church? Where? While they hold up their hands and turn up their eyes toward heaven, they make all their vows to Satan, or at least to the fair devils, his representatives, whom I shall speak of in their place.

Do not the sons of God make arrangements with the daughters of men in the very house of worship? Do they not talk to them in the language of the eyes? And what is at the bottom of it, while one eye is upon the prayer-book and the other adjusting their dress? Are they not sacrificing to Venus and Mercury, indeed, and the very Devil they dress for?

Let any man impartially survey the church-gestures, the air, the postures and the behavior. Let him keep an exact roll, and if I do not show him two Devil worshipers for every one true saint, then the word "saint" must have another signification than I ever yet understood it by.

The church (as a place) is the *receptacle of the dead* as well as the assembly of the living. What relates to those below, I doubt Satan (if he would be so kind), could give a better account of them than I can. But as to the appearances, I pretend to so much penetration as to tell you that there are more specters, more apparitions always there than you who know nothing of the matter may be aware of.

I happened to be at an eminent place of God's most devout worship the other day with a gentleman of my acquaintance, who, I observed, minded very little the business he ought to have come for. First, I saw him always busy staring about him and bowing this way and that way. Indeed, he made two or three bows and scrapes[23] when he was repeating the responses to the Ten Commandments. And I assure you he made it correspond strangely so the harmony was not so broken in upon as you would expect it should.

Thus, "Lord (and a bow to a fine lady just approaching her seat), have mercy upon us ____ (then three bows to a throng of ladies that came together into the next pew), and incline ____ (then stopping to make a great bow to my Lord ____), our hearts . . ."

Just then the hearts of all the church were gone off from the subject, for the response was over, so he huddled up the rest in whispers, for God Almighty could hear him well enough, he said—indeed, as well as if he had spoken as loud as his neighbors did.

After we arrived home, I asked him what he meant by all that, and what he thought of it.

"How could I help it?", said he. "I must not be rude."

"What," says I, "rude to who?"

"Why," says he, "there came in so many she-devils I could not help it."

23 Scraping the floor with his foot as he moved his foot while bowing (Ed.).

"What," said I, "could you not help bowing when you were saying your prayers?"

"Oh sir!" says he, "the ladies would have thought I had slighted them. I could not avoid it."

"Ladies!" said I, "I thought you called them devils just now.

"Yes, yes, devils," said he, "little charming devils, but I must not be rude to them, however."

"Very well," said I, "then you would be rude to God Almighty, because you could not be rude to the Devil?"

"Why that's true," said he. "But what can we do? There's no going to church as the case stands now if we must not worship the Devil a little between whiles."

This is the case indeed, and Satan carries his point on every hand. For if the fair speaking world and the fair looking world are generally devils, that is to say, are in Satan's management, we are sure that the foul speaking and the foul doing world are all on his side. And you have then only the fair-doing part of the world that is out of his class, and when we speak of them, oh how few!

But I return to the Devil's managing our wicked part, for this he does with most exquisite subtlety. And this is one part of it, viz., he thrusts our vices into our virtues, by which he mixes the clean and the unclean, and thus by the corruption of the one, poisons and debauches the other so the slave he governs cannot account for his own common actions and is inclined to be obliged to his maker to accept the heart without the hands and feet—to take, as we commonly express it, the will for the deed. And if heaven were not so good to come into that half-in-half service, I don't see but what the Devil would carry away all his servants. Here indeed I should enter into a long detail of involuntary wickedness, which in short is neither more or less than the devil in everybody, indeed, in every one of you, (our governors excepted); take it as you please.

What is our language when we look back with reflection and reproach on past follies? "I think I was bewitched." "I was possessed." "Certainly the Devil was in me, or else I had never been such a sot."

Devil in you, sir! Indeed, who doubts it; you may be sure the Devil was in you, and there he is still. And next time he can catch you in the same snare. You'll be just the same sot that you say you were before.

In short, the Devil is too cunning for us and manages us his own way. He governs the vices of men by his own methods. Though every crime will not make a man a devil, yet it must be acknowledged that every crime puts the criminal in some measure into the Devil's power and gives him a title to the man. And he treats him magisterially ever after.

Some tell us every single man, every individual, has a Devil attending him to execute the orders of the Devil (Grand Signior) of the whole clan and that this attending evil angel, for so he is called, sees every step you take, is with you in every action, prompts you to every mischief, and leaves you to do everything that is pernicious to yourself. They also allege that there is a good spirit which attends him too, which latter is always accessary to everything that we do that is good and reluctant to evil.

If this is true, how comes it to pass that those two opposite spirits do not quarrel about it when they are pressing us to contrary actions, one good and the other evil? And why does the evil tempting spirit so often prevail? Instead of answering this difficult question, I shall only tell you that as to this story of good and evil angels attending every particular person, 'tis a good allegory indeed to represent the struggle in the mind of man between good and evil inclinations. But as to the rest, the best thing I can say of it is that I think 'tis a fib.

But to take things as they are and only talk by way of natural consequence, to argue from nature is certainly the best way to find out the Devil's story. If there are good and evil spirits attending us, that is to say, a good angel and a devil, then 'tis no unjust reproach upon anybody to say, when they follow the dictates of the latter, that the Devil is in them, or they are devils. Indeed, I must carry it farther still, namely, that since the generality and greatest number of people do follow and obey the evil spirit and not the good, and that the predominate power is allowed to be the nominating power, you must then admit that, in short, the greater part of mankind has the Devil in them, and so I come to my text.

To this purpose allow me to borrow a few lines of a friend on this very part of the Devil's management.

To places and persons he suits his disguises,
And dresses up all his banditti,
Who as pickpockets flock to a country assizes,
Crowd up to the court and the city.

They're at every elbow and every ear,
And ready at every call, sir;
The vigilant scout plants his agents about,
And has something to do with us all, sir.

In some he has part, and in some he's the whole,
And of some (like the Vicar of Baddow)
It can neither be said they have body or soul,
But only are devils in shadow.

The pretty and witty, are devils in masque,
The beauties are mere apparitions;
The homely alone by their faces are known,
And the good by their ugly conditions.

The beaus walk about like the shadows of men.
And wherever he leads 'em they follow,
But tak'em and shak'em, there's not one in ten
But's as light as a feather and hollow.

Thus all his affairs he drives on in disguise,
And he tickles mankind with a feather:
Creeps in at our ears, and looks out at our eyes,
And jumbles our senses together.

He raises the vapours, and prompts the desires,
And to every dark deed holds the candle;
The passions enflames and the appetite fires,
And takes everything by the handle.

Thus he walks up and down in complete masquerade,
And with every company mixes,
Sells in every shop, works at every trade,
And everything doubtful perplexes.

How Satan comes by this governing influence in the minds and upon the actions of men is a question I have not yet come to, nor indeed does it so particularly belong to the Devil's history. It seems rather a polemic so it may pass at school among the metaphysics and puzzle the heads of our masters. Wherefore I think to write to the learned Dr. B____ about it, imploring his most sublime haughtiness, that when his other more momentous avocations of pedantry and pedagogism give him an interval from wrath and contention, he will set apart a moment to consider human nature devilized and give us a mathematical anatomical description of it with a map of Satan's kingdom in the microcosm of mankind along with such other illuminations as to him and his contemporaries in their great wisdom shall deem appropriate.

5

OF THE DEVIL'S MANAGEMENT IN THE PAGAN HIERARCHY BY OMENS, ENTRAILS, AUGURS, ORACLES, AND SUCH LIKE PAGEANTRY OF HELL; AND HOW THEY AT LAST WENT OFF THE STAGE BY THE INTRODUCTION OF TRUE RELIGION.

I have adjourned, not finished, my account of the Devil's secret management by possession and shall resume it in its place. But I must take leave to mention some other parts of his retired scheme by which he has hitherto managed mankind, and the first of these is by that fraud of all frauds called oracle.

Here his trumpet yielded an uncertain sound for some ages, and like what he was and according to what he practiced from the beginning, he delivered out falsehood and delusion by promoting gossip. The priests of Apollo performed this farce for him to a great nicety at Delphi. There were divers others at the same time, and some of which, to give the Devil his due, he had very little hand in, as we shall see presently.

There were also some smaller and some greater, some more and some less famous places where those oracles were seated and audience was given to the enquirers, in all of which the Devil or somebody for him, *permissu superiorum* [of superior education], for either vindictive or other hidden ends and purposes, was allowed to make at least a pretension to the knowledge of things to come. But as public cheats generally do, they acted in masquerade and gave such uncertain and inconsistent responses that they were obliged to use the utmost art to reconcile events to the prediction, even after things had come to pass.

Here the Devil was a lying spirit in a particular and extraordinary manner in the mouths of all the prophets. And yet he had the cunning to express himself in such a way that whatever happened, the oracle was supposed to have been meant that way as it fell out. And all their augurs,[24] omens and voices, by which the Devil amused the world, not at that time only, but since, have been likewise interpreted.

Julian the Apostate dealt mightily in these amusements, but the Devil, who neither wished his fall or presaged it to him, evidenced that he knew nothing of Julian's fate. For as he sent almost to all the oracles of the east and summoned all the priests together to inform him of the success of his Persian Expedition, they all, like Ahab's prophets, having a lying spirit in them, encouraged him and promised him success.

Indeed, they presaged good from the ill omens that disturbed him. For example, he was at a prodigious expense when he was at Antioch to buy up white beasts and white fowls for sacrifices and for predicting from the entrails whence the Antiochians, in contempt, called him Victimarius [the victim]. But whenever the

24 An "augur" was an official diviner in ancient Rome (Ed.).

entrails foreboded evil, the cunning Devil made the priests put a different construction upon them and promise him good.

When he entered into the Temple of the *Genij* [Genius] to offer sacrifice, one of the priests dropped down dead. This, had it had any signification more than a man falling dead of an apoplectic, would have signified something fatal to Julian, who made himself a brother sacrist or priest, whereas the priests turned it presently to signify the death of his colleague, the Consul Sallust, which happened just at the same time, though eight hundred miles off.

So in another case, Julian thought it ominous that he, who was Augustus, should be named with two other names of persons, both already dead. The case was thus: The title of the emperor was Julianus Fœlix Augustus, and two of his principal officers were Julianus and Fœlix. Now both Julianus and Fœlix died within a few days of one another, which disturbed him much, who was the third of the three names. But his flattering Devil told him it all imported good to him, viz., that though Julianus and Fœlix should die, Augustus should be immortal.

Thus, whatever happened and whatever was foretold, and howsoever much they differed from one another, the lying spirit was sure to reconcile the prediction and the event and make them at least seem to correspond in favor of the person enquiring.

Now we are told oracles have ceased and the Devil is further limited for the good of mankind, not being allowed to vent his delusions by the mouths of the priests and augurs, as formerly. I will not take upon myself to say how far they have really ceased more than they were before. I think 'tis much more reasonable to believe there was never any reality in them at all, or that any oracle ever gave out any answers but what were the invention of the priests and the delusions of the Devil. I have a great many ancient authors on my side in this opinion, such as Eusebius, Tertullian, Aristotle, and others, who since they lived so near the pagan times, and when even some of those rites were yet in use, they had much more reason to know and could probably pass a better judgment upon them.

Indeed, Cicero himself ridiculed them in the most open manner. And again, other authors descended to particulars and show how the cheating was managed by the heathen sacrists and priests, and in what enthusiastic manner they spoke, namely, by going into the hollow images (such as the brazen bull and the image of Apollo), and how subtly they gave out dubious and ambiguous answers—and that when the people did not find their expectations answered by the event, they might be imposed upon by the priests and confidently be told they did not rightly understand the oracle's meaning.

However, I cannot say but that indeed there are some authors of good credit, too, who will have it that there was a real prophetic spirit in the voice or answers given by the oracles, and that oftentimes they were miraculously exact in those answers. And for an example they offer that of the Delphic oracle answering the question that was given about Crœsus, viz., what Crœsus was doing at that time—to wit, that he was boiling a lamb and the flesh of a tortoise together, in a brass vessel, or boiler with a cover of the same metal, that is to say, in a kettle with a brass cover.

To affirm therefore that they were all frauds, a man must encounter with antiquity and set his private judgment up against an established opinion, but 'tis no matter. If I do not see anything in that received opinion capable of evidence, much less of demonstration, I must be allowed still to think as I do. Others may believe as they are inclined; I see nothing hard or difficult in the thing. The priests, who were always historically informed of the circumstances of the enquirer, or at least something about them, might easily find some ambiguous speech to make and put some double entendre upon them, which upon the event solved the credit of the oracle were it one way or other. And this they certainly did, or we have room to think the Devil knows less of things now than he did in former days.

It is true that by these delusions the priests got infinite sums of money, and this makes it still probable that they would labor hard and use the utmost of their skill to uphold the credit of their oracles. And 'tis a full discovery as well of the subtlety of the sacrists, as of the ignorance and stupidity of the people in those early days of Satan's witchcraft, to see what merry work the Devil made with the world and what gross things he put upon mankind. Such was the story of the Dordonian oracle in Epirus, viz., that two pigeons flew out of Thebes (N.B. it was the Egyptian Thebes) from the Temple of Belus, erected there by the ancient sacrists, and that one of these fled eastward into Lybia and the deserts of Africa while the other into Greece, namely, to Dordona. And these communicated the divine mysteries to one another and afterward gave mystical solutions to the devout enquirers. First the Dordonian pigeon perching upon an oak spoke audibly to the people there that the gods commanded them to build an oracle, or temple, to Jupiter in that place, which was accordingly done. The other pigeon did the like on the hill in Africa, where it commanded them to build another to Jupiter, Ammon, or Hammon.

Wise Cicero condemned all this and, as authors tell us, ridiculed the answer, which, as I have hinted above, the oracle given to Crœsus proved that the oracle itself was a liar, that it could not come from Apollo because Apollo never spoke Latin. In a word, Cicero rejected them all, and Demosthenes also mentions the deceptions of the oracles. When speaking of the oracle of Apollo, he said, Pithia Philippized. That is, when the priests were bribed with money, they always gave their answers in favor of Philip of Macedon.

But that which is most strange to me is that in this dispute about the reality of oracles, the heathen who made use of them are the people who expose them and who insist most positively upon their being frauds and impostors, as in particular those mentioned above, while the priests who reject them outwardly yet believe they did really foretell things, answer questions, and so forth only with this difference: that the heathen authors who oppose them insist that 'tis all delusion and deception, and charge it upon the priests. And the Christian opposers insist that it was real, but that the Devil, not the gods, gave the answers, and that he was permitted to do it by a superior power to magnify that power in the total silencing of them at last.

But as I said before, I am with the heathen here against the Christian writers. For I take it all to be a deception and delusion. I must give my reason for it, or I do nothing. My reason is this: I insist Satan is as blind in matters of futurity as we are and can tell nothing of what is to come. These oracles often pretending to predict could be nothing else, therefore, but a deception formed by the money-getting priests to amuse the world and bring grist to their mill. If I meet with anything in my way to open my eyes to a better opinion of them, I shall tell it to you as I go on.

On the other hand, whether the Devil really spoke in those oracles or set the cunning priests to speak for him, whether they predicted or only made the people believe they predicted, whether they gave answers that came to pass or prevailed upon the people to believe that what was said came to pass, it was much at one and fully answered the Devil's design—namely, to amuse and delude the world. And as to do or to cause to be done is the same part of speech, since whoever did it, the Devil's interest was carried on by it, his government preserved, and all the mischief he could desire was effectually brought to pass so that every way they were the Devil's oracles, that's out of the question.

Indeed, I have wondered sometimes why, since by this sorcery the Devil performed such wonders (that is, played so many tricks in the world and had such universal success) that he should set up no more of them. But there might be a great many reasons given for that (too long to tire you with at present). 'Tis true, there were not many of them, and yet considering what a great deal of business they dispatched, it was enough; for six or eight oracles were more than sufficient to amuse all the world. The chief oracles we meet with in history are among the Greeks and the Romans, viz.:

- That of *Jupiter Ammon,* in *Lybia,* as above.
- The *Dordonian,* in *Epirus.*
- *Apollo Delphicus,* in the Country of *Phocis* in *Greece.*
- *Apollo Clavius,* in *Asia Minor.*
- *Serapis,* in *Alexandria* in *Egypt.*
- *Trophomis,* in *Bæotia.*
- *Sybilla Cumæa,* in *Italy.*
- *Diana,* at *Ephesus.*
- *Apollo Daphneus,* at *Antioch.*
- Besides many of lesser note, in several other places, as I have hinted before.

I have nothing to do here with the story mentioned by Plutarch of a voice being heard at sea from some of the islands called the Echinades, and calling upon one Thamuz, an Egyptian who was on board a ship, instructing him when he came to the Palodes, other islands in the Ionian Seas, to tell them there that the great god Pan was dead. And when Thamuz performed it, great groanings, howling, and lamentation were heard from the shore.

This tale tells it but indifferently, though indeed it looks more like a Christian fable than pagan. Because it seems as if made to honor the Christian worship and blast all the pagan idolatry. And for that reason, I reject it, the Christian profession needing no such fabulous stuff to confirm it.

Nor is it true in fact that the oracles ceased immediately upon the death of Christ. But as I noted before, the sum of the matter is this—the Christian religion spreading itself universally, as well as miraculously, and that too by the *foolishness of preaching* into all parts of the world, the oracles ceased. That is to say, their trade ceased, their rogueries were daily detected, and the deluded people being better taught came no more after them, and being ashamed as well as discouraged, they sneaked out of the world as well as they could. In short, the customers fell off, and the priests who were the shopkeepers, having no business to do, shut up their shops, broke, and went away. The trade and the tradesmen were hissed off the stage together. So the Devil, who, it must be confessed prospered infinitely by the deception, became bankrupt and was obliged to set other engines at work, such as other frauds and deceivers do, who when one trick grows stale and will serve no longer, are forced to try another.

Nor was the Devil to seek new measures. For though he could not give out his delusive trash as he did before in pomp and state with the solemnity of a temple and a set of enthusiasts called priests, who played a thousand tricks to amuse the world, he then had recourse to his old Egyptian method, which indeed was more ancient than that of oracles, and that was by magic, sorcery, familiar spirits, witchcraft, and the like.

Of this we find the people of the South, that is, of Arabia and Chaldea, were the first, whence we are told of the wise men, that is to say, magicians, who were called Chaldeans and Soothsayers. Hence also we find that Ahaziah, the king of Israel, sent to Baalzebub, the god of Ekron, to enquire whether he should live or die. Some think this was a kind of an oracle, though others think it was only some over-grown magician who counterfeited himself to be a Devil and obtained in that idol-hunting age to make a cunning man of him. And for that purpose he got himself made a priest of Baalzebub, the god of Ekron, and gave out answers in his name.

Thus, those merry fellows in Egypt, Jannes and Jambres, are said to mimic Moses and Aaron when they worked the miraculous plagues upon the Egyptians. And we have some instances in Scripture that support this, such as the Witch of Endor, the king, Manasseh, who dealt with the Devil openly and had a familiar spirit, and the woman mentioned in Acts 16:16 who had a spirit of divination and who got money by playing the oracle, that is, by answering doubtful questions, and so forth, and which spirit or devil the Apostles cast out.

Now though it is true that the old women in the world have filled us with tales, some improbable, others impossible, some weak, and some ridiculous, and that this puts a general discredit upon all the graver matrons who entertain us with stories better put together, yet 'tis certain, and I must be allowed to affirm, that the Devil does not disdain to take into his service many troops of old women (men, too, whom he finds 'tis for his service to keep in constant pay). To these he is found frequently to communicate his mind, and oftentimes we find them so proficient that they know much more than the Devil can teach them.

I confess it is not very incongruous with the Devil's temper, or with the nature of his business, to shift hands. He possibly found that he had taxed the world with oracular deceptions, that men began to suffer loss from them and grew sick of the frauds that were so frequently detected, so that it was time to take new measures and contrive some new trick to bite the world so he might not be exposed to contempt. Or perhaps he saw the approach of new light, which the Christian doctrine bringing with it began to spread in the minds of men, that it would outshine the dim burning ignis fatuus with which he had so long cheated mankind and was afraid to continue lest he should be mobbed off the stage by his own people when their eyes should begin to open (that upon this foot he might in policy withdraw from those old retreats the oracles and restrain those responses before they lost all their credit). For we find the people seemed to be at a mighty loss for some time for lack of them, so it made them run up and down to conjurers and man-gossips, to brazen heads, speaking calves, and innumerable simple things so gross that they are scarcely fit to be named, to satisfy the itch of having their fortunes told them, as we call it.

Now as the Devil is very seldom blind to his own interest and therefore thought it fit to quit his old way of imposing upon the world by his oracles (only because he found the world began to be too wise to be imposed upon that way), but on the other hand finding there was still a possibility to delude the world, though by other instruments, he no sooner laid down his oracles and the solemn pageantry, magnificent appearances, and other frauds of his priests and adherents in their temples and shrines, but he set up a new trade. And having, as I have said, agents and instruments sufficient for any business that he could have to employ them in, he began in corners, as the learned and merry Dr. Brown says, and exercised his minor trumperies by way of his own contriving, lifting up a great number of new-found operators such as witches, magicians, diviners, figure-casters, astrologers, and such inferior seducers.

Now, it is true, as that doctor says, this was running into corners as if he had been expelled from his more triumphant way of giving audience in form, which for so many ages had been allowed him. Yet I must add that as it seemed to be the Devil's own doing from a right judgment of his affairs, which had taken a new turn in the world since the shining of new lights from the Christian doctrine, so it must be acknowledged that the Devil made himself amends upon mankind by the various methods he took and the multitude of instruments he employed, and perhaps deluded mankind in a more fatal and sensible manner than he did before, though not so universally.

Before, he had indeed more pomp and figure put upon it, and he cheated mankind then in a way of magnificence and splendor. But this was not in over eight or ten principal places, and not fifty places in all, public or private. Whereas now, fifty thousand of his angels and instruments, visible and invisible, hardly may be said to suffice for one town or city. But in short, as his invisible agents fill the air and are at hand for mischief on every emergence, so his visible fools swarm in every village, and you have scarce a hamlet or a town where his emissaries are not at hand for business. And which is still worse, in all places he finds business, indeed, even where religion is planted and seems to flourish, he yet keeps his ground and pushes his interest according to what has been said elsewhere upon the same subject, so that wherever religion plants, the Devil plants close by it.

Nor, as I say, does he fail to succeed. Delusion spreads like a plague, and the Devil is sure of adherents. Like a true charlatan, he can always bring a crowd about his stage, and sometimes faster than other people.

What I observe upon this subject is this: that the world is at a strange loss for lack of the Devil. If it were not so, what's the reason that upon the silencing of the oracles and religion telling them that miracles have ceased and God has finished speaking by prophets, they never enquire whether heaven has established any other or new way of revelation, but away they run with their doubts and difficulties to these dreamers of dreams, tellers of fortunes, and personal oracles to be resolved as if when they acknowledge the Devil is dumb, these could speak, and since if the wicked spirit could do more than the good, the *diabolical* can do more than the *divine*, or that heaven, having taken away the Devil's voice, had furnished him with an equivalent by allowing scolders, shrews, and old weak and superannuated wretches to speak for him. For these are the people many go to now in their doubts and emergencies.

While this blindness continues among us, 'tis nonsense to say that oracles are silenced, or the Devil is dumb, for the Devil still gives audience by his deputies. As Jeroboam made priests of the basest of the people, so he is grown a little humble and makes use of lesser instruments than he did before. For whereas the priests of Apollo and of Jupiter were splendid in their appearance, of grave and venerable aspect, and sometimes of no small quality, now he makes use of scoundrels and rabble, beggars and vagabonds, old hags, superannuated, miserable hermits, gypsies and strollers, all the pictures of envy and ill luck.

Either the Devil is grown an ill master and gives such meager wages that he can get no better servants, or else common sense has grown to be very low-prized and contemptible in that such as these are fit tools to continue the succession of fraud and carry on the Devil's interest in the world. For were not the passions and temper of mankind deeply pre-engaged in favor of this dark prince, we could never suffer ourselves to accept his favors by the hands of such contemptible agents as these! How do we receive his oracles from an old witch of particular eminence and whom we believe to be more than ordinarily inspired from hell? I say, do we receive the oracle with reverence, that is to say, with a kind of horror, with regard to the black prince it comes from and at the same time turn our faces away from the wretch who mumbles out the answers, lest she should cast an evil eye, as we call it, upon us and put a devil into us when she plays the devil before us? How do we listen to the chant of those worst of vagabonds, the gypsies, when at the same time we watch our hedges and hen-roosts for fear of their thieving?

Either the Devil uses us more like fools than he did our ancestors, or we really are worse fools than those ages produced; for they were never deluded by such low-prized devils as we are.

We have heard much of magicians, soothsayers, devil-raisers, and such people, but seldom above the degree of the least of the basest people and the lowest of the lowest rank. Indeed the words, *Wise Men,* which the Devil would be pleased to have had his agents honored with, was used a while in Egypt and in Persia among the Chaldeans, but it continued only a little while and never reached so far northward as our country. Nor, however the Devil has managed it, have many of our great men who have been most acquainted with him ever been able to acquire the title of wise man.

I have heard that in older times, I suppose in good Queen Bess's days, or beyond (for little is to be said here for anything on this side of her time), there were some counsellors and statesmen who merited the character of *wise* in the best sense, that is to say, good and wise as they stand in conjunction. But as to what has happened since then, or as we may call it, from that queen's funeral to the late revolution, I have little to say. But I'll tell you what honest Andrew Marvel said of those times, and by that you may, if you please, make your calculation or let it alone; 'tis all one.

> To see a white staff-maker, a beggar, a lord,
> And scarce a wise man at a long council-board.

But I may be told this relates to wise men in another constitution, or wise men as they are opposed to fools, whereas we are talking of them now under another class, namely, as wise men or magicians, soothsayers, and so forth such as were in former times called by that name.

But to this I answer that, take them in which sense you please, it may be the same. For if I were to ask the Devil the character of the best statesman he had employed among us for many years past, I am apt to think that though oracles have ceased, he would honestly, according to the old ambiguous way, when I asked if they were Christians, answer they were (his) privy-counsellors.

It was but a little while ago that I happened (in conversation) to meet with a long list of the magistrates of that age in a neighboring country, that is to say, the men of fame among them. And it was a very diverting thing to see the judgment that was passed upon them among a great deal of good company. It is not for me to tell you how many white staves, golden keys, marshals' batons, cordons blue, gordon rouge, and gordon blanc there were among them, or by what titles such as dukes, counts, marquis, abbots, bishops, or justices they were to be distinguished.

But to return to the subject, to such meager things is the Devil now reduced in his ordinary way of carrying on his business in the world that his oracles are delivered now by the bellmen, the chimney sweepers, and by the least of those who speak in the dark. And if he operates by them, you may expect it accordingly. His agents seem to me as if the Devil had singled them out by their deformity, or that there was something particular required in their aspect to qualify them for their employment. Whence, when our looks are very dismal and frightful, it has become proverbial to say I look like a witch, or in other cases to say, *as ugly as a witch,* and in another case to look as envious as a witch. Now whether there is anything particularly required in the looks of the Devil's modern agents that is assisting in the discharge of their offices and making their answers appear more solemn, this the Devil has not yet revealed, at least not to me. And therefore, why it is that he singles out such creatures as are fit only to frighten the people who come to them with their enquiries, I do not take upon myself to determine.

Perhaps it is necessary that they should be thus extraordinary in their aspect so they might strike an awe into the minds of their adherents as if they were Satan's true and real representatives and that the said adherents may think when they speak to the witches they are really talking to the Devil. Or perhaps 'tis necessary to the witches themselves that they should be so exquisitely ugly that they might not be surprised at whatever figure the Devil makes when he first appears to them, being certain they can see nothing uglier than themselves.

Some are of the opinion that the communication with the Devil, or between the Devil and those creatures who are his agents, has something assimilating in it, and that if they were tolerable before, they are, *ipso facto,* turned into devils by talking with him. I will not say but that a tremor in the limbs, a horror in the aspect, and a surprising stare in the eyes may seize upon some of them when they really see the Devil, and that the frequent repetition may make those distortions that we so constantly see in their faces becomes natural to them (by which, if it does not continue always upon the countenance, they can at least, like the posture-masters, cast themselves into such figures and frightful dislocations of the features in their faces and so assume a Devil's face suitable to the occasion).

But be it which of these the enquirer pleases, 'tis all one to the case in hand. This is certain: such deformed devil-like creatures, which most of those we call hags and witches, are in their shapes and aspects that allow them to give out their sentences and frightful messages with an air of revenge for some injury received; for witches are famous chiefly for doing mischief.

It seems the Devil has always picked out the most ugly and frightful old women to do his business. Mother Shipton, our famous English witch or prophetess, is very much wronged in her picture if she was not of the most terrible image imaginable. And if it be true that Merlin, the famous Welsh fortune-teller was a frightful figure, it will seem the more rational to believe, if we credit another story, viz., that he was begotten by the Devil himself, of which I shall speak by itself. But to go back to the Devil's instruments being so ugly, it may be observed that the Devil has always dealt in such sort of cattle. The Sibyls,[25] of whom so many strange prophetic things are recorded (whether true or not is not to the question), are all represented as very old women if the Italian painters may have any credit given to them. And as if ugliness were a beauty to old age, they seem to paint them out as ugly and frightful as the Devil himself could make them. Not that I believe there are any original pictures of them really extant, but it is not unlikely that the Italians might have some traditional knowledge of them, or some remaining notions of them.

I had thoughts indeed here to have entered into a learned discourse of the excellency of old women in all diabolical operations, and particularly of the necessity of having recourse to them for Satan's more exquisite administration, which also may serve to solve the great difficulty in the natural philosophy of hell, namely, why it comes to pass that the Devil is obliged for lack of old women, properly so called, to turn so many ancient fathers, grave counsellors both of law and state, and especially civilians or doctors of the law into old women, and how the extraordinary operation is performed. But this is a thing of great consequence in Satan's management of human affairs, and particularly as it may lead us into the necessary history, as well as characters of some of the most eminent of these sects among us.

---

25 Prophetesses usually accepted as 10 in number and credited to widely separate parts of the ancient world (such as Babylonia, Egypt, Greece, and Italy). (Ed.).

6

OF THE EXTRAORDINARY APPEARANCE OF THE DEVIL, AND PARTICULARLY OF THE CLOVEN FOOT.

Some people would gladly have us treat this tale of the Devil's appearing with a cloven foot with more solemnity than I believe the Devil himself does. Satan, who knows how much of a deception it is, must certainly ridicule it in his own thoughts to the last degree. But as he is glad of any way to hoodwink the understandings and bubble the weak part of the world, so, if he sees men willing to take every scarecrow for a devil, it is not his business to undeceive them. On the other hand, he finds it his interest to foster the deception and serve himself with the consequence. Nor could I doubt that the Devil, if any mirth be allowed him, often laughs at the many frightful shapes and figures we dress him up in, and especially to see how willing we are first to paint him as black, make him appear as ugly as we can, and then stare and be startled at the spectrum of our own making.

The truth is, among all the horrible things that we dress up Satan in, I cannot but think that of all the rest, we show the least of creativity in this of a goat, or a thing with a goat's foot.

For though a goat is a creature made use of by our Savior in the allegory of the Day of Judgment and is said there to represent the wicked, rejected party, yet it seems to be only on account of their similitude to the sheep, and so to represent the just fate of hypocrisy and hypocrites, and in particular to form the necessary antithesis in the story. For else, our whimsical fancies excepted, a sheep or a lamb has a cloven foot as well as a goat. If the Scripture be of any value in the case, 'tis to the Devil's advantage; for the dividing the hoof was the distinguishing character or mark of a clean beast, and how the Devil can be brought into that number is pretty hard to say.

One would have thought if we had intended to have given a just figure of the Devil, it would have been more appropriate to have ranked him among the cat-kind and given him a foot (if he is to be known by his foot) like a lion, or like a red dragon, being the same creatures by which he is represented in the text, and so his claws would have had some terror in them as well as his teeth.

But the goat is not a true representative of the Devil at all, for we do not rank the goats among the subtle or cunning part of the brutes. He is counted a fierce creature indeed of his kind, though nothing like those others mentioned above, and he is emblematically used to represent a lustful temper, but even that part does not fully serve to describe the Devil, whose operation lies principally another way.

Besides, it is not the goat himself that is made use of, 'tis the cloven hoof only, and that so particularly that the cloven foot of a ram or a swine, or any other creature, may serve as well as that of a goat, only that history gives us some cause to call it the goat's foot.

In the next place 'tis understood by us not as a bare token to know Satan by but as if it were a brand upon him, and that like the mark God put upon Cain, it was given him for a punishment so he cannot keep from appearing without it. Indeed, he cannot conceal it whatever other clothing or disguise he may put on. And as if it was to make him as ridiculous as possible, they will have it be that whenever Satan has occasion to dress himself in any human shape, be it of whatsoever degree from the king to the beggar, be it of a fine lady or of an old woman (the latter it seems he most often assumes), yet still he not only must have this cloven foot about him but also he is obliged to show it too. Indeed, they will not allow him any clothing without the cloven foot being shown from under them. They will not so much as allow him an artificial shoe or a jack-boot, as we often see contrived to conceal a club foot or a wooden leg. But so the Devil may be known wherever he goes, he is bound to show his foot, and so they might as well oblige him to set an announcement upon his cap and have it written in capital letters, "I am the Devil."

It must be confessed, this is very particular and would be very hard for the Devil if it had not another article in it, which is some advantage to him. And that is, that the thing is not true. But the belief of this is so universal that all the world runs away with it, by which mistake the good people miss the Devil many times where they look for him and meet him as often where they did not expect him, when for lack of this cloven foot they do not recognize him.

Upon this very account I have sometimes thought that this has not been put upon him by mere fancy and the deception of a heavy imagination propagated by fable, but that it has been a contrivance of his own and that, in short, the Devil raised this scandal upon himself so he might keep his disguise the better and might go on visiting among his friends without being known. For if it were really so that he could go nowhere without this particular brand of infamy, he could not come into company, could not dine with my lord mayor, nor drink tea with the ladies, could not go to the drawing room at ______, could not have gone to Fontainebleau to the King of France's wedding, or to the Diet of Poland to prevent the grandees there from coming to an agreement. And which would be still worse than all, he could not go to the masquerade nor to any of our balls. The reason is plain: he would always be discovered, exposed and forced to leave the good company. Or which would be as bad, the company would all cry out, "The Devil!" in fright and run out of the room.

Nor could all the help of invention do him any service. No clothing he could put on would cover him. Not all our friends at Tavistock Corner could furnish him with a habit that would disguise or conceal him, as that unhappy foot would spoil it all. Now this would be such a great a loss to him that I question whether he could carry on any of his most important affairs in the world without the necessary disguise. For though he has access to mankind in his complete disguise, I mean that of his invisibility, yet (the learned very much to agree in this), his corporeal presence in the world is absolutely necessary upon many occasions to support his interest and keep up his correspondences, and particularly to encourage his friends when numbers are requisite to carry on his affairs.

As I have thus suggested, that the Devil himself has politically spread about this false notion concerning his appearing with a cloven foot, so I doubt not that he has thought it for his purpose to paint this cloven foot so lively in the imaginations of many of our people (and especially of those clear-sighted folks who see the

Devil when he is not to be seen) that they would make no scruple to say, and, indeed, make affidavit too, even before Satan himself whenever he sat upon the bench, that they had seen his worship's foot at such and such a time. This I the rather advance because 'tis very much for his interest to do this. For if we had not many witnesses, viva voce, to testify to it, we should have had some obstinate fellows always among us who would have denied the fact, or at least would have spoken doubtfully of it, and so would have raised disputes and objections against it as impossible, or at least as improbable—buzzing one ridiculous notion or other into our ears as if the Devil is not so black as he was painted and that he had no more a cloven foot than a Pope (whose apostolic toes have so often been reverentially kissed by kings and emperors). But now, alas, this part is out of the question.

Things as certain as death and taxes can be more firmly believed: ***The Devil does not have a cloven foot!***

I doubt not but I could, in a short time, bring you a thousand old women together who would as soon believe there were no devil at all. Indeed, they will tell you he could not be a devil without it any more than he could come into the room and the candles not burn blue, or go out and not leave a smell of brimstone behind him.

Since then the certainty of the thing is so well established, and there are so many good and substantial witnesses ready to testify that he has a cloven foot, and that they have seen it too, indeed, and that we have antiquity on our side, for we have this truth confirmed by the testimony of many ages, why should we doubt it any longer? We can prove that many of our ancestors have been of this opinion, and divers learned authors have left it upon record—particularly, that learned Mother Hazel, whose writings are to be found in MS. in the famous library at Pye-Corner, also the admired Joan of Amesbury, the history of the Lancashire witches, and the Reverend Exorcist of the devils of London, whose history is extant among us to this day. All these and many more may be quoted and their writings referred to for the confirmation of the antiquity of this belief. There seems to be no occasion for further evidence, but 'tis enough. Satan himself, if he did not raise the report, yet tacitly owns the fact. At least he appears willing to have it believed and be received as a general truth for the reasons above.

But besides all this, and as much a jest as some unbelieving people would have this story pass for, who knows but that if Satan is empowered to assume any shape or body and to appear to us visibly (as if really so shaped), I say, who knows but he may by the same authority be allowed to assume the addition of the cloven foot? And why not a cloven foot as well as any other foot if he thinks fit? For if the Devil can assume a shape and can appear to mankind in a visible form, it may, I doubt not with as good authority be advanced, that he is left at liberty to assume whatever shape he pleases, and to choose what case of flesh and blood he'll be pleased to wear, whether real or imaginary. And if this liberty be allowed him, it is an admirable disguise for him to come generally with his cloven foot, that when he finds it for his purpose, on special occasions to come without it, as I said above, he may not be suspected. But take this with you as you go, that all this is upon a supposition that the Devil can assume a visible shape and make a real appearance, which however I do not yet think fit to grant or deny.

Certain it is, the first people who bestowed a cloven foot upon the Devil were not so despicable as you may imagine but were real favorites of heaven. For did not Aaron set up the Devil as a calf in the congregation and set the people a dancing about it for a god? Upon which occasion, Bible expositors tell us that particular command was given: *"They shall no more offer their sacrifices unto devils, after whom they have gone a whoring"* (Lev.17:7). Likewise, King Jeroboam set up the two calves, one at Dan and the other at Bethel, and we find them charged afterward with setting up the worship of devils instead of the worship of God.

After this we find some nations actually sacrificed to the Devil in the form of a ram, and others of a goat, as some think also that the Devil most ordinarily appeared to the Egyptians and Arabians, whence it was derived.

Also, in the old writings of the Egyptians, I mean their hieroglyphic writing before the use of letters was known, we are told this was the mark that he was known by. The figure of a goat was the hieroglyphic of the Devil. Some will affirm that the Devil was particularly pleased to be so represented. Though how they came by their information, and whether they had it from him directly, authors have not yet determined.

But be this as it will, I do not see that Satan could have been at a loss for some extraordinary figure to have bantered mankind with, but as I said above, 'tis none of his business to solve doubts or remove difficulties out of our heads but to perplex us with more as much as he can.

But neither is this all, for other would-be-wise people take upon themselves to make further and more considerable improvements upon this belief of the cloven foot and treat it as a most significant instrument of Satan's private operation, and that it had a kind of hellish inspiration in it and a separate and magical power by which he wrought his infernal miracles. That is, the cloven foot had a superior significance and was not only emblematic of the conduct of men but really guided their conduct in the most important affairs of life. And the agents the Devil employed to influence mankind to delude them and draw them into all the snares and traps that he lays continually for their destruction were equipped with this foot in aid of their other powers for mischief.

Here they read us learned lectures about the sovereign operations that the Devil is at present master of in the government of human affairs, and how the cloven foot is an emblem of the true *double entendre* or divided aspect that the great men of the world generally act with, and by which all their affairs are directed. Whence it comes to pass that there is no such thing as a single-hearted integrity or an upright meaning to be found in the world—that mankind, worse than the ravenous brutes, preys upon his own kind and devours them by all the laudable methods of flattery, wine, deception, and treachery, devours its own kind, which the very beasts refuse to do, and that by all the ways of fraud and allurement that hell can invent, holds out a cloven, divided hoof or hand, pretending to save when the very pretense is made use of to ensnare and destroy.

Thus the divided hoof is the representative of a divided, double tongue and heart, an emblem of the most exquisite hypocrisy and the most fawning and fatally deceiving flattery. And here they give us very diverting histories (tragic in themselves) of the manner in which some of the Devil's inspired agents have managed themselves under the especial influence of the cloven foot, and how they have made war under the pretense of peace, murdered garrisons under the most sacred capitulations, and massacred innocent multitudes after surrenders to mercy.

Again, they tell us the cloven foot has been made use of in all treasons, plots, assassinations, and secret as well as open murders and rebellions. Thus, Joab under the treason of an embrace showed how dexterously he could manage the cloven foot and struck Abner under the fifth rib. Thus, David played the cloven foot upon poor Uriah when he had a mind to lie with his wife. Thus, Brutus played it upon Cæsar.

Now to come nearer home, we have had a great many retrograde motions in this country by this magical implement, the foot, such as that of the Earl of Essex's fate, the beheading the Queen of Scots, and diverse others in Queen Elizabeth's time, and those of the Earl of Shrewsbury, Sir Thomas Overbury, Count Gondamor, and Sir Walter Raleigh, and many others in King James the I.'s time. And some have thought the innocent branches of the royal house of Stuart did not fare the better in the ages that followed.

It must be confessed, the cloven foot was in its full exercise in the next reign, and the generation that rose up immediately after them arrived to the most exquisite skill for the management of it. Here they fasted and prayed, and there they plundered and murdered. Here they raised war for the king, and there they fought against him, cutting throats *for God's sake* and deposing both king and kingly government according to law.

This mutilated apparition has been so public in other countries, too, that it seems to convince us the Devil is not confined to England only, but that as his empire extended to all the temporal world, so he gives them all room to see he is qualified to manage them his own way.

What abundant use did that prince of dissemblers, Charles V, make of this foot? 'Twas by the help of this apparition of the foot that he baited his hook with the city of Milan and tickled Francis I of France so well with it that when he passed through France and was in that king's power, he let him go and never got the bait off of the hook either.

How cruelly did Philip II of Spain manage this foot in the murder of the nobility of the Spanish Netherlands, the assassination of the Prince of Orange? And yet such was the Devil's craft, and so nicely did he bestir his cloven hoof, that this monarch died consoled (though impenitent) in the arms of the Church and with the benediction of the clergy too (who are the second best managers of the said hoof in the world).

I must acknowledge, I agree with this opinion thus far, namely, that the Devil, acting by this cloven foot as a machine, has done a great many things in the world for propagating his dark empire among us. And history is full of such examples as we have already seen.

In a word, this *opera* of the cloven foot has been acted all over the Christian world ever since Judas betrayed the Son of God with a kiss. Indeed, our Savior said expressly of him, *"One of you is a Devil"* (John 6:70). And the sacred text says in another place, *"Then entered Satan into Judas"* (Luke 22:3).

It would take up a great deal of time and paper, too, to give you a full account of the travels of this cloven foot, its progress into all the courts of Europe, and with what most accurate hypocrisy Satan has made use of it upon many occasions and with what success.

It remains to tell you that this merry story of the cloven foot is very essential to the history that I am now writing, since it has been all along the great emblem of the Devil's government in the world, and by which all his most considerable engagements have been answered and executed—for as he is said not to be able to conceal this foot, but that he carries it always with him. The Devil would be no Devil if he were not a dissembler, a deceiver, and did not carry a *double entendre* in all he does or says, and if he could not say one thing and mean another, promise one thing and do another, engage and not perform, declare and not intend, and act like a true Devil as he is with a countenance that is no index of his heart.

I might indeed go back to originations and derive this cloven foot from Satan's primitive state as a cherubim or a celestial being, which cherubims, as Moses is said to have seen them about the throne of God in Mount Sinai, and as the same Moses, from the beginning represented them as afterward covering the Ark, and which beings had the head and face of a man, wings of an eagle, body of a lion, and legs and feet of a calf.[26]

But this is not so much to our present purpose, for as we are to allow, whatever Satan had of heavenly beauty before the Fall, he lost it all when he commenced being the Devil. So to fetch his origin so far up would be only to say that he retained nothing but the cloven foot, and that all the rest of him was altered and deformed to become frightful and horrible as the Devil. But his cloven foot, as we now understand it, is rather mystical and emblematic, and describes him only as the fountain of mischief and treason, the prince of hypocrites, and as such we are now to speak of him.

---

26 For clarity, it is not the Scripture that testifies to Moses seeing angelic beings around the throne but something said by others apart from the biblical account. Also, the reference to the "head and face of a man, wings of an eagle . . . and legs and feet of a calf" cannot be Scripturally traced to either a description by Moses, the Ark of the Covenant, or even a cherubim, but instead only to a manifestation seen by Ezekiel of "four living creatures"—as described in Ezekiel chapter one and again by the Apostle John in Revelation 4:6-8. (Ed.).

So, every dissembler, every false friend, and every secret deceiver, has a cloven foot and, so far, hands on the Devil's interest by the same powerful agency of art as the Devil himself uses to act when he appears in person, or would act if he were just now upon the spot. For this foot is a machine that is to be wound up and wound down as the cause it appears for requires. And there are agents and engineers to act in it by directions of Satan (the grand engineer), who lies still in his retirement, only issuing out his orders as he sees convenient.

Again, every class, every trade, every shopkeeper, every peddler, indeed, that least of tradesmen, and that church peddler, the Pope, has a cloven foot, with which he wishes them all well, and at the same time deceives them, wishes them all fed and at the same time starves them, and wishes them all in heaven and at the same time marches before them directly to the Devil, *a-la-mode de cloven foot.*

Indeed, the very bench, the ever-living foundation of justice in the world, how often has it been made the tool of violence, the refuge of oppression, and the seat of bribery and corruption by this monster in masquerade, and that everywhere? They had much better wipe out the picture of justice blinded with the sword and scales in her hand, which in foreign countries is generally painted over the seat of those who sit to do justice, and place instead thereof a naked, unarmed cloven hoof, a proper emblem of that spirit that influences the world, and of the justice we often see administered among them. Human imagination cannot form an idea more suitable, nor the Devil propose an engine better qualified for an operation of justice by the influence of bribery and corruption. It is this magnipotent[27] instrument in the hands

27 Possessing great power. (Ed.).

of the Devil that under the closest disguise agitates every passion, bribes every affection, blackens every virtue, gives a double face to words and actions to all persons who have any concern in them, and in a word, makes us all devils to one another.

Indeed, the Devil has taken but a dark emblem to be distinguished by, for this of a goat was said to be a creature hated by mankind from the beginning and that there is a natural antipathy in mankind against them. Hence, the scapegoat was to bear the sins of the people and go into the wilderness with all that burden upon him.

But we have a saying among us, in defense of which we must enquire into the proper sphere of action that may be assigned to this cloven foot, as hitherto described. The Proverb is this: *Every Devil has not a cloven foot.* This Proverb, instead of giving us some more favorable thoughts of the Devil, confirms what I have said already—that the Devil raised this scandal upon himself, I mean, the report that he cannot conceal or disguise his Devil's foot, or hoof, but that it must appear under whatever clothing he shows himself.

And the reason I gave holds good still, namely, that he may be more effectually concealed when he goes abroad without it. For if the people were fully persuaded that the Devil could not appear without this badge of his honor, or mark of his infamy, take it as you will, and that he was bound also to show it upon all occasions, it would be natural to conclude that whatever frightful appearances might be seen in the world, if the cloven foot did not also appear, we had no occasion to look for the Devil or so much as to think of him much less to apprehend he was near us. And as this might be a mistake, and that the Devil might be there while we thought ourselves so secure, it might on many occasions be a mistake of very ill consequence, and particularly so since it would give the Devil room to act in the dark and not be discovered where it might be most needful to know him.

From this short hint, thus repeated, I draw a new thesis, namely, *that devil is most dangerous that has no cloven foot*; or if you will have it in words more to the common understanding, the Devil seems to be most dangerous when he goes without his cloven foot.

And here a learned speculation offers itself to our debate, and which indeed I ought to call a council of moral reasoners and men learned in the Devil's politics to determine:

Which is most hurtful to the world, the Devil walking about without his cloven foot, or the cloven foot walking about without the Devil?

It is indeed a nice and difficult question and merits to be well enquired into; for which reason, and diverse others, I have referred it to be treated with some decency and as a dispute of dignity sufficient to take up a chapter by itself.

7

WHICH IS MOST HURTFUL TO THE WORLD, THE DEVIL WALKING ABOUT WITHOUT HIS CLOVEN FOOT, OR THE CLOVEN FOOT WALKING ABOUT WITHOUT THE DEVIL?

In discussing this most critical distinction of Satan's private motions, I must, as the pulpit gentlemen direct us, explain the text and let you know what I mean by several dark expressions in it so I may not be understood to talk (as the Devil walks) in the dark.

1. As to the Devil's walking about.
2. His walking without his cloven foot.
3. The cloven foot walking about without the Devil.

Now as I study brevity, and yet would be understood too, you may please to understand me as I understand myself, thusly:

1. That I must be allowed to suppose the Devil really has a full interaction in, through, and about this globe, with egress and regress, for carrying on his special affairs when, how, and

where it shall seem appropriate, that sometimes he appears and becomes visible, and that he does not always carry his cloven foot with him. This will necessarily bring me to some debate over the most important question of apparitions, hauntings, walkings, and so forth, whether of Satan in human shape, or of human creatures in the Devil's shape, or in any other manner whatsoever.

2. I must also be allowed to tell you that Satan has a great deal of wrong done to him by the general embracing of common errors, and that there is a cloven foot oftentimes without a Devil, or, in short, that Satan is not guilty of all the wicked things we charge him with.

These two heads well settled will fully explain the title of this chapter, answer the query mentioned in it, and at the same time correspond very well with, and give us a further aspect into the main and original design of this work, namely, *The History of the Devil.* We are so fond of and pleased with the general notion of seeing the Devil that I am loth to disoblige my readers so much as calling into question his visibility. Nor is it my business, any more than it is his, to undeceive them where the belief is so agreeable to them, especially since upon the whole it matters not one farthing either on one side or on the other whether it be so or not, or whether the truth of fact be ever discovered or not.

Certain it is, whether we see him or not, here he is, and I make no doubt but he is looking on while I am writing this part of his story. Whether behind me, or at my elbow, or over my shoulder is not material to me, nor have I once turned my head about to see whether he is there or not. For if he be not in the inside, I have so mean an opinion of all his disruptive powers, that it seems of very little consequence to me what shape he takes up, or in what posture he appears. Nor indeed can I find in all my enquiry that ever the Devil appeared (Qua Devil) in any of the most dangerous or important of his designs in the world—the most of his projects, especially of the significant part of them, having been carried on another way.

However, as I am satisfied nobody will be pleased if I should dispute the reality of his appearance, and the world runs away with it as a received point and admits no dispute, I shall most readily grant the generalities and give you some account of the particulars.

History is fruitful of particulars. Whether invention has supplied them or not, I will not say where the Devil is brought upon the stage in plain and undeniable apparition. The story of Samuel being raised by the woman of Endor, I shall leave quite out of my list, because there are so many scruples and objections toward that story, and I shall not dispute with the Scripture (1 Samuel 28). On the other hand, I have so much deference for the gravity of the Devil as not to determine rashly how far it may be in the power of every old woman to call him up whenever she pleases, and that he must come, whatever the pretense is or whatever business of consequence he may be engaged in.

Nor will I undertake to tell you how far the Devil is concerned to discover frauds, detect murders, reveal secrets, and especially to tell where any money is hidden and show folks where to find it. 'Tis an odd thing that Satan should think it of consequence to come and tell us where such a miser hid a treasure or where such an old woman buried her pot full of money, the value of all which is perhaps but a trifle, when at the same time he lets so many veins of gold, so many unexhausted mines, and mountains of silver remain hidden in the bowels of the earth, and which it would be so much to the good of whole nations to discover and never say one word of them to anybody. Besides, how does the Devil's doing things so foreign to himself, and so out of his way, agree with the rest of his character, namely, showing a kind of a friendly disposition to mankind or doing beneficent things? This is so beneath Satan's nature that I scarce know what to say to it. But that which is still more pungent in the case is that these things are so out of his road, and so foreign to his calling that it shocks our faith in them and seems to clash with all the just notions we have of him, and of his business in the world.

But where he is more intimate, we are told he appears in a manner less disagreeable, and there he is more properly a familiar spirit—that is, in short, a Devil of their acquaintance. It is true, the ancients understand the words, a familiar spirit, to be one of the kinds of possession. But if it serves our turn as well under the denomination of an intimate devil, or a devil visitant, it must be acknowledged to be as near in the literal sense and acceptation of the word as the other. Indeed, it must be allowed, 'tis a very great piece of familiarity in the Devil to make visits and show none of his disagreeables, not appear formidable, or in the shape of what he is, respectfully withholding his dismal part in compassion to the infirmities of his friends.

We have many solid tales well attested in history as well as in the reports of honest people who could not be deceived, intimating the Devil's personal appearance, some in one place, some in another, as also sometimes in one habit or dress, and sometimes in another, and it is to be observed that in none of those that are most likely to be real, and in which there is least of fancy and vapor, you have any mention of the cloven foot, which rather seems to be a mere invention of men (and perhaps chiefly of those who had a cloven understanding), I mean a shallow kind of craft, the effect of an empty and simple head, thinking by such a well-meant, though weak fraud, to represent the Devil to the old women and children of the age, with some addition suitable to the weakness of their intellects and suited to making them afraid of him.

Now it is unworthy of the occasion to take notice that we really wrong the Devil and speak of him very much to his disadvantage when we say of such a great lord, or of such a lady of quality, "I think the Devil is in your Grace." No, no, Satan has other business, he very rarely possesses F___ls. Besides, some are so far from having the Devil in them that they are themselves really transmigrated into the very essence of the Devil. And others again are not transmigrated, or assimilated, but indeed and in truth show us that they are to have mere native devils in every part and parcel of them, and that the rest is only masque and disguise.

Thus if rage, envy, pride and revenge can constitute the parts of a Devil, why should not a lady of such quality, in whom all those extraordinaries abound, have a right to the title of being a devil really and substantially, and to all intents and purposes in the most perfect and absolute sense according to the most exquisite descriptions of devils already given by me or anybody else—and even just as Joan of Arc, or Joan Queen of Naples were, who were both sent home to their native country as soon as it was discovered that they were real devils, and that Satan acknowledged them in that quality.

This would do nicely, and as I who am originally a projector have spent some time upon this study, and doubt not in a little time to finish my engine that I am contriving to screw the Devil out of every body, or any body, I question not when I have brought it to perfection but I shall make most excellent discoveries by it. And besides the many extraordinary advantages of it to human society, I doubt not but it will make good sport in the world too.

In a word, a secret power of discovering what devils we have among us, and where and what business they are doing, would be a vast advantage to us all so we might know among the crowd of devils who walk about streets who are apparitions [pretend], and who are not.

I had a long discourse upon this subject one day with a beautiful young lady of my acquaintance, who the world very much admired, and as the world judges no farther than they can see (and how should they, you would say). They took her to be, as she really was, a most charming creature.

To me indeed she revealed herself many ways besides the advantage I had of my extraordinary penetration by the "magic powers" [insights] which I am vested with. To me, I say, she appeared a fury, a satyr, a fiery little fiend as could possibly be dressed up in the flesh. In short, she appeared to me what really she was, a very devil. It is natural to human creatures to desire to discover any extraordinary powers they are possessed of superior to others, and this itch prevailing in me, among the rest, I was impatient to let this lady know that I understood her composition perfectly well, indeed, as well as she did herself.

Happening to be in the family once for some days and having the honor to be very friendly with her and her husband too, I took an opportunity on an extraordinary occasion, when she was in the height of good humor, to talk with her. You must note that as I said the lady was in an extraordinary good humor, there had been a great deal of mirth in the family for some days. But one evening, Sir Edward, her husband, upon some very sharp turn she gave to another gentleman, with a passion of good humor took her in his arms, and turning to me, said, "This wife of mine is full of wit and good humor, but when she has a mind to be smart, she is the keenest little devil in the world"—alluding to the quick turn she had given the other gentleman.

"Is that the best language you can give your wife?" said my lady.

"O madam," said I, "such devils as you are all angels."

"Ay, ay," said my lady, "I know that he has only let a truth fly out that he does not understand."

"Look there now," said Sir Edward. "Could anything but such a dear devil as this have said a thing so pointed? Well, well," he added, "devil to a lady in a man's arms, is a word of divers interpretations."

Thus, they rallied for a good while, as he was holding her fast all the while in his arms, and frequently kissing her, and at last, it went off all in sunshine and mirth.

But the next day I had the honor to lodge in the lady's father's house, where my lady began with me upon the subject, and that very smartly, so that first I did not know whether she was in jest or earnest.

"Ay, ay," she said, "you men make nothing of your wives after you have them," alluding to the discourse with Sir Edward the night before.

"Why Madam," said I, "we men, as you are pleased to term it, if we meet with good wives, we worship them and make idols of them, what would you have more of us?"

"No, no," she said, "before you have them, they are angels, but when you have been in heaven," she added with a smile, "then they are devils."

"Why madam," said I, "devils are angels, you know, and were the highest sort of angels once."

"Yes," she said, very smartly, "all devils are angels, but all angels are not devils."

"But madam," said I, "you should never take it ill to be called devil, you know."

"I know," she said, hastily. "What do you mean by that?"

"Why madam," said I, and looked very gravely and serious, "I thought you had known that I knew it, or else I would not have said so, for I would not offend you. But you may depend on it, I shall never reveal it unless you order me to do so for your particular service."

Upon that she looked hard and wild, and bid me explain myself.

I told her I was ready to explain myself if she would give me her word that she would not resent it and would take nothing ill from it.

She gave me her word solemnly that she would not, though like a true devil she broke her promise with me all at once.

Well however, being unconcerned whether she kept her word or not, I began by telling her that I had not long since obtained much insight into these matters by which I could penetrate into many things that to ordinary perception were invisible and had some special glasses, by the help of which I could see into all visionary or imaginary appearances in a different manner than other people did.

"Very well," she said, "suppose you can, what's that to me?"

I told her it was nothing to her any further than that as she knew herself to be originally not the same creature she seemed to be, but was of a sublime angelic origin. So by the help of my recited art I knew it too, and so far as it might relate to her.

"Very fine," she said, "so you would make a devil of me indeed."

I took that occasion to tell her I would make nothing of her but what she was, that I supposed she knew well enough God Almighty never thought fit to make any human creature so perfect and completely beautiful as she was, but that such were also reserved for figures to be assumed by angels of one kind or another.

She rallied me upon that and told me that would not bring me off, for I had not determined her for anything angelic, but a mere devil. And she asked how I could flatter her with being handsome and being a devil both at the same time?

I told her Satan, whom we abusively called the Devil, was created by God as an immortal seraph and of an original angelic nature so abstracted from anything wicked. He was a most glorious being that when he thought fit to encase himself with flesh and walk about in disguise, it was in his power equally with the other angels to make the form he took upon himself be as he thought fit, beautiful, or deformed.

Here she disputed the possibility of that, and after charging me faintly with flattering her face she told me the Devil could not be represented by anything handsome, alleging our constant picturing the Devil in all the most frightful appearances imaginable.

She insisted that angels did not always assume beautiful appearances. That sometimes they appeared in terrible shapes, but that when they did not, it was at best only amiable faces, not exquisite, and that therefore it would not hold that to be handsome should always render them suspect.

I told her the Devil had more occasion to form beauties than other angels had, his business being principally to deceive and ensnare mankind. And then I gave her some examples upon the whole.

I found by her discourse that she was willing enough to pass for an angel, but 'twas the hardest thing in the world to convince her that she was a devil, and she would not come into that by any means. She argued that I knew her father, and that her mother was a very good woman and she was delivered of her in the ordinary way, and that there was such and such ladies who were present in the room when she was born, and they had often told her so.

I told her that was nothing in such a case as hers, and that when the old gentleman had occasion to transform himself into a fine lady, he could easily dispose of a child and place himself in the cradle instead of it when the nurse or mother were asleep. Indeed, or when they were wide awake too, it was the same thing to him. And upon that occasion I quoted to her Martin Luther, who affirmed that it had been so. However I said to convince her that I knew it (for I would have it that she knew it already), if she pleased I would go to my chamber and fetch her my special "magic looking-glass," where she could see her own picture, not only as it was an angelic picture for the world to admire, but a devil also frightful enough to anybody but herself and me who understood it.

"No, no," she said, "I'll look in none of your conjuring glasses. I know myself well enough, and I desire to look no different than I am."

"No, madam," said I, "I know that very well. Nor do you need any better shape than that you appear in. 'Tis most exquisitely fine. All the world knows you are a complete beauty, and that is clear evidence what you would be if your present appearing form was reduced to its proper personality."

"Appearing form!" she said. "Why would you make an apparition of me?"

"An apparition! Madam," said I. "Yes, to be sure. Why you know you are nothing else but an apparition. And what else would you be when it is so infinitely to your advantage?"

With that, she turned pale and angry and then rose up hastily and looked into the glass (a large peer-glass being in the room), where she stood, surveying herself from head to foot, with vanity not a little.

I took that time to slip away, and running up into my apartment, I fetched my magic glass, as I called it, in which I had a hollow case so framed behind a plain looking glass, so that in the first, she would see her own face only. But in the second, she would see the devil's face, ugly and frightful enough, but dressed up with a lady's head-clothes in a circle, the devil's face in the center, and as it were at a little distance behind.

I came down again so soon that she did not think the time long, especially having spent it in surveying her fair self. When I returned, I said, "Come, madam, do not trouble yourself to look there, that is not a glass capable of showing you anything; come, take *this* glass."

"It will show me as much of myself," she said, a little scornfully, "as I desire to see." So she continued looking in the peer-glass. After some time more (for seeing her a little out of humor, I waited to see what observations she would make), I asked her if she had viewed herself to her satisfaction? She said she had, and she had seen nothing of a devil about her.

"Come, madam," said I, "look here." And with that I opened the looking-glass, and she looked in it but saw nothing but her own face.

"Well," she said, "the glasses agree well enough, I see no difference. What can you make of it?"

With that I took it a little away. "Don't you?" said I. "Then I should be mistaken very much." So I looked in it myself, and giving it a turn imperceptible to her, I showed it to her again, where she saw a devil indeed, dressed up like a fine lady, but ugly and as devil-like as could be expected for a devil to be.

She started, cried out most horribly, and told me she thought I was more of a devil than she, for that she knew nothing of all those tricks, and I did it to frighten her. She believed I had raised a devil.

I told her it was nothing but her own natural picture and that she knew well enough, and that I did not show it to her to inform her of it but to let her know that I knew it too, and that so she might make no pretenses of being offended when I talked familiarly to her of a thing of this nature.

"Very well. So," said she, "I am a real frightful devil, am I?"

"O, madam," said I, "don't say, am I? Why you know what you are, don't you? A devil! Indeed, certainly, as sure as the rest of the world believes you a lady."

I had a great deal of further discourse with her upon that subject, though she would like to have beaten me off of it, and two or three times she put the talk off and brought something else on. But I always found means to revive it and to attack her upon the reality of her being a devil, till at last I made her downright angry, and then she showed it.

First, she cried and told me I came to affront her, that I would not talk so if Sir Edward were by. I endeavored to pacify her and told her I had not treated her with any indecency, nor would I, because while she thought fit to walk around incognito, it was none of my business to reveal her, and that if she thought fit to tell Sir Edward anything of the discourse, she was very welcome, or to conceal it (which I thought the wisest course). She should do just as she pleased. But I left no question that I should convince Sir Edward, her husband, that what I said was just. Whether or not it was best for her for him to know it was for her to consider.

This calmed her a little, and she looked hard at me a minute without speaking a word, when suddenly she broke out thusly:

"And you will undertake," she said, "to convince Sir Edward that he has married a devil, will ye? A fine story indeed! And what follows? Why then it must follow that the child I carry (for she was big with child) will be a devil too, will it? A fine story for Sir Edward, indeed! Isn't it?"

"I don't know that madam," said I. "That's as you order it, by the father's side," said I. "I know not but what it may by the mother's side. That's a doubt I can't resolve till the devil and I talk further about it."

"You and the Devil talk together!" she said and looked ruefully at me. "Why do you talk with the devil then?"

"Ay, madam," said I, "as sure as ever you did yourself. Besides can you question that? Pray who am I talking to now?"

"I think you are mad," she said. "Why you will make devils of all the family, it may be, and particularly I must be with child of a devil, that's certain."

"No, madam," said I, "'tis not certain. As I said before, I question it."

"Why you say I am the devil. The child, you know, has always most of the mother in it. Then that must be a devil too I think; what else can it be?" she said.

"I can't tell that, madam," said I. "That's as you agree among yourselves. This kind does not go by generation. That's a dispute foreign to the present purpose."

Then I entered into a discourse with her of the ends and purposes for which the Devil takes up such beautiful forms as hers, and why it always gave me a suspicion when I saw a lady handsomer than ordinary, and set me upon the search to be satisfied whether she was really a woman or an apparition, a lady or a devil. Allowing all along that her being a devil was quite out of the question.

Upon that very foot, she took me up again roundly, and so, she said, "You are very civil to me through all your discourse, for I see it ends all in that, and you take it as a thing confessed, that I am a devil! A very pretty piece of good usage indeed!" she said, "I thank you for it."

"Indeed, madam," said I, "do not take it ill of me, for I only reveal to you that I knew it. I do not tell it to you as a secret, for you are satisfied of that another way."

"Satisfied of what?" she said. "That I am a devil? I think the devil is in you." And so she began to be hot.

"A devil! Yes, madam," says I, "without doubt a mere devil; take it as you please. I can't help that." And so, I began to take it ill that she should be disgusted at opening such a well-known truth to her.

With that she discovered it all at once, for she turned furious, in the very letter of it, flew out in a passion, railed at me, cursed me most heartily, and immediately disappeared.

We had a great deal of discourse besides this relating to several other young ladies of her acquaintance, some of which, I said, were mere apparitions like her. And I told her which were so, and which not, and the reason why they were so, and for what uses and purposes—some to delude the world one way, and some another—and she was pretty well pleased to hear that, but she could not bear to hear her own true character, which, however as cunning as she was, made her act the devil at last, as you have heard, and then vanished out of my sight.

I hope all the enamored beaus, all the beauty-hunters and fortune-hunters, will take heed, for I suppose if they get a devil they will not complain for lack of a fortune. And there's danger enough, I assure you, for the world is full of apparitions, *non rosa sine spinis* [not a rose without thorns], and not a beauty without a devil. Lord have mercy and may a cross be set on the man's door who goes a courting.

THE TEMPTATION OF CHRIST

8

OF THE CLOVEN FOOT WALKING ABOUT THE WORLD WITHOUT THE DEVIL, VIZ., OF WITCHES MAKING BARGAINS FOR THE DEVIL, AND PARTICULARLY OF SELLING THE SOUL TO THE DEVIL.

I have dwelt long upon the Devil in masque as he goes about the world incognito, and especially without his cloven foot, and have touched upon some of his disguises in the management of his interest in the world. I must say *some* of his disguises only, for who can give a full account of all his tricks and arts in so narrow a compass as I am prescribed to?

I have had some thought of making a full and complete discovery here of that great doubt which has so long puzzled the world, namely, whether there is any such thing as secret-making bargains with the Devil. And the first positive assurance I can give you in the case is that if there is not, 'tis not his fault. 'Tis not for lack of his effort. And 'tis plain if you will permit me to quote Scripture. I say, 'tis evident he would gladly have made a contract with our Savior, and he boldly offered (give him his due), namely, all the kingdoms of the world for one bend of His knee (Matt. 4:9). Impudent Seraph! To think your Lord should pay you homage!

But how many would agree with him here for a less price!

Besides, he is a knave in his dealing, for he really promises what he cannot perform. Witness his impudent proposal to our Lord mentioned above. *"All these things will I give thee!"* Lying Spirit! Why they were none of his to give, no not one of them, for the earth is the Lord's and the kingdoms thereof. Nor were they in his power any more than in his right. So (I have heard that) some poor dismal creatures have sold themselves to the Devil for a sum of money, for so much cash, and yet even in that case, when the day of payment came I never heard that he brought the money or paid the purchase. So he is a scoundrel in his treaties. For you shall trust for your bargain but not be able to get your money. And yet for your part, he comes for you still the same.

In a word, let me caution you all that when you trade with the Devil, either get the price or quit the bargain. The Devil is a cunning swindler. He will wriggle himself out of the performance on his side if possible, and yet expect you should be punctual on your side.

We have a very remarkable example of a man selling himself to the Devil in the Bible, and I do not find what the Devil did for him in payment of the purchase price. The person selling was Ahab, of whom the text says expressly, *"There was none like unto Ahab, which did sell himself to work wickedness in the sight of the Lord,"* (1 Kings 21: 25). I think it might have been rendered, if not translated, *in spite of the Lord,* or in defiance of God, for certainly that's the meaning of it. And now allowing me to preach a little upon this text, my sermon shall be very short. Ahab sold himself. Who did he sell himself to? I answer that question by a question: Who would buy him? Who, as we say, would give anything for him? And the answer to that is plain also. You may judge the purchaser by the work he was to do. He who buys a slave in the market, buys him to work for him and to do such business as he has for him to do. Ahab was bought to work wickedness, and who would buy him for that but the Devil?

I think there's no room to doubt but Ahab sold himself to the Devil. The text is plain that he sold himself, and the work he was sold to do points out the master who bought him. What price he agreed with the Devil for, that indeed the text is silent on, so we may let it alone. Nor is it much to our purpose, unless it be to enquire whether or not the Devil stood to his bargain, and whether he paid the money according to the agreement or cheated him.

This buying and selling between the Devil and us is, I must confess, an odd kind of speculative exchange, and indeed the Devil may be said to sell the bearskin,[28] whatever he buys. But the strangest part is when he comes to demand the transfer. For as I hinted before, whether he performs or not, he expects his bargain to a title. There is indeed some difficulty in resolving how and in what manner payment is made. The stories we meet with in our chimney-corner histories, and which are in so many ways used to make the Devil frightful to us and our heirs forever, are generally so foolish and ridiculous (whether true or not), as to have materially nothing in them. They are of no significance, or else so impossible in their nature that they make no impression

28 From an old saying, "Don't sell the bearskin until you have caught the bear." (Ed.).

upon anybody above twelve years old and under seventy. Or else they are so deplorable that antiquity has fabled them down to our taste, so we might be able to hear them and repeat them with less horror than is due to them.

However, to speak a little more gravely to it, I cannot say but that since, by the two eminent instances of it above about Ahab and about Christ, the fact is evidently ascertained—that the Devil attempted to make such a bargain with one, and actually did make it with the other. The possibility of it is not to be disputed. But then I must explain the manner of it a little and bring it down nearer to our understanding so it may be more intelligible than it is. As for this selling of the soul and making a bargain to give the Devil possession by allowance and title on the day appointed, that I cannot come into by any means, no, nor into the other part, namely, of the Devil coming to claim his bargain and to demand the soul according to agreement, and upon default of a fair delivery, taking it away by violence, case and all, of which we have many historical relations pretty current among us. Some of which, for ought I know, we might have hoped had been true if we had not been sure they were false. And others we had reason to fear were false because it was impossible they should be true.

The bargains of this kind, according to the best accounts we have of them, used to consist of two main articles according to the ordinary stipulations in all covenants, namely:

1. Something to be performed on the Devil's part—buying.
2. Something to be performed on the man's part—selling.

The Devil's Part: This was generally some poor trifle, for the Devil generally bought good bargains and oftentimes like a complete swindler agreed to give what he was not able to procure. That is to say, he would bargain for a price he could not pay, for example, Long Life. This, though the deluded peddler has often had folly enough to contract for, the Devil never had power to make good. And we have a famous story, how true I know not, of a wretch who sold himself to the Devil on condition that he, Satan, should assure him that (1.) he should never lack food, (2.) he should never be cold, (3.) he should always come to him when he called him, and (4.) he should let him live one and twenty years, and then Satan was at liberty to have him—that is, I suppose to take him wherever he could find him.

It seems the fellow's desire to be assured of 21 years of life was chiefly that, during that time, he might be as wicked as he wanted and should yet be sure not to be hanged, indeed, to be free from all punishment. Upon this base, 'tis said he commenced roguery and committed a great many robberies and other villainous things. Now it seems the Devil was pretty true to his bargain in several of those things, particularly, that two or three times when the fellow was taken up for petty crimes and called for his old friend, he came and frightened the constables so, that they let the offender get away from them. But at length, having done some capital crime, he was seized by a set of constables, or such like officers, who were not to be frightened by the Devil in whatsoever shape he appeared. So they carried him off, and he was committed to Newgate or some other prison.

Nor could Satan with all his skill unlock his fetters, much less the prison doors. But he was tried, convicted, and executed. The fellow in his extremity, they say, expostulated with the Devil for his bargain since the term of 21 years seems not to have expired. But the Devil, it is said, shuffled with him, told him a good while he would get him out, bid him have patience and stay a little, and thus led him on till he came, as it were, within sight of the gallows, that is to say, within a day or two of his execution. The Devil then objected to the conditions of his bargain and told him he agreed to *let* him live 21 years, and he had not hindered him, but that he did not covenant to *cause* him to live that time, and there was a great deal of difference between doing and suffering. He told him he was to suffer him to live, and that he did, but he could not make him live when he had brought himself to the gallows.

Whether this story was true or not, for you must not expect we historians should answer for the discourse between the Devil and his chaps, because we were not privy to the bargain. I say, whether it was true or not, the inference is to our purpose several ways.

1. It confirms what I have said of the knavery of the Devil in his dealings with us on the best conditions he can get. He very seldom performs his bargain.
2. It confirms what I have likewise said, that the Devil's power is limited, with this addition: He not only cannot destroy the life of man, but he also cannot preserve it. In short, he can neither prevent nor bring on our destruction.

I may be allowed, I hope, for the sake of the present discourse, to suppose that the Devil would have been so just to this wicked, though foolish creature, as to have saved him from the gallows if he could. But it seems he at last acknowledged that it was not in his power. Indeed, he could not keep him from being taken and carried to prison after he fell into the hands of a bold fellow or two who were not to be frightened by his bluster, as some foolish creatures had been before.

And how simple, how weak, how unlike anything of an angelic nature it was to attempt to save the poor wretch only by little noises and sham appearances, putting out the candles, rushing and jostling in the dark, and the like! If the Devil was that mighty seraph which we have heard of, if he is a god of this world, a prince of the air, a spirit able to destroy cities and make havoc in the world, if he can raise tempests and storms, throw fire about the world, and do wonderful things, as an unchained Devil no doubt could do, what need of all this pretentious show? And what need he try so many ridiculous ways, by the emptiness, indeed, the silly nonsensical manner of which he shows that he is able to do no better, and that his power is extinguished? In a Word, he would certainly act otherwise if he could. *Sed caret pedibus*, he lacks power.

How weak a thing is it then for any man to expect performance from the Devil? If he has not power to do mischief, which is his element, his very nature, and on many accounts the very sum of his desires, how should he have power to do good? How should he have power to deliver from danger or from death, which deliverance would be in itself a good, when we know it is not in his nature to do good to or for any man?

In a word, the Devil is strangely impudent to think that any man should depend on him for the performance of an agreement of any kind whatsoever when he himself knows that he is not able, if he were honest enough, to be as good as his word.

Next we come to his expecting our performance to him. Though he is not so just to us, yet it seems he never fails to come and demand payment from us at the very day appointed. He was but a weak trader in things of this nature, who having sold his soul to the Devil (so our old women's tales call the thing), and when the Devil came to demand his bargain, put it off as a thing of no force. For it was done so long ago he thought he (the Devil) had forgotten it. It was a better answer, which they tell us, that a Lutheran divine gave the Devil in the name of a poor wretch who had sold himself to the Devil, and who was in a terrible fright about his coming for his bargain, as he might well be indeed if the Devil had such a power as really to come and take it by force. The story (if you can bear a serious one) is this:

The man was in great horror of mind, and the family feared he would destroy himself. At length they sent for a Lutheran minister to talk with him, and who after some labor with him got out the truth, viz., that he had sold himself to the Devil, and the time was almost expired when he expected the Devil would come and fetch him away. And he was sure he would not fail coming at the time to a minute.

The minister first endeavored to convince him of the horrid crime, and to bring him to a true repentance for that part. And having as he thought made him a sincere penitent, he then began to encourage him. And particularly, he desired of him that when the time came for the Devil to fetch him away, he, the minister, should be in the house with him. Accordingly, to make the story short, the time came. The Devil came. And the minister was present when the Devil came.

What shape he was in, the story does not say. But the man said he saw him and cried out. The minister could not see him, but the man affirming he was in the room, the minister said aloud, "In the name of the living God, Satan, what comest thou here for?"

The Devil answered, "I come for my own."

The minister answered, "He is not thy own, for Jesus Christ

has redeemed him, and in His name, I charge thee to avoid and touch him not." At which, says the story, the Devil gave a furious stamp and went away, and was never known to molest him afterward.

For Satan, it seems, as the story says, had the impudence to demand his agreement notwithstanding he had failed in the performance on his part. What the answer was I do not pretend to have seen, but it seems it was something like what is mentioned above, viz., that he was in better hands, and that he durst not touch him.

I have heard of another person who had actually signed a contract with the Devil. And during a fast kept by some Protestant or Christian divines, while they were praying for the poor man, the Devil was obliged to come and throw the contract in at the window.

But I vouch for none of these stories. There may be much in them, and much use made of them, even whether or not they are related exactly such in fact. The best use I can make of them is this: If any wicked, desperate wretches have made a bargain and sale with Satan, their only way out is to repent, if they know how, and that before he comes to claim them. Then batter him with his own guns. Play religion against devilism, and perhaps they may drive the Devil out of their reach. At least he will not come at them, which is as well.

On the other hand, how many stories have we handed around of the Devil's really coming with a terrible appearance at the time appointed, and powerfully or by violence carrying away those who have given themselves up to him, indeed, and sometimes a piece of the house along with them, as in the famous instance of *Sudbury*, anno 1662. It seems he comes with rage and fury upon such occasions, pretending he only comes to take his own, or as if he had permission given him to come and take his goods, as we say, where he could find them, and would strike a terror into all who should oppose him.

The greatest part of the terror we are usually in upon this occasion is from a supposition that when this hell-fire contract is once made, God allows the Devil to come and take the wicked creature how and in what manner he thinks fit, as being given up to him by his own act and deed. But in my opinion there's no divinity at all in that. For in our law, we punish a *felo de se*, or self-murderer, because, as the law suggests, he had no right to dismiss his own life. He being a subject of the commonwealth, the government claims the ward or custody of him, and so 'twas not murder only, but robbery, and is a felony against the state, robbing the king of his liege-man, as 'tis justly called. So neither has any man a right to dispose of his soul, which belongs to his Maker in property and in right of creation. The man then having no right to sell, Satan has no right to buy, or at best he has made a purchase without a title and, consequently, has no just claim to the possession.

It is therefore a mistake to say that when any of us have been so mad as to make such a pretended contract with the Devil that God gives him permission to take it as his due. 'Tis no such thing. The Devil has bought what you had no right to sell, and therefore, as an unlawful oath it is to be repented of and then broken. So your business is to repent of the crime and then tell the Devil you have better considered it, and that you won't stand to your bargain, for you had no power to sell. And if he pretends to violence after that I am mistaken, I believe the Devil knows better.

Thus they tell us the Devil carried away Dr. Faustus and took a piece of the wall of his garden along with them. Thus at Salisbury, the Devil, as it is said, and publicly printed, carried away two fellows who had given themselves up to him and carried away the roof of the house with them, and the like, all which I believe my share of. Besides, if these stories were really true, they are all against the Devil's true interest. Satan must be a fool, which is indeed what I never took him to be for the most part. This would not be the way to increase the number of desperadoes who should thus put themselves into his hand only to make himself a terror to them. And this is one of the most powerful objections I have against the thing, for the Devil, I say, is no fool. That must be acknowledged. He knows his own game, and generally plays it confidently.

I might, before I quit this point, seriously reflect here upon our *Beau mond*, viz., the lighthearted, jovial part of mankind (especially those of the times we live in) who walk about in a composure and tranquility inexpressible and, yet as we all know, must certainly have all sold themselves to the Devil for the power of performing the foolish things with the greater applause. It is true, to be a fool is the most pleasant life in the world if the fool has the particular felicity that few fools want, viz., to think themselves wise. The learned say it is the dignity and perfection of fools that they never fail trusting themselves. They believe themselves sufficient and able for everything, and hence their lack or waste of brains is no grievance to them, but they hug themselves in the satiety of their own wit. But to bring other people to have the same notion of them that they have of themselves, and to have their apish and ridiculous conduct make the same impression on the minds of others as it does on their own, this requires a general infatuation, and must either be a judgment from heaven, or a mist of hell. Nothing but the Devil can make all the men of brains applaud a fool. And can any man believe that the Devil will do this for nothing? No, no, he will be well paid for it, and I know no other way they have to compound with him, but this of bargain and sale.

It may be true that under the powerful guard and protection of the Devil, men do sometimes go a great way in crime, and that perhaps farther in these our days of boasted morals than was known among our fathers. The only difference that I meet with between the sons of Belial in former days and those of our ages seems to be in the Devil's management, not in theirs. The sum of which amounts to this, that Satan seems to act with more cunning and they with less. For in the former ages of Satan's dominion, he had much business upon his hands. All his art and engines, and engineers also, were kept fully employed to beguile, allure, betray, and circumvent people, and draw them into crimes. And they found him, as we may say, a full employment. I doubt not he was called the tempter on that very account. But the case seems quite altered now. The tables are turned. Then, the Devil tempted men to sin, but now, in short, they tempt the Devil. Men push into crimes before he pushes them. They out shoot him with his own bow and outrun him on his own ground. And as we say of some hot spurs who ride post, they whip the postboy. In a word, the Devil seems to have no business now but to sit still and look on.

I must confess, this seems to intimate some secret compact between the Devil and them. But then it looks not as if they had contracted with the Devil for permission to sin, but that the Devil had contracted with them so they should sin so and so, up to such a degree, without giving him the trouble of daily solicitation, private management, and artful screwing up their passions, their affections, and their most retired faculties, as he was before obliged to do.

This also appears more agreeable to the nature of the thing. And as it is a most exquisite part of Satan's cunning, so 'tis an undoubted testimony of his success. If it were not so, he could never bring his kingdom to such a height of absolute power as he has done. This also solves several difficulties in the affair of the world's present way of sinning, which otherwise it would be very hard to understand, as particularly, how some eminent men of quality among us, whose upper rooms are not extraordinary or well-furnished in other cases, yet are so very witty in their wickedness that they gather admirers by hundreds and thousands, who, however heavy, lumpish, slow, and backward, even by nature and in force of constitution in better things, yet in their race devil-wards, they are suddenly grown nimble, light of foot, and outrun all their neighbors.

Fellows who are as empty of sense as beggars are of honesty, and as far from brains as a whore is of modesty, you shall find suddenly dip into polemics and study Michael Servetus, Socinus, and the most learned of their disciples. They shall reason against all religion as strongly as a philosopher, blaspheme with such a keenness of wit, and satirize God and eternity with such a brightness of fancy as if the soul of a Rochester or a Hobbs was transmigrated into them. In a little length of time more, they banter heaven, burlesque the Trinity, and jest with every sacred thing. And all are so sharp, so ready, and so terribly witty, as if they were born buffoons and were singled out by nature to be champions for the Devil.

Whence can all this come? How is the change wrought?

Who but the Devil can inject wit in spite of natural dullness, create brains, fill empty heads, and supply the vacuities in the understanding? And will Satan do all this for nothing? No, no, he is too wise for that. I can never doubt a secret compact, if there is such a thing in nature. When I see a head where there was no head, sense in power where there is no sense in existence, wit without brains, and sight without eyes, 'tis all devil-work. Who could neither read Latin or spell English, like old Sir William Read, who wrote a book on optics, which when it was printed, he did not know which was the right side uppermost, and which the wrong? Could this eminent uninformed beau turn atheist and make wise speeches against that being who made him a fool if the Devil had not sold him some wit in exchange for that trifle of his captivated soul? Had he not bartered his inside with that son of the morning (Isa. 14:12), to have his tongue tipped with blasphemy (he who knew nothing of a God but only to swear by Him), he could never have set up for a wit to burlesque His providence and ridicule His government of the world.

But the Devil, as he is god of the world, has one particular advantage, and that is that when he has work to do he very seldom lacks instruments. With this circumstance also, that the degeneracy of human nature supplies him, as the late King of France said of himself when they told him what a calamity was about to befall his kingdom by the famine, "Well," said the king, "then I shall not lack soldiers." And it was so, lack of bread supplied his army with recruits, so lack of grace supplied the Devil with reprobates for his work.

Another reason why I think the Devil has made more bargains of that kind we speak of in this age, is, because he seems to have laid aside his cloven foot. All his old emissaries, the tools of his trade, the engineers that he employed in his mines, such as witches, warlocks, magicians, conjurers, astrologers, and all the hellish train or rabble of human devils, who did his drudgery in former days, seem to be out of work. I shall give you a fuller enumeration of them in the next chapter.

These, I say, seem to be laid aside; not that his work is abated, or that his business with mankind for their delusion and destruction is not the same, or perhaps more than ever. But the Devil seems to have changed hands. The temper and genius of mankind is altered, and they are not to be taken by fright and horror as they were then. The figures of those creatures were always dismal and horrible, and that is what I mean by the cloven foot. But now wit, beauty, and jovial things are the sum of his craft. He manages by the soft and the smooth, the fair and the artful, the kind and the cunning, not by the frightful and terrible, the ugly and the odious.

When the Devil for weighty dispatches,
Wanted messengers cunning and bold,
He pass'd by the beautiful faces,
And pick'd out the ugly and old.

Of these he made warlocks and witches,
To run of his errands by night,
Till the over wrought hag-ridden wretches,
Were as fit as the Devil, to fright.

But whoever has been his adviser,
As his kingdom increases in growth;
He now takes his measures much wiser,
And traffics with beauty and youth.

Disguis'd in the wanton and witty,
He haunts both the Church and the court,
And sometimes he visits the city,
Where all the best Christians resort.

Thus dress'd up in full masquerade,
He the bolder can range up and down,
For he better can drive on his trade,
In anyone's name than his own.

9

OF THE TOOLS THE DEVIL WORKS WITH, VIZ., WITCHES, WIZARDS OR WARLOCKS, CONJURERS, MAGICIANS, DIVINES, ASTROLOGERS, INTERPRETERS OF DREAMS, TELLERS OF FORTUNES, AND, ABOVE ALL THE REST, HIS PARTICULAR MODERN PRIVY-COUNSELLORS CALLED WITS AND FOOLS.

Though, as I have advanced in the foregoing chapter, the Devil has very much changed hands in his modern management of the world, and that instead of the rabble and long train of implements reckoned up above, he now walks about in beaus, beauties, wits and fools, yet I must not omit to tell you that he has not dismissed his former regiments, but like officers in time of peace, he keeps them all in half pay, or like extraordinary men at the custom-house, they are kept on call to be ready to fill up vacancies, or to employ when he is more than ordinarily full of business.

Therefore, it may not be amiss to give some brief account of them, from Satan's own memoirs, their performance being no inconsiderable part of his history.

Nor will it be an unprofitable digression to go back a little to the primitive institution of all these orders, for they are very ancient, and I assure you, it requires great knowledge of antiquity to give a particular of their origin. I shall be very brief in it.

In order then to this enquiry, you must know that it was not for lack of servants that Satan took this sort of people into his pay. He had, as I have observed in its place, millions of diligent devils at his call, whatever business and however difficult things he had for them to do. But as I have said above, our modern people are forwarder than even the Devil himself can desire them to be. And they come before they are called, run before they are sent, and crowd themselves into his service. And so it seems it was in those early days, when the world was one universal monarchy under his dominion, as I have at large described in its place.

In those days the wickedness of the world keeping a just pace with their ignorance, this inferior sort of low prized instruments did the Devil's work mighty well. They drudged on in his black art so laboriously, and with such good success, that he found it was better to employ them as tools to delude and draw in mankind than to send his invisible implements about and oblige them upon every trifling occasion, which, perhaps, was more costly than worship, and more pains than pay.

Having then a set of these volunteers in his service, the true Devil had nothing to do but to keep an exact correspondence with them and communicate some needful powers to them to make them be and do something extraordinary and give them a reputation in their business. And these, in a word, did a great part of almost all the Devil's business in the world.

To this purpose he gave them power (if we may believe old Glanville, Baxter, Hicks, and other learned consultors) to walk invisible, to fly in the air, to interpret dreams, answer questions, betray secrets, to talk the universal language (gibberish), bring up spirits, and torment the living with a thousand other needful tricks to amuse the world, keep themselves in veneration, and carry on the Devil's empire in the world.

Among the first nations in whom these infernal practices were found were the Chaldeans. And that I may do justice in earnest, as well as in jest, it must be allowed that the Chaldeans, or those of them so called, were not at first conjurers or magicians but only philosophers and studiers of nature, wise, sober and studious men. And we have an extraordinary account of them. And if we may believe some of our best writers of fame, Abraham was himself famous among them.

Now granting this, it is all to my purpose, namely, that the Devil drew these wise men in to search after more knowledge than nature could instruct them in. And the knowledge of the true God being at that time sunk very low, he debauched them all with dreams, apparitions, conjurers, and so forth, till he ruined the just notions they had and made devils of them all, like him.

The learned Senensis, speaking of this *Chaldean* kind of learning, gives us an account of five sorts of them. You will pardon me for being so grave as to go this length back.

1. Chascedin or Chaldeans, properly so called, being astronomers.
2. Asaphim or magicians, such was Zoroastres and Balaam, the son of Beor.
3. Chatumim or interpreters of dreams and hard speeches,

enchanters, and so forth.

4. Mecasphim or witches, Malefici or Venefici, poisoners.
5. Gazarim or Auruspices, and diviners, such as mentioned in Ezekiel or as others, called Augurs.

Now, as to all these, I suppose I may do them no wrong if I say, however justifiable they were in the beginning, the Devil got them all into his service at last, and that brings me to my text again, from which the rest was a Digression.

1. The Chascedin or Chaldean astronomers turned astrologers, fortune-tellers, and vile deluders of the people, as if the wisdom of the holy God was in them, as Nebuchadnezzar said of Daniel on that very Account.
2. The Asaphim or Magi, or Magicians: Sixtus Senensis says they were such as wrought by covenants with devils, but turned to it from their wisdom, which was to study the practical part of natural philosophy, working admirable effects by the mutual application of natural causes.
3. The Chartumim, from being reasoners or disputers upon difficult points in philosophy, became enchanters and conjurers.
4. The Mecasphim or prophets: They turned to be sorcerers and raisers of spirits, such as wounded by an evil eye, and by bitter curses, and were afterward famed for having familiar conversation with the Devil and were called witches.
5. The Gazarim, from the bare observations of the good and bad omens, by the entrails of beasts, flying of birds, and so forth, were turned to sacrists or priests of the heathen idols and sacrificers.

Thus, I say, first or last, the Devil engrossed all the wise men of the east, for so they are called, made them all his own, and by them worked wonders. That is, he filled the world with lying wonders as if wrought by these men, when indeed it was all his own from beginning to the end and set on foot merely to propagate delusion and impose upon blinded and ignorant men. The god of this world blinded their minds, and they were led away by the subtlety of the Devil (to say no worse of it) till they became devils themselves as to mankind. For they carried on the Devil's work upon all occasions, and the race of them still continue in other nations, and some of them among ourselves, as we shall see presently.

The Arabians followed the Chaldeans in this study, while it was kept within its due bounds, and after them, the Egyptians. And among the latter we find that Jannes and Jambres were famous for leading Pharaoh by their pretended magic performances to reject the real miracles of Moses (2 Tim. 3:8-10). And history tells us of strange pranks the wise men, the magicians, and the soothsayers played to delude the people in the most early ages of the world.

But, as I say the Devil has improved himself now, so he also did then. For the Grecian and Roman heathen rites coming on, they outdid all the magicians and soothsayers by establishing the Devil's lying oracles, which, as a masterpiece of hell, did the Devil more honor and brought more homage to him than ever he had before or could arrive to since.

Again, as by the setting up of the oracles, all the magicians and soothsayers grew out of credit. So at the ceasing of those oracles, the Devil was pleased to go back to the old game again and take up with the agency of witches, divinations, enchantments and conjurings, as I hinted before, answerable to the four sorts mentioned in the story of Nebuchadnezzar, viz., magicians, astrologers, the Chaldeans and the soothsayers. How these began to be out of request, I have mentioned already. But as the Devil has not quite given them over, only laid them aside a little for the present, we may venture to ask what they were, and what use he made of them when he did employ them.

The truth is, I think as it was a very meager employment for anything that wears a human countenance to take up, so, I must acknowledge, I think 'twas a meager, low prized business for Satan to take up with—below the very Devil, below his dignity as an angelic, though condemned creature, below him even as a devil to go to talk to a parcel of ugly, deformed, spiteful, malicious old women, to give them power to do mischief who never had a will after they entered into the state of old womanhood to do anything else. Why the Devil always chose the ugliest old women he could find, whether wizardism made them ugly (who were not so before), and whether the ugliness (as it was a beauty in witchcraft) did not increase according to the meritorious performance in the black trade, these are all questions of moment to be decided in ages to come (if human learning can arrive to so much perfection).

The strange work that the Devil has made in the world by this sort of his agents called witches, is such, and so extravagantly wild, that except our hope that most of those tales happen not to be true, I know not how anyone could be easy to live near a widow after she was five and fifty.

All the other sorts of emissaries whom Satan employs come short of these ghosts, and sometimes (we err to believe) they come and show themselves on particular accounts. And some of those particulars respect doing justice, repairing wrongs, preventing mischief, and sometimes in matters very considerable, and on things so necessary to public benefit that we are tempted to believe they proceed from some vigilant spirit who wishes us well. But in reality they are never concerned in anything but mischief. Indeed, if what they do portends good to one, it results in hurt to many. The whole tenor of their existence, their design in general, is to do mischief, and they are only employed in mischief and nothing else. How far they are furnished with ability suitable to the horrid will they are vested with, remains to be described.

These witches, 'tis said, are furnished with power suitable to the occasion that is before them, and particularly that which deserves to be considered as prediction and foretelling events, which I insist the author of witchcraft is not accomplished with himself, nor can he communicate it to any other. How then witches come to be able to foretell things to come, which, 'tis said, the Devil himself cannot know, and which, as I have shown 'tis evident he does not know himself, is yet to be determined. But that witches do foretell is certain from the Witch of Endor, who foretold things to Saul (1 Sam. 28) that he knew not before, namely, that he should be slain in battle the next day, which accordingly came to pass (1 Sam. 31).

There are, however, and notwithstanding this particular case, many instances wherein the Devil has not been able to foretell approaching events, and that in things of the utmost consequence. And he has given certain foolish or false answers in such cases. The Devil's priests, who were summoned by the prophet Elijah to decide the dispute between God and Baal—had the Devil been able to have informed them of it, they would certainly have received notice from him of what was intended against them by Elijah, that is to say, that they would be all cut in pieces. For Satan was not such a fool as to not know that Baal was a non-entity, a nothing, at best a dead man, perished and rotting in his grave. For Baal was Bell or Belus, an ancient king of the Assyrian monarchy, and he could no more answer by fire to consume the sacrifice than he could raise himself from the dead.

But the priests of Baal were left of their master to their just fate, namely, to be a sacrifice to the fury of a deluded people. Hence I infer his inability, for it would have been very unkind and ungrateful in him not to have answered them if he had been able. There is another argument raised here most justly against the Devil relative to his being under restraint, and that of greater eminence than we imagine. And it is drawn from this very passage, thus: 'Tis not to be doubted but that Satan, who has much of the element put into his hands as prince of the air (Eph. 2:2), had a power, or was able potentially speaking, to have answered Baal's priests by fire. Fire being in virtue of his airy principality a part of his dominion. But he was certainly withheld by the Superior Hand that gave him that dominion, I mean withheld for the occasion only.

And so, in another case, it was plain that Balaam, who was one of those sorts of Chaldeans mentioned above, who dealt in divinations and enchantments, was withheld from cursing Israel. Some are of opinion that Balaam was not a witch or a dealer with the Devil because 'tis said of him, or rather he says it of himself, that he saw the visions of God. *"He hath said, which heard the words of God, and knew the knowledge of the most High, which saw the vision of the Almighty, falling into a trance, but having his eyes open"* (Num. 24:16). Hence, they allege he was one of those Magi whom St. Augustine speaks of, *de Divinatione*, who by the study of nature, and by the contemplation of created beings came to the knowledge of the creature, and that Balaam's fault was, that being tempted by the rewards and honors that the king promised him, he intended to have cursed Israel. But when his eyes were opened, and he saw they were God's own people, he durst not do it.

They will have it therefore, that except as above, Balaam was a good man, or at least that he had the knowledge of the true God, that the fear of that God was upon him, and that he honestly declares this. *"If Balak would give me his house full of silver and gold, I cannot go beyond the commandment of the Lord"* (Num. 24:13). Where though he is called a false prophet by some, he evidently owns God and assumes a property in him, as other prophets did: *The commandment of the Lord,* and *I cannot go beyond.* But that which gives me a better opinion of Balaam than all this is, his plain prophecy of Christ, where he calls him the *Star of Jacob,* and declares, *"I shall see him, but not now: I shall behold him, but not nigh: there shall come a Star out of Jacob, and a Scepter shall rise out of Israel, and shall smite the corners of Moab, and destroy all the children of Seth"* (Num. 24:17). All of these express not only a knowledge but also a faith in Christ; but I have done preaching. This is all by the by. I return to my business, which is the history.

ANGELS DOING BATTLE IN HEAVEN.

10

OF THE VARIOUS METHODS THE DEVIL TAKES TO CONVERSE WITH MANKIND.

Having spoken something of persons, and particularly of such as the Devil thinks fit to employ in his affairs in the world, it comes next, of course, to say something of the manner in which he communicates his mind to them, and by them to the rest of his acquaintance in the world.

In his access to converse with mankind, I take the Devil to be under great difficulties in his affairs on his part, especially occasioned by the bounds that are set for him, or that policies oblige him to set for himself. 'Tis evident he is not permitted to fall upon them with force and arms, that is to say, to muster up his infernal troops and attack them with fire and sword. If he were free to act in that manner as he was able, by his own seraphic power to destroy the whole race, and even the earth they dwelt upon, he would certainly, and long ago, have effectually done it. His particular interests and inclinations are well enough known.

But in the next place, as he is thus restrained from violence, so prudence restrains him in all his other encounters with mankind. And being confined to stratagem and soft sell methods, such as persuasion, allurement, feeding the appetite, prompting, and then gratifying corrupt desires, and the like, he finds it for his purpose not to appear in person, except very rarely, and then in disguise, but to perform all the rest in the dark under the visor of art and craft, making use of persons and methods concealed, or at least not fully understood or discovered.

As to the persons whom he employs, I have taken some pains, you see, to discover some of them. But the methods he uses with them either to inform and instruct and give orders to them, or to converse with other people by them, these are very particular and deserve some place in our memoirs, particularly as they may serve to remove some of our mistakes. And to take off some of the frightful ideas we are apt to entertain in prejudice of this hellish manager, as if he were no more to be matched in his politics than he would be matched in his power if it were let loose, which is so much a mistake that on the contrary we read of several people who have abused and cheated the Devil (a thing which I cannot say is very honest or just, notwithstanding the old Latin Proverb, *Fallere fallentem non est fraus,* which men construe, or rather render, by way of banter upon Satan that 'tis no sin to cheat the Devil), which for all that, upon the whole I deny and allege that, let the Devil act how he will by us, we ought to deal fairly by him.

But to come to the business without excessive narrative, I am to enquire how Satan issues out his orders, gives his instructions, and fully delivers his mind to his emissaries, of whom I have mentioned some in the title to Chapter IX. In order to do this, you must form an idea of the Devil sitting in great state, in open campaign, with all his legions about him in the height of the atmosphere, or if you will, at a certain distance from the atmosphere and above it, so the plan of his encampment might not be hurried round its own axis with the earth's daytime activity, which might be some disturbance to him.

By this fixed situation, the earth performing its rotation, he has every part and parcel of it brought to a direct opposition to him and, consequently, to his view once in twenty-four hours. The last time I was there, if I remember right, he had this quarter of the world, which we call Christendom, just under his eye. And as the motion is not so swift but what his piercing optics can take a strict view of it *en passant* [by the way], for the circumference of it being but twenty one thousand miles, and its circular motion being a full twenty-four hours in performing, he has something more than an hour to view every thousand miles, which, to his supernatural penetration, is not worth naming.

As he takes thus a daily view of all the circle, and an hourly view of the parts, he is fully master of all transactions, at least such as are done above board by all mankind. And then he dispatches his emissaries or *Aides de Camp* to every part with his orders and instructions. Now these emissaries, you are to understand, are not the witches and diviners, of whom I spoke above, for I call them also emissaries. But they are all devils or (as you know they are called) Devil's angels. And these may, perhaps, come and converse personally with the sub-emissaries I mentioned to be ready for their support and assistance on all occasions of business. These are those devils that the witches are said to call upon, for we can hardly suppose Satan comes himself at every summons.

These run about into every nook and corner, wherever Satan's business calls them, and are never lacking to him but are the most diligent devils imaginable. These are those with whom they tell us our witches, sorcerers, wizards, and such sorts of folks converse freely.

History has not yet enlightened us in this part with useful knowledge, or at least not sufficiently for a description of the persons or habits of these sorts, as to what shapes they take up, what languages they speak, and what particular works they perform. So we must refer it to further enquiry. But if we may credit history, we are told many famous stories of these appearances.

For example, the famous Mother Lakland, who was burnt as a supposed witch at Ipswich in 1646, confessed at the time of her execution, or a little before it, that she had frequent conversations with the Devil himself. She, being very poor, and withal of a devilish, passionate, cruel, and revengeful disposition, used to wish she had it in her power to do such and such mischievous things to some whom she hated. And the Devil himself, who it seems knew her temper, came to her one night as she lay in her bed. And as she was between sleeping and waking, she heard a deep hollow voice, supposing she heard from the Devil, that if she would serve him in some things, she should have her will over all her enemies and should lack for nothing. She was much afraid at first, but soliciting her very often, he bade her not be afraid of him, and still urged her to yield. And as she says, he struck his claw into her hand. And though it did not hurt her, it made it bleed, and with the blood he wrote the covenants, that is to say, the bargain between them. And being asked what was in them, and if he required her to curse or deny God or Christ, she said no.[29]

Then she claimed the Devil furnished her with three devils, I suppose to wait upon her, for she confessed they were to be

29 N. B. I do not find she told them whether the Devil wrote it with a pen, or whether on paper or parchment, nor whether she signed it or not, but it seems he carried it away with him. I suppose, if Satan's register were examined, it might be found among the archives of hell, the rolls of his acta Publica, and when his historiographer royal publishes them, we may look for it among them. (Defoe).

employed in her service. The first she bewitched was her own husband, by which he lay a while in great misery and died. Then she sent to one Captain Beal and burnt a new ship of his just built, which had never been at sea. These and many other horrid things she did and confessed. And having been twenty years as a witch, at last the Devil left her, and she was burnt for her crimes.

That some extraordinary occasions may bring these agents of the Devil, indeed, sometimes the Devil himself, to assume human shapes and appear to other people we cannot doubt, as he did thus in the case of our Savior, as a tempter, and some think he did so to Manasseh, whom the Scripture charges with sorcery and having a devil.

But in these modern ages of the world, he finds it much more to his purpose to work underground, as I have observed, and to keep upon the reserve so that we have no authentic accounts of his personal appearance except those very ancient or very remote from our faith, as well as our enquiry.

It seems to me, though, that generally speaking, the Devil finds it more for his purpose to have his interest in the world propagated another way, namely, in private. And his personal appearances are reserved for things only of extraordinary consequence and, as I may say, of evident necessity where his honor is concerned and where his interest could be carried on no other way, not forgetting to take notice that this is very seldom.

Next to spirits and apparitions, we find mankind disturbed by the abundance of little odd, reserved ways in which the Devil is shrewdly suspected of having a hand, such as dreams, noises, voices, and the like.

As to dreams, I have nothing to say in Satan's prejudice at all there. I make no question but he deals very much in that kind of intelligence, and why should he not? We know heaven itself formerly conversed very often with the greatest of men by the same method, and the Devil is known to mimic the methods as well as the actions of his Maker. Whether heaven has not quite left off that way of working, we are not certain. But we pretty well know the Devil has not left it. And I believe some instances may be given where his worship has been really seen and talked to in sleep as much as if the person had been awake with his eyes open.

These are to be distinguished, too, pretty much by the goodness or badness of the subject. How often have men committed murder, robbery, and adultery in a dream while at the same time the head has never been removed from the pillow, or the body so much as turned in the bed (except when with an extraordinary agitation of the soul it is expressed by extraordinary noises in the sleep, by violent sweating, and by other such ways)?

In such cases where the soul with all the passions and affections are agitated, and with him giving his full assent to the facts of whatsoever kind there are, is not the man as guilty as if the sins so dreamed of his committing had actually been committed? Though it be no doubt to me that it is so, yet as it is foreign to the present affair and not at all relating to the Devil's history, I leave it to the reverend doctors of the Church as properly belonging to them to decide.

In short, I take dreams to be the second best of the advantages the Devil has over mankind. The first, I suppose, you all know, viz., the treachery of the garrison within. By dreams he may be said to get inside of us without opposition. Here he opens and locks without a key, and like an enemy laying siege to a fortified city, reason and nature (the governor of the city) keep him out by day and keep the garrison true to their duty. But in the dark he gets in and parleys with the garrison (the affections and passions), debauches their loyalty, and stirs them up to disloyalty and rebellion so they betray their trust, revolt, mutiny, and go over to the besieger.

Thus he manages his interest, I say, and insinuates himself into the inside of us without our consent, indeed, without our knowledge. For whatever speculation may do, 'tis evident demonstration does not assist us to discover which way he gets access to the soul while the organ tied up, and dozing with sleep, has locked it up from action. That it is so, is clear, but how he does it is a secret, which I do not find the ancients or moderns have yet made a discovery of.

As to the difference between the several devils who appear, it relates to the office of the persons who employ them—as conjurers who seem to command the particular devil who waits upon them with more authority and raise them and lay them at pleasure, drawing circles, casting figures, and the like. But the witch, in a more familiar manner, whispers with the Devil, keeps the Devil in a bag or a sack, and sometimes in her pocket, and the like.

But all these kinds deal much in dreams, talk with the Devil in their sleep, and make other people talk with him in their sleep too. And 'tis on this occasion I mention it here. In short, the Devil may well take this opportunity with mankind. For not half the world that came into his measures would comply if they were awake. But of that, hereafter.

And yet his thus insinuating himself by dream does not seem sufficient, in my opinion, to answer the Devil's end and carry on his business. And therefore, we must be forced to allow him a kind of actual possession in particular cases, and that in the souls of some people by different methods from others. Luther was of the opinion that the Devil gets a familiarity with some souls just at, or rather before, their being embodied. As to the manner and method how he gets in, that is another question and may be spoken of by itself. Besides, why may not He, who at Satan's request to enter into the herd of swine said go (Matt. 8:31-32), give the same commission to possess a sort of creatures so many degrees below the dignity of the Gadarenian swine, and open the door too? But as for that, when our Lord said go, the Devil never enquired which way he should get in.

When, then, I see nations, or indeed herds of nations set on fire of hell, and as I may say, enflamed by the Devil—when I see towns, parties, factions and rabbles of people visibly possessed—'tis enough to me that the great master of the devils [Satan] has said to him, *go*. There's no need to enquire which way he finds open, or at what postern gate he gets in. As to his appearing, 'tis plain he often gets in without appearing, and therefore the question about his appearing still remains a doubt and is not very easy to be resolved.

In the Scripture we have some light into it, and that is all the help I find from antiquity. And it goes a great way to solve the phenomena of Satan's appearing. What I mean by the Scripture giving some light to it, is this: 'Tis said in several places, and of several persons, God came to them in a Dream. *"God came to Abimelech in a dream by night"* (Gen. 20:3). *"And God came to Laban the Syrian in a dream"* (Gen. 31:24). *"The angel of the Lord appeareth to Joseph in a dream"* (Matt. 2:13).

Short comments are sufficient to plain texts. Applying this to my friend when he wanted to be satisfied about the how, relating to his dream, viz., how he should come to dream such wicked things, I told him, in short, the case was plain, the Devil came to him in a dream by night. How and in what manner he formed the wicked representations and spread debauched appearances before his fancy, by real whispers and voice, according to Milton, or by what other methods, the learned are not arrived to any certainty about it.

This leads me necessarily to enquire whether or not the Devil or some of his agents are always in our company, and whether or not they make any visible appearances. For my part, I make no question of it. How else could he come to the knowledge of what we do? For as I can allow him no prescience at all, as for many reasons I have observed already, he must be able to see and know us and what we are about when we know nothing of him, or else he could know nothing of us and our affairs, which yet we find otherwise. And this gives him infinite advantage to influence our actions, to judge our inclinations, and to bring our passions to clash with our reason, as they often do, and get the better of it too.

All this he obtains by being able to walk about invisibly and see when he is not seen, of which I have spoken already.

There are indeed many things that are laid to the Devil's charge, though he really may know nothing of the matter. And this would bring me to defend Satan in some things, wherein he may truly be said to suffer wrongfully. And if I thought it would oblige him, I might say something to his advantage this way. However, I'll venture a word or two for an injured devil, take it as you will.

First, it is certain that as this invisibility of the Devil is very much to our prejudice, so the doctrine of his visibility is a great prejudice to him, as we make use of it.

By his invisibility he is certainly vested with infinite

advantages against us. While he can be present with us, and we know nothing of the matter, he informs himself of all our measures and arms himself in the best and most suitable manner to injure and assault us so he can counteract all our secret, concerted designs, disappoint all our schemes, and (except when heaven apparently concerns itself to overrule him) defeat all our enterprises, break all our measures, and do us mischief in almost every part of our life—and all this, because we are not privy to all his motions as he is to ours.

But now for his visibility and his real appearance in the world, and particularly among his disciples and emissaries. Here, I think Satan has a great deal of loss, suffers manifest injury, and has great injustice done to him. And therefore, I ought to clear this matter up a little, if it be possible, and set matters right in the world about him, according to that useful old maxim of setting the saddle upon the right horse, or giving the Devil his due.

First, as I have said, we are not to believe every idle head who pretends even to converse face to face with the Devil and who tells us they have thus seen him and been acquainted with him every day. Many of these pretenders are manifest cheats. And however they would have the honor of a private interest in him and boast how they have him at their beck, can call him this way and send him that way as they please, raise him and lay him when, and how, and as often as they find it for their purpose, I say, whatever boasts they make of this kind, there is really nothing of truth in them.

Now the injuries and injustice done to the Devil in these cases are manifest, namely, they entitle the Devil to all the mischief they are pleased to do in the world. And if they commit a murder or a robbery, set fire to a house, or do any act of violence in the world, they presently are said to do it by the agency of the Devil, and the Devil helps them. So Satan bears the reproach, and they have all the guilt. This is (1.) a grand fraud upon the world, and (2.) a notorious slander upon the Devil. And it would be a public benefit to mankind to have such would-be-devils as these turned inside out so we might know when the Devil was really at work among us and when not, what mischiefs were of his doing and which were not, and so these fellows might not slip their necks out of the halter by continually laying the blame of their wickedness upon the Devil.

Not that the Devil is not very willing to have his hand in any mischief, or in all the mischief that is done in the world, but there are some low prized rogueries that are too little for him, beneath the intentions of his operation, and which 'tis really a scandal to the Devil to charge upon him.

In some cases he may encourage them in these little frauds and deceptions, and give them authority to make use of his name to bring them afterwards, and by degrees, to have a real acquaintance with him. So bringing the jest of their trade into earnest, till at length prompting them to commit some great villainy, he secures them to be his own by their very fear of him leaving them to be exposed to the world.

But this is not the only way the devil is injured either, for we have often found people pretend upon him in other cases, and of nearer concern to him a great deal, and in articles weightier, as in particular, the great business of possession. It is true this point is not thoroughly understood among men, neither has the Devil thought fit to give us those illuminations about it as I believe he might do. Particularly, that great and important article is not, for ought I can see, rightly explained, namely, whether there are not two several kinds of possession, viz., some wherein the Devil possesses us, and some in which we really possess the Devil, the nicety of which I doubt this age, with all its penetration, is qualified to explain. And a dissertation upon it is too long for this work, especially so near its conclusion.

But to come back to the point in hand, and to consider the injustice done to the Devil in the various turns and tricks that men put upon him very often in this one article, viz., pretending to possession and to have the Devil in them when really it is not so, certainly the Devil must take it very ill to have all their demented, lunatic tricks charged upon him. Some of which, indeed, most of which, are so gross, so simple, so empty, and so little to the purpose, that the Devil must be ashamed to see such things pass in his name, or that the world should think he was concerned with them.

Thus you see the Devil may be wronged and falsely accused in many particulars, and often has been so. There are likewise some other sorts of counterfeit devils in the world, such as gypsies, fortune-tellers, foretellers of good and bad luck, false prophets, raisers of storms, and many more, some practiced among us, some in foreign parts, too many almost to reckon up. Indeed, I almost doubt whether the Devil himself knows all the sorts of them, for 'tis evident he has little or nothing to do with them, I mean not in the way of their craft.

11

OF DIVINATION, SORCERY, THE BLACK ART, POWWOWING, AND SUCH LIKE PRETENDERS TO DEVILISM, AND HOW FAR THE DEVIL IS OR IS NOT CONCERNED WITH THEM.

Though I am writing the history of the Devil, I have not undertaken to do the same of all the kinds of people, male or female, who pretend to be devils in the world. This would be a task for the Devil indeed, and fit only for him to undertake, for their number is and has been prodigiously great and may with his other legions be ranked among the innumerable.

What a world do we inhabit! where there is not only with us a great Roaring-Lion-Devil, daily seeking whom of us he may devour (1 Peter 5:8), but also innumerable millions of lesser devils hovering in the whole atmosphere over us (indeed, and for ought we know, other millions always invisibly moving about us and perhaps in us, or at least in many of us). Besides all these, the world has a vast many counterfeit hocus pocus devils (human devils) who are visible among us, of our own species and fraternity, conversing with us upon all occasions, and who set up their stages in every town, chat with us at every tea-table, converse with us in every coffee-house, and impudently tell us to our faces that they are devils, boast of it, and use a thousand tricks and arts to make us believe it too, and that too often with success.

It must be confessed, there is a strong propensity in man's nature, especially the more ignorant part of mankind, to resolve every strange thing, whether really strange or not (but if it be but strange to us), into devilism, and to say everything that they can give no account of is the Devil.

Wonderful operations astonish the mind, especially where the head is not over-burdened with brains. And custom has made it so natural to give the Devil either the honor or scandal of everything that we cannot otherwise account for, that it is not possible to put the people out of the road of it.

The magicians were, in the Chaldean monarchy, called the wise men. And though they are joined with the sorcerers and astrologers in the same place (Dan. 2:4), yet they were generally so understood among those people. But in our language, we understand them to be people who have an art to reveal secrets, interpret dreams, foretell events, and so forth, and who use enchantments and sorceries, by all which we understand the same thing, which now in a more common way we express by one general coarse expression: *Dealing with the Devil.*

The Scripture speaks of a spirit of divination, and a wench who was possessed by this Spirit *"brought her masters much gain by soothsaying"* (Acts 16:16), that is to say, according to the learned, by oracling or answering questions. Whence you will see in the margin that this soothsaying devil is there called Python, that is, Apollo, who is often called Python, and who at the oracle of

Delphi gave out such answers and double entendres as this wench possibly did. And hence, all those spirits that were called spirits of divination were in another sense called Pythons.

Now when the Apostle Paul came to see this creature, this spirit took upon itself to declare that *"These men,"* meaning Paul and Timotheus, *"are the servants of the most high God, which shew unto us the way of salvation"* (Acts 16:17). This was a good turn of the Devil to preserve his authority in the possessed girl. She brought them gain by soothsaying, that is to say, by resolving difficult questions, answering doubts, interpreting dreams, and so forth. Among these doubts, he made her give testimony to Paul and Timotheus, to flatter the new Christians, and perhaps (though very ignorantly) even with Paul and Timotheus themselves, to gain a kind of credit and respect to her for speaking.

But the Devil, who never speaks truth without some sinister end, was discovered here and detected. His flattering recognition not accepted, and he himself uncovered as he deserved, there the Devil was overshot with his own bow again.

Here now was a real possession, and the evil spirits who possessed her stooped to sundry little acts of servitude that we could give little or no reason for, only that the girl's master might get money by her. Perhaps this was a particular case and prepared to honor the authority and power the apostles had over evil spirits.

But we find these things carried a great way farther in many cases, that is to say, where the parties are thus really possessed. Namely, the Devil makes agents of the possessed parties to do many things for the propagating of his interest and kingdom, and particularly for the carrying on of his dominion in the world. But I am for the present not so much concerned with the real possession as the pretended, and particularly, we have had many who have believed themselves possessed when the Devil never believed it of them and perhaps knew them better. Some of these are really poor devils to be pitied and are what I call *Diables Imaginaire.* These have, notwithstanding, done the Devil good service and brought their masters good gain by soothsaying.

We find possessions acknowledged in Scripture to be really and personally the Devil, or according to the text, legions of devils in the plural. The Devil, or rather devils, that possessed the man among the tombs, is positively affirmed to be the Devil in the Scripture. All the evangelists agree in calling him so, and his very works show it, namely, the mischief he did to the poor creature among the tombs (who was made so fierce that he was the terror of all the country) as well as to the herd of swine, and to the country in the loss of them.

I might preach you a lecture here of the Devil's terror upon the approach of our Savior, the dread of his government, and how he acknowledged that there was a time for his torment that was not yet come: *"Art thou come hither to torment us before our time?"* (Matt. 8:29). It is evident the Devil comprehended that Christ would chain them up before the Day of Judgment, and therefore some think the Devil here, being as it were, caught out of his due bounds by possessing the poor man in such a furious manner, was afraid and petitioned Christ not to chain him up for it. And as the text says, they *"besought him [to] suffer them to go away,"* and so forth—that is to say, when they said, *art thou come hither to torment us before the time?* The meaning is, they begged that He would not cast them into torment before the time, which was already fixed, but that if He would cast them out of the man, He would let them go away, and so forth.

The evangelist, Luke, says they [*Legion,* many devils]

"besought him that he would not command them to go out into the deep" (Luke 8:31). Our learned annotators think that part is not rightly rendered, adding that they do not believe the Devil fears drowning. But I submit, I believe the meaning is that they would not be confined to the vast ocean, where no inhabitants being to be seen, they would be effectually imprisoned and tied down from doing mischief, which would be a hell to them. As to their going into the swine, that might afford us some allegory, but I am not disposed to jest with the Scripture, no, neither with the Devil, further than needs must.

It is evident the Devil makes use of very small instruments sometimes, such as the damsel possessed with a spirit of divination (Acts 16:16) and several others.

The Devil has often found fools very necessary agents for propagating his interest and kingdom, but we never knew the good spirits to do so. On the other hand, it does not seem likely that heaven should deprive a poor creature of its senses and, as it were, take her soul from her, and then make her an instrument of instruction to others and an oracle to declare His decrees. This does not seem to be rational.

The Devil seems to do most of his work himself, and by shorter methods. For he has so complete an influence among those he now lists in his service, that he brings all the common affairs of mankind into a narrower compass in his management with a dexterity particular to him, and by which he carries on his interest silently and surely much more to the detriment of virtue and good government, and consequently much more to his satisfaction than ever he did before.

There is a kind of sorcery, or what else you may be pleased to call it, that, though unknown to us, is yet, it seems, still very much encouraged by the Devil. But this is a great way off and in countries where the politer instruments that he finds here are not to be had, namely, among the Indians of North America. This is called powwowing, and they have their divines, which they call powwows, who use strange gestures, distortions, horrid smokes, and scents, and several such things which the sorcerers in ancient times are said to have used in determining or, as they pretended, directing the fate of persons. And the Devil is pleased, it seems (or is permitted), to fall in with these things and, as some people think, appears often to them for their assistance upon those occasions.

The age has grown too wise to be agitated by these dull scarecrow things that their forefathers were tickled with. Satan has been obliged to lay aside his puppet-shows and his morris-dancing[30] devils. Those things, as they may be supposed to be very troublesome to him (and but that he has servants enough would be chargeable too), are now of no great use in the new management of his affairs.

In a word, men are too much devils themselves, in the sense that I have called them so, to be frightened with such little, low prized appearances as these. They are better acquainted with the old archangel than to be so. And they seem to tell him they must be treated after another manner, and then, as they are good-natured and docile, he may deal with them upon better terms.

Hence the Devil goes to work with mankind a much shorter way. For instead of the art of flattering and whining, together with the laborious part of tricking and sharping, hurrying and driving, frightening and terrifying, all which the Devil was put

30 Morris—a vigorous English dance traditionally performed by men wearing costumes and bells. (Ed.).

to the trouble of before, he, in short, acts the Grand Manner as the architects call it (I don't know whether our Freemasons may understand the word), and therefore, I may hereafter explain it as it is to be diabolically as well as mathematically understood.

At present my meaning is, he acts with them immediately and personally by a magnificent transformation, making them mere devils to themselves upon all needful occasions, and devils to one another, too, whenever he (Satan) has need of their service.

This way of embarking mankind in the Devil's particular engagement is really very modern. And though the Devil himself may have been long acquainted with the method and, as I have heard, began to practice it toward the close of the Roman Empire, when men began to act upon very polite principles and were capable of the most refined wickedness, and afterward with some popes, who likewise were a kind of church devils (such as Satan himself could hardly expect to find in the world), yet I do not find that he was ever able to bring it into practice, at least not so universally as he does now. But now the case is altered, and men being generally more expert in wickedness than they were formerly, they suffer the smaller alteration of the species in being transmigrated. In a word, they turn into devils with hardly any trouble at all to either the Devil or to themselves.

This particular would need much less explanation could I obtain a license from Sir Hellebore Wormwood, Bart., or from my Lord Thwartover, Baron of Scoundrel Hall in the Kingdom of Ireland to write the true history of their own conduct and how early, and above all, how easily they commenced being devils without the least impeachment of their characters as wise men, and without any diminution of that part of their denomination that established them for fools.

How many mad fellows appear among us every day in the critical juncture of their transmigration just when they have so much of the man left as to be known by their names, and enough of the Devil taken up to settle their characters? This ease of the Devil's access to these people, and the great convenience it is to him in his general business, is a proof to me that he has no more occasion to need diviners, magicians, sorcerers, and whatever else we please to call those people who were formerly so great with him. For what occasion has he to employ devils and wizards to confound mankind, when he has arrived to such a perfection of art as to bring men, at least in these parts of the world, to do it all themselves?

Upon this account we do not find any of the old sorcerers and diviners, magicians, or witches appearing among us. Not that the Devil might not be as well able to employ such people as formerly he did, and qualify them for the employment too, but really, there is no need of them hereabout—the Devil now having a shorter way, and mankind being much more easily possessed. The old *herd of swine* were not sooner agitated, though there was full 2,000 of them together. Nature has opened the door, and the Devil has egress and regress at pleasure, so that witches and diviners are quite out of the question.

Nor let any man be alarmed at this alteration in the case as it stands between mankind and the Devil and think the Devil having gained so much ground may in time, by encroachment, come to a general possession of the whole race, and so we should all come to be devils incarnate. I say, let us not be alarmed, for Satan does not get these advantages by encroachment and by his infernal power or art, no not at all. But 'tis the man himself who does it by his indolence and negligence on one hand, and his complaisance to the Devil on the other. And he, as it were, opens the door to him both ways, beckons him with his very hand to come in, and the Devil has nothing to do but enter and take possession. Now if it be so, and man is so frank to him, you know the Devil is no fool not to take the advantage when 'tis offered him. And therefore 'tis no wonder if the consequences that I have been just now naming follow.

But let no man be discouraged by this from reaffirming his natural and religious powers and venturing to shut the Devil out. For the case is plain that he may be shut out. The soul is a strong castle and has a good garrison placed within to defend it. If the garrison behave well and do their duty, it is impregnable, and the cowardly Devil must raise his siege and be gone. Indeed, he must flee or, as we call it, make his escape, lest he be laid by the heels, that is, lest his weakness be exposed along with all his lurking and lying in wait. This part would bear a great enlargement, but I have no room to be witty about him, so you must take it in general, the Devil lies at Blye Bush, as our country people call it, to watch your coming out of your hold. And if you happen to go abroad unarmed, he seizes upon and masters you with ease.

Unarmed! you'll say, what arms should I take? What fence against a flail? What weapons can a man take to fight the Devil? I could tell you what to fight him with, and what you might frighten him with, for the Devil is to be frightened with several things besides Holy Water. But 'tis too serious for you, and you'll tell me I am a preaching and the like. So I must let the Devil manage you rather than displease you with talking Scripture and religion.

Well, but may not the Devil be fought with some of his own weapons? Is there no dealing with him in a way of human nature? This would require a long answer, and some religion and philosophy might be dealt with and applied. Therefore, if you are afraid he should charge upon you and attack you, if you won't make use of those Scripture weapons I have already mentioned in this history, and which you may hear of, if you enquire at Eph. 6:16, *"Above all, taking the shield of faith, wherewith ye shall be able to quench all the fiery darts of the wicked,"* you must look for things better where you think you can find them.

But be it one way or another, the historical part seems to be a little against me. For 'tis certain, the Devil both wanted and made use of legions of agents, human as well as infernal, visible and invisible, in that great and important affair, and we cannot doubt but he has innumerable instruments still at work about it.

I might anticipate all your objections by granting the busy Devil at this time employing all his agents and instruments (for I never told you they were idle and useless) in striving to enflame the Christian world and bring a new war to overspread Europe. I might, perhaps, point out to you some of the measures he takes, the provocatives that his state physicians administer to the courts and counsellors of princes to foment and ferment the spirits and members of nations, kingdoms, empires and states in the world in order to bring these glorious ends of blood and war to pass. For you cannot think that he who knows so much of the Devil's affairs as to write his history must know something of all these matters more than those who do not know so much as he.

But all this is remote to the present case; for this is no impeachment of Satan's new methods with mankind in this part of the world, and in his private and separate capacity. All this only signifies that in his more general and national affairs, the Devil still acts by his old methods. And when he is to seduce or embroil nations, he, like other conquerors, subdues them by armies, employs mighty squadrons of devils, and sends out strong detachments with generals to lead them, some to one part of the world, some to another, some to influence one nation, some to manage and direct another, according as business presents and his occasions require, so his affairs may be carried on currently and to his satisfaction.

If it were not thus, but that the Devil by his new and exquisite management, of which I have said so much, had brought mankind in general to be the agents of their own mischiefs, and that the world were so at his beck that he need but command them to go and fight, declare war, raise armies, destroy cities, kingdoms, countries and people, the world would be a field of blood indeed, and all things would presently run into confusion.

But this is not the case at all. Heaven has not let go the government of the Creation to His subdued enemy, the Devil. That would overturn the whole system of God and give Satan more power than ever he was or will be vested with. When, therefore, I speak of a few forward wretches in our day, who are so warm in their wickedness that they anticipate the Devil, save him the trouble to tempt, turn devils to themselves, and gallop hellward faster than he drives, I speak of them as single persons acting in their own personal and private capacity. But when I speak of nations and kingdoms, there the Devil is obliged to go on in the old road and act by stratagem, by his proper machinery, and to make use of all his arts, and all his agents, just as he has done in all ages from the beginning of his politic government to this day.

And if it were not thus, what too would become of all his numberless legions of which all ages have heard so much, and with which all parts of the world have had so much fatal experience? They would seem to be quite out of employment and be rendered useless in the world of spirits where it is to be supposed they reside. Not even the Devil himself could find any business for them, which by the way, to busy and mischievous spirits as they are, would be a hell to them, even before their time. They would be, as it were, doomed to a state of inactivity, which we may suppose was one part of their expulsion from blessedness and the creation of man, or as they were for the surprising interval between the destruction of mankind by the Deluge and Noah's coming out of the ark, when indeed they might be said to have nothing at all to do.

But this is not Satan's case, and therefore let me tell you, too, so you may not think I treat the case with more levity than I really do, and I am sure I intend to do, though it is so true that our modern and modish sinners have arrived to more exquisite ways of being wicked than their fathers and really seem, as I have said, to need no devil to tempt them, they do Satan's work for him as to others also, and make themselves devils to their neighbors, tempting others to crime even faster than the Devil desires them, running before they are sent, and going about the Devil's errands *gratis*, by which means Satan's work is, as to them, done to his hand, and they may be said to save him a great deal of trouble. Yet after all, the Devil has still a great deal of business upon his hands, and he as well as all his legions find themselves a full employment in disturbing the world and opposing the glory and kingdom of their great Superior, whose kingdom it is their whole business, however vain in its end, to overthrow and destroy, if they were able, or at least to endeavor it.

This being the case, it follows of course that the general mischiefs of mankind, public as well national, as family mischiefs, and even personal (except as before excepted), still all lie at the Devil's door as much as ever, and let his advocates bring him off of it if they can. And this brings us back again to the manner of the Devil's management and the way of his working by human agents or, if you will, the way of human devils working in affairs of low life, such as we call divination, sorcery, black-art, necromancy, and the like, all which I take to consist of two material parts, and both very necessary for us to be rightly informed of.

1. The part that Satan by himself or his inferior devils empowers such people to do, as he is in confederacy with here on earth. To whom he may be said, like the master of an opera or comedy, to give their parts to act and to qualify them to act them. Whether he obliges them to a rehearsal in his presence to try their talents and see that they are capable of performing, that indeed I have not enquired into.
2. That part that these empowered people do volunteer or go beyond their commission to show their diligence in the service of their new master and either (a.) to bring grist to their own mill and make their market of their employment in the best manner they can, or (b.) to gain applause, be admired, wondered at, and applauded, as if they were ten times more devils than really they are.

In a word, the matter consists of what the Devil does by the help of these wicked people and what they do in his name without him. The Devil is sometimes cheated in his own business, as there are pretenders to witchcraft and black art, who Satan never made any bargain with, but who he connives with because at least they do his cause no harm, though their business is rather to get money than to render him any service, of which I gave you a remarkable instance before.

But to go back to his real agents, of which I reckon two:

1. Those who act by direction and confederacy, as I have said already many do.
2. Those whom he acts in and by, and they (perhaps) know it not, of which sort history gives us plenty of examples, from Machiavelli's first disciple to the famous Cardinal Alberoni, and even to some more modern than his eminence, of whom I can say no more till further occasion offers.

Those who act by immediate direction of the Devil and in confederacy with him are such as I've already mentioned, whose arts are truly black, because they are really infernal. It will be very hard to decide the dispute between those who really act thus in confederacy with the Devil and those who only pretend to it. So, I shall leave that dispute where I find it. But there are, or at least have been, a set of people in the world who really are of his acquaintance and very intimate with him. And though, as I have said, he has much altered his schemes and changed hands of late, yet that there are such people, perhaps of all sorts, and that the Devil keeps up his correspondence with them, I must not venture to deny that part lest I bring upon me the whole posse of the conjuring and bewitching crew, male and female, and they should mob me for pretending to deny them the honor of dealing with the Devil, by which they are so exceedingly willing to have such fame.

Not that I am hereby obliged to believe all the strange things the witches and wizards who have been allowed to be such (indeed, who have been hanged for it) have said of themselves—indeed, that they have confessed of themselves, even at the gallows. And if I come to have an occasion to speak freely of the matter, I may perhaps convince you that the Devil's possessing power is much lessened of late, and that he either is limited and his fetter shortened more than it has been, or that he does not find the old way (as I said before) so fit for his purpose as he did formerly, and therefore takes other measures. But I must adjourn that to a time and place by itself. But we are told that there is another sort of people, and, perhaps, a great many of them too, in whom and by whom the Devil really acts, and they know it not.

It would take up a great deal of time and room, too much for this place so near the close of this work, to describe and mark out the involuntary devils that there are in the world; of whom it may be truly said, that really the Devil is in them, and they know it not. Now, though the Devil is cunning and managing, and can be very silent where he finds it for his interest not to be known, yet it is very hard for him to conceal himself and give so little disturbance in the house, since the family should not know who lodged in it. Yet, I say, the Devil is so subtle and so mischievous an agent that he uses all manner of methods and craft to reside in such people as he finds for his purpose, whether they will or not, and which is more, whether they know it or not.

And let none of my readers be angry or think themselves ill-used when I tell them the Devil may be in them, and may act them, and by them, and they not know it. For I must add, it may perhaps be one of the greatest pieces of human wisdom in the world for a man to know when the Devil is in him and when not, when he is a tool and agent of hell, and when he is not, and, in a word, when he is doing the Devil's work and under his direction, and when he is not.

It is true, this is a very weighty point and might deserve to be handled in a more serious way than I seem to be talking in all this book, but permit me to talk of things my own way, and withal, to tell you that there is no part of this work so seemingly ludicrous but what a grave and well-weighed mind may make a serious and solid application of it, if they please. Nor is there any part of this work in which a clear sight and a good sense may not see that the author's intention is that they should do so. And as I am now so near the end of my book, I thought it was important to tell you so and lead you to it as far as I can.

I say, 'tis a great part of human wisdom to know when the Devil is acting in us and by us, and when he is not. The next and still greatest part would be to oppose him and prevent him, put a stop to his progress, bid him go about his business, and let him know he should carry on his designs no farther in that manner, that we will be his tools no longer, and in short, turn him out of doors, and bring a stronger power to take possession. But this, indeed, is too solid a subject, and too great to begin with here.

But now, as to the basic knowing of when he is at work with us, I say this: Though it is considerable, it may be done, nor is it so very difficult. For example, you have no more to do but look a little into the microcosm of the soul and see there how the passions that are the *blood*, and the affections that are the *spirit*, move in their particular vessels—how they circulate, and in what temper the pulse beats there. And you may easily see who turns the wheel. If a perfect calm possesses the soul, if peace and temper prevail and the mind feels no tempests rising, if the affections are regular and exalted to virtuous and sublime objects, the spirits cool, and the mind sedate, the man is in a general rectitude of mind, and he may be truly said to be his own man. Heaven shines upon his soul with its holy and benign influences, and he is out of the reach of the evil spirit. For the divine Spirit is an influence of peace, all calm and bright, happy and sweet like itself, and tending to everything that is good both present and future.

But on the other hand, if at any time the mind is ruffled, if vapors rise and clouds gather, if passions swell the breast, if anger, envy, revenge, hatred, wrath, strife (if these, or any of these) hover over you (much more if you feel them within you), if the affections are possessed and the soul is hurried down the stream to embrace low and base objects, if those spirits which are the life and enlivening powers of the soul are drawn off to parties and to be engaged in a vicious and corrupt manner (shooting out wild and wicked desires and running the man headlong into crime), the case is easily resolved, the man is possessed. The Devil is in him. And having taken the fort, he is making his shelter to cover and secure himself in his hold so that he may not be dispossessed.

Nor can he be easily dispossessed when he has got such hold as this. And 'tis no wonder that being lodged thus upon the out-works of the soul, he continues to sap the foundation of the rest and, by his incessant and furious assaults, reduces the man at last to a surrender.

If the allegory be not as just and opposite as you would have it be, you may, however, see by it in a full view that, in the state of the man and how the Devil carries on his designs, nothing is more common. And I believe there are few thinking minds but may reflect upon it in their own compass, that for our passions and affections to flow out of the ordinary channel, the spirits and blood of the soul to be extravasated, the passions grow violent and outrageous, the affections impetuous, corrupt, and violently vicious. Whence does all this proceed? We can't pretend it comes from heaven. If we must not say, 'tis the Devil, whose door must it lie at? Pride swells the passions. Avarice moves the affections. And what is pride, and what is avarice, but the Devil inside the man? Indeed, as personally and really as ever he was in the herd of swine (Luke 8:32).

Let not any man then who is a slave to his passions, or who is chained down to his covetousness, pretend to take it ill when I say he has the Devil in him, or that he is a devil. What else can it be, and how comes it to pass that passion and revenge so often dispossess the man of himself as to lead him to commit murder, to lay plots and snares for the life of his enemies, and so to thirst for blood? How comes this but by the Devil putting those spirits of the soul into so violent a ferment, into a fever? That the circulation is precipitated to that degree, and that the man too is precipitated into mischief, and at last into ruin, 'tis all the Devil, though the man does not know it.

Thus, the Devil has his involuntary instruments as well as those who act in confederacy with him. He has a very great share in many of us, and acts us, and in us unknown to us though we know nothing of it, and indeed, though we may not suspect it of ourselves. Like Hazael the Assyrian, who, when the prophet told him how he would act the Devil upon the poor Israelites, answered with detestation, *"is thy servant a dog that he should do this great thing?"* (2 Kings 8:13). And yet he was that dog and did all those cruel things for all that, the Devil acting him, or acting in him, to make him wickeder than ever he thought it was possible for him to be.

THE LAST JUDGMENT

12—THE CONCLUSION

OF THE DEVIL'S LAST SCENE OF LIBERTY AND WHAT MAY BE SUPPOSED TO BE HIS END, WITH WHAT WE ARE TO UNDERSTAND OF HIS BEING TORMENTED FOR EVER AND EVER.

As the Devil is a *prince of the power of the air*, his kingdom is mortal, and must have an end. And as he is called the *god of this world*, that is, the great usurper of the homage and reverence that mankind ought of right to pay to their Maker, so his usurpation also, like the world itself, must have an end. Satan is called the god of this world, as men too much prostrate and prostitute themselves to him. Yet he is not the governor of this world, and therefore the homage and worship he has from the world is an usurpation, and this will have an end, because the world itself will have an end. And all mankind, as they had a beginning in time, so must expire and be removed before the end of time.

Since then the Devil's empire is to expire and come to an end, and that the Devil himself and all his host of devils are immortal seraphs, spirits that are not embodied and cannot die, but are to remain in being, the question before us next will be, what is to become of him? What is his state to be? Where is he to wander, and in what condition is he to remain in that eternity in which he is still to exist?

I hope no man will mistake me so much in what I have said as to spirits, which are all flame, not being affected with fire, as if I supposed there were no place of punishment for the Devil, nor any kind of punishment that could affect them, and so, of our spirits also when transformed.

I must be allowed to speak there of that material fire, by which, as by an allegory, all the terrors of an eternal state are represented to us in Scripture, and in the writings of the learned Bible commentators, and by which the pain of sense is described. This, perhaps, I do not understand as they seem to, and therefore have said:

When we're all flame (that is all spirit), we shall all fire (that is, all such fire as this) despise. And thus, I claim to be understood.

It does not follow from that, neither do I suggest, or so much as think, that infinite power cannot form a something (though inconceivable to us here) that shall be as tormenting, and as insupportable to a devil, an apostate seraph, and to a spirit, though exalted, unembodied and rarified into flame, as fire would be to other bodies, in which I think I am orthodox, and do not give the least occasion to an enemy to charge me with profane speaking in those words, or to plead for thinking profanely himself.

It must be atheistic to the last degree to suggest, that whereas the Devil has been heaping up and amassing guilt ever since the creation of man, increasing in hatred of God and rebellion against Him, and in all possible endeavors to dethrone and depose the Majesty of Heaven, that yet heaven had not prepared, or could not prepare a just penalty for him, and that it should not all end in

God's entire victory over hell, and in Satan's open condemnation. Heaven could not be just and God to His own glory if He should not avenge himself upon this rebel, Satan, for all his superlative wickedness in his modern as well as ancient station and for the blood of so many millions of God's faithful subjects and saints whom the Devil has destroyed. And if nothing else offered itself to prove this part, it would appear undoubted to me. But this, I confess, does not belong to Satan's history, and therefore I have reserved it to this place, and shall also be the shorter in it.

That his condition is to be a state of eternal punishment, and that by torment, the Devil himself has owned, and his calling out to our blessed Lord when he cast him out of the furious man among the tombs, is a proof of it (*"What have we to do with thee,* [and] *art thou come hither to torment us before the time?"* Matt. 8:29), where the Devil acknowledges four things, and three of them are directly to my present purpose. And if you won't believe the Word of God, I hope you will believe the Devil, especially when 'tis an open confession against himself.

1. He confess Christ to be the *Son of God*
2. He acknowledges he may be tormented.
3. He acknowledges Christ was able to torment him.
4. He acknowledges that there is a time appointed when he shall be tormented.

As to how, in what manner, and by what means this tormenting of the Devil is to be performed or executed, that I take to be as needless to us as 'tis impossible to know. And being not at present inclined to fill your heads and thoughts with weak and imperfect guesses, I leave it where I find it.

It is enough to us that this torment of the Devil is represented to us by fire, it being impossible for our confined thoughts to conceive of torment by anything in the world more exquisite. Whence I conclude, that devils shall at last receive a punishment suitable to their spirit nature, and as exquisitely tormenting as a burning fire would be to our bodies.

Having thus settled my own belief of this matter, and stated it so, as I think will let you see 'tis rightly sounded, the matter stands thusly:

Satan, having been let loose to play his game in this world, has improved his time to the utmost. He has not failed on all occasions to exert his hatred, rage, and malice at his Conqueror and Enemy, namely, his Maker. He has not failed from principles of mere envy and pride to pursue mankind with all possible rancor in order to deprive him of the honor and felicity that he was created for, namely, to succeed the Devil and his angels in the state of glory from which they fell.

This hatred of God and envy at man, having broken out in so many several ways in the whole series of time from the Creation, must necessarily have greatly increased his guilt. And as Heaven is righteous to judge him, it must terminate in an increase of punishment adequate to his crime and sufficient to his nature.

Some have suggested that there is yet a time to come when the Devil shall exert more rage and do more mischief than ever yet he has been permitted to do. Whether he shall break his chain, or be unchained for a time, they cannot tell, nor can I. And 'tis happy for my work that even this part, too, does not belong to his history. If ever it shall be given an account of by mankind, it must be after it has come to pass. For my part is not dealing with prophecy of foretelling what the Devil shall do but the history of what he has done.

Thus, good people, I have brought the history of the Devil down to your own times. I have, as it were, raised him for you, and set him in your view so you may know him and have a care of him.

If any more cunning men among you think they are able now to lay him again, and so dispose of him out of your sight so you shall be troubled no more with him, either here or hereafter, let them go to work with him their own way. You know things future do not belong to an historian, so I leave him among you, wishing you may be able to give no worse an account of him for the time to come than I have done for the time past.

ALSO AVAILABLE FROM BRIDGE-LOGOS

PRACTICAL RELIGION

by J. C. Ryle
Compilation and Biography by Gene Fedele

Practical Religion, by J. C. Ryle was first published in 1878 and is renowned as a theological and apologetic Christian "classic"—esteemed for its clear, profoundly growing and penetrating narrative on the practice of genuine Christian living. Within its pages, Ryle masterfully unfolds practical biblical truths in a series of papers written to address critical aspects of where personal faith in Christ and the practice of that faith in holy living unite and are essential for Christian growth and effectiveness as a witness for Christ in the world. Ryle's unique style penetrates the heart and challenges the mind of its readers, not for the faint of heart. No wonder Charles Spurgeon called him "an evangelical champion."

ISBN: 978-1-61036-264-1

Facebook.com/genefedele

ISBN: 978-0-88270-934-5

ALSO AVAILABLE FROM BRIDGE-LOGOS

SECRET POWER

D. L. Moody

Dwight L. Moody wrote, "The result is lack of power in testimony and work. If we would work, 'not as one that beats the air,' but to some definite purpose, we must have this power from on high. Without this power, our work will be drudgery. With it, it becomes a joyful task, a refreshing service. May God make this book a blessing to many. This is my prayer."

- Revised into modern English
- Rare photos from the Moody family album
- Biography
- Index

ISBN: 978-0-88270-114-1

ALSO AVAILABLE FROM BRIDGE-LOGOS

SPURGEON ON THE PSALMS: BOOK FOUR

Charles Spurgeon

Spurgeon called this work The Treasury of David, and it truly is a treasury that is filled with jewels, gems, and nuggets of gold from the Book of Psalms. In many ways, this is Spurgeon's Magnum Opus. His wife, Susannah, said that if her husband had never written any other work, his writings on the Psalms would have become a permanent literary memorial to him. This is the fourth volume in a six-book series. Senior Editor Beverlee Chadwick has sensitively updated and revised this Pure Gold Classic for the modern reader. As you will see, Spurgeon delighted in his study of the Psalms, and it was his desire that readers would search the Psalms further for themselves. Reading this book leads one right into the heart of God.

ISBN: 978-1-61036-152-1

ALSO AVAILABLE FROM BRIDGE-LOGOS

THE HOLY WAR

John Bunyan

A classic struggle for the human soul, The Holy War, John Bunyan's second-most popular book, has now been translated from the original seventeenth-century text and further edited and annotated by L. Edward Hazelbaker—editor of two other Pure Gold Classics by Bunyan (*The Pilgrim's Progress* and *Grace Abounding to the Chief of Sinners*). Hazelbaker's well-crafted works have proven to be bestsellers. This classic allegory illustrates the struggle between good and evil and the ultimate battle for the human soul. Though the battle continues to rage, this book will show the reader what the enemy's intentions are and what God is doing to overcome him.

ISBN: 978-1-61036-153-8